ALL MY GHOSTS

A GRAPHIC NOVEL BY JEREMY MASSIE

THIS BOOK IS DEDICATED TO
BONNIE MILLER
AND
SCOTT GLASS
WHO BOTH BECAME GHOSTS
DURING ITS PRODUCTION.

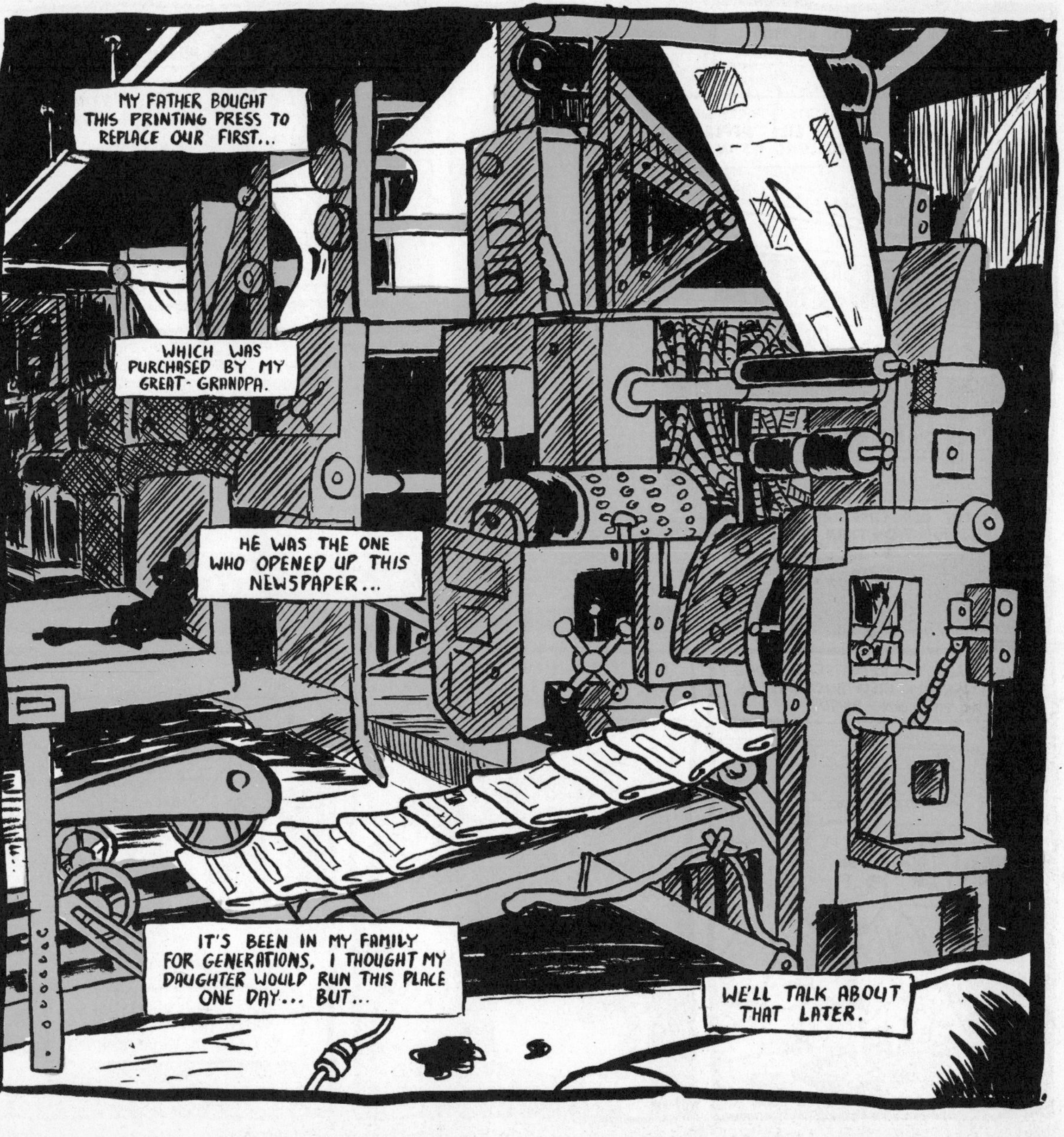
MY FATHER BOUGHT THIS PRINTING PRESS TO REPLACE OUR FIRST...
WHICH WAS PURCHASED BY MY GREAT-GRANDPA.
HE WAS THE ONE WHO OPENED UP THIS NEWSPAPER...
IT'S BEEN IN MY FAMILY FOR GENERATIONS. I THOUGHT MY DAUGHTER WOULD RUN THIS PLACE ONE DAY... BUT...
WE'LL TALK ABOUT THAT LATER.

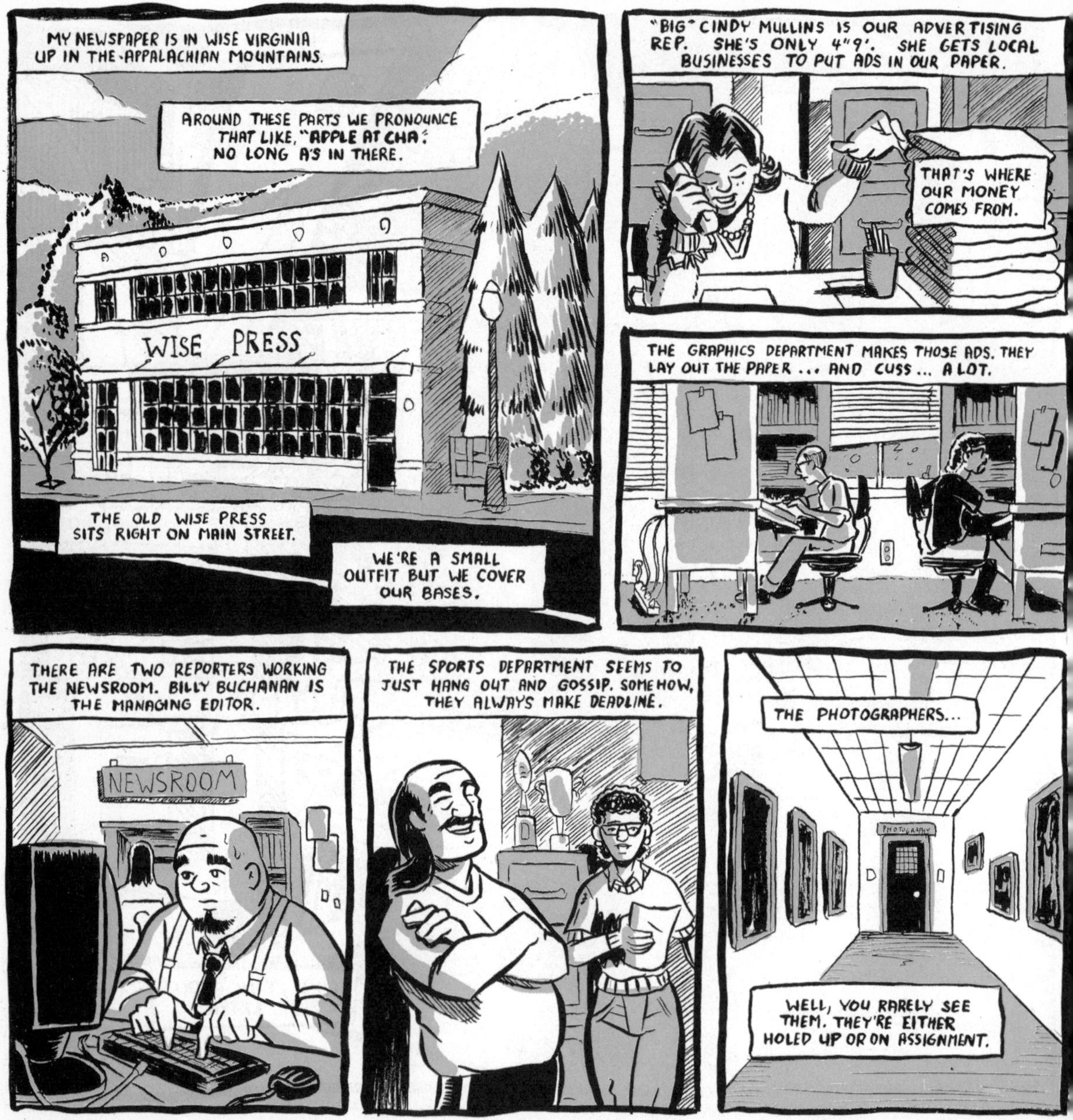
MY NEWSPAPER IS IN WISE VIRGINIA UP IN THE APPALACHIAN MOUNTAINS.
AROUND THESE PARTS WE PRONOUNCE THAT LIKE, "APPLE AT CHA." NO LONG A'S IN THERE.
WISE PRESS
THE OLD WISE PRESS SITS RIGHT ON MAIN STREET.
WE'RE A SMALL OUTFIT BUT WE COVER OUR BASES.
"BIG" CINDY MULLINS IS OUR ADVERTISING REP. SHE'S ONLY 4"9'. SHE GETS LOCAL BUSINESSES TO PUT ADS IN OUR PAPER.
THAT'S WHERE OUR MONEY COMES FROM.
THE GRAPHICS DEPARTMENT MAKES THOSE ADS. THEY LAY OUT THE PAPER ... AND CUSS ... A LOT.
THERE ARE TWO REPORTERS WORKING THE NEWSROOM. BILLY BUCHANAN IS THE MANAGING EDITOR.
NEWSROOM
THE SPORTS DEPARTMENT SEEMS TO JUST HANG OUT AND GOSSIP. SOMEHOW, THEY ALWAYS MAKE DEADLINE.
THE PHOTOGRAPHERS...
PHOTOGRAPHY
WELL, YOU RARELY SEE THEM. THEY'RE EITHER HOLED UP OR ON ASSIGNMENT.

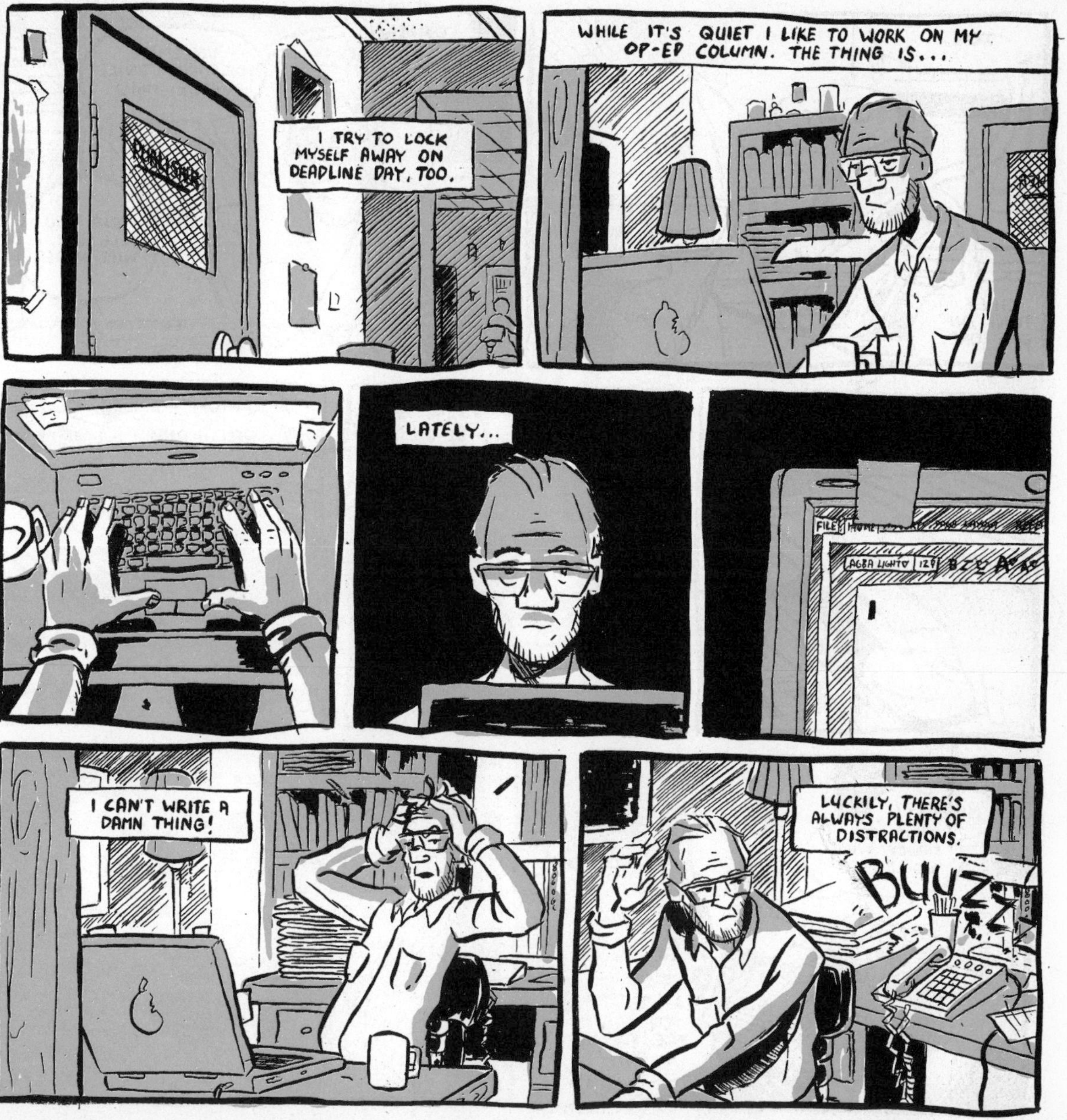
I TRY TO LOCK MYSELF AWAY ON DEADLINE DAY, TOO.
WHILE IT'S QUIET I LIKE TO WORK ON MY OP-ED COLUMN. THE THING IS...
LATELY...
FILE HOME
AGBA LIGHTO 12
I CAN'T WRITE A DAMN THING!
LUCKILY, THERE'S ALWAYS PLENTY OF DISTRACTIONS.
BUUZZ

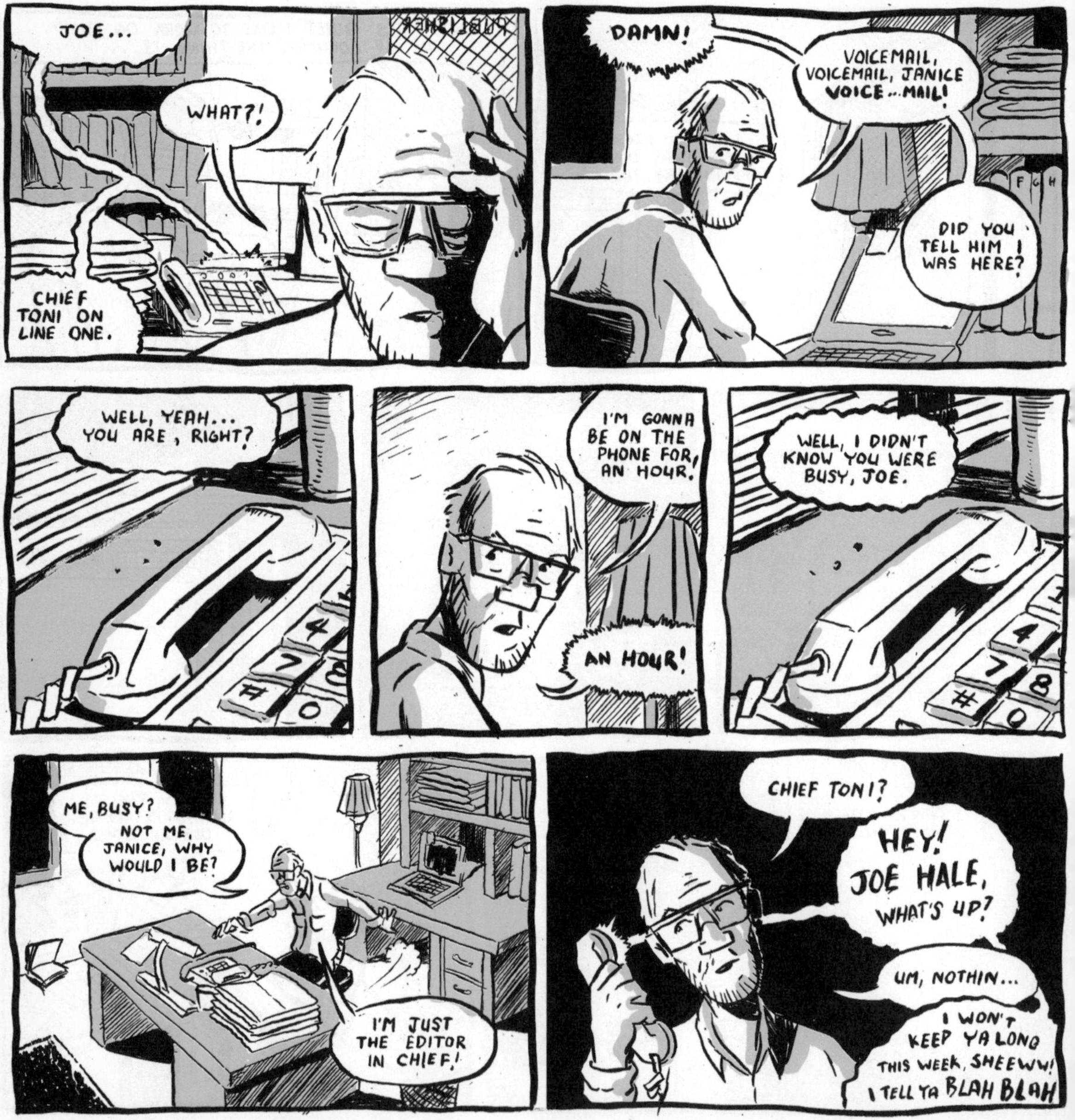
JOE...
WHAT?!
CHIEF TONI ON LINE ONE.
PUBLISHER
DAMN!
VOICEMAIL, VOICEMAIL, JANICE VOICE...MAIL!
DID YOU TELL HIM I WAS HERE?
WELL, YEAH... YOU ARE, RIGHT?
I'M GONNA BE ON THE PHONE FOR AN HOUR.
AN HOUR!
WELL, I DIDN'T KNOW YOU WERE BUSY, JOE.
ME, BUSY?
NOT ME, JANICE, WHY WOULD I BE?
I'M JUST THE EDITOR IN CHIEF!
CHIEF TONI?
HEY! JOE HALE, WHAT'S UP?
UM, NOTHIN...
I WON'T KEEP YA LONG THIS WEEK, SHEEWW! I TELL YA BLAH BLAH

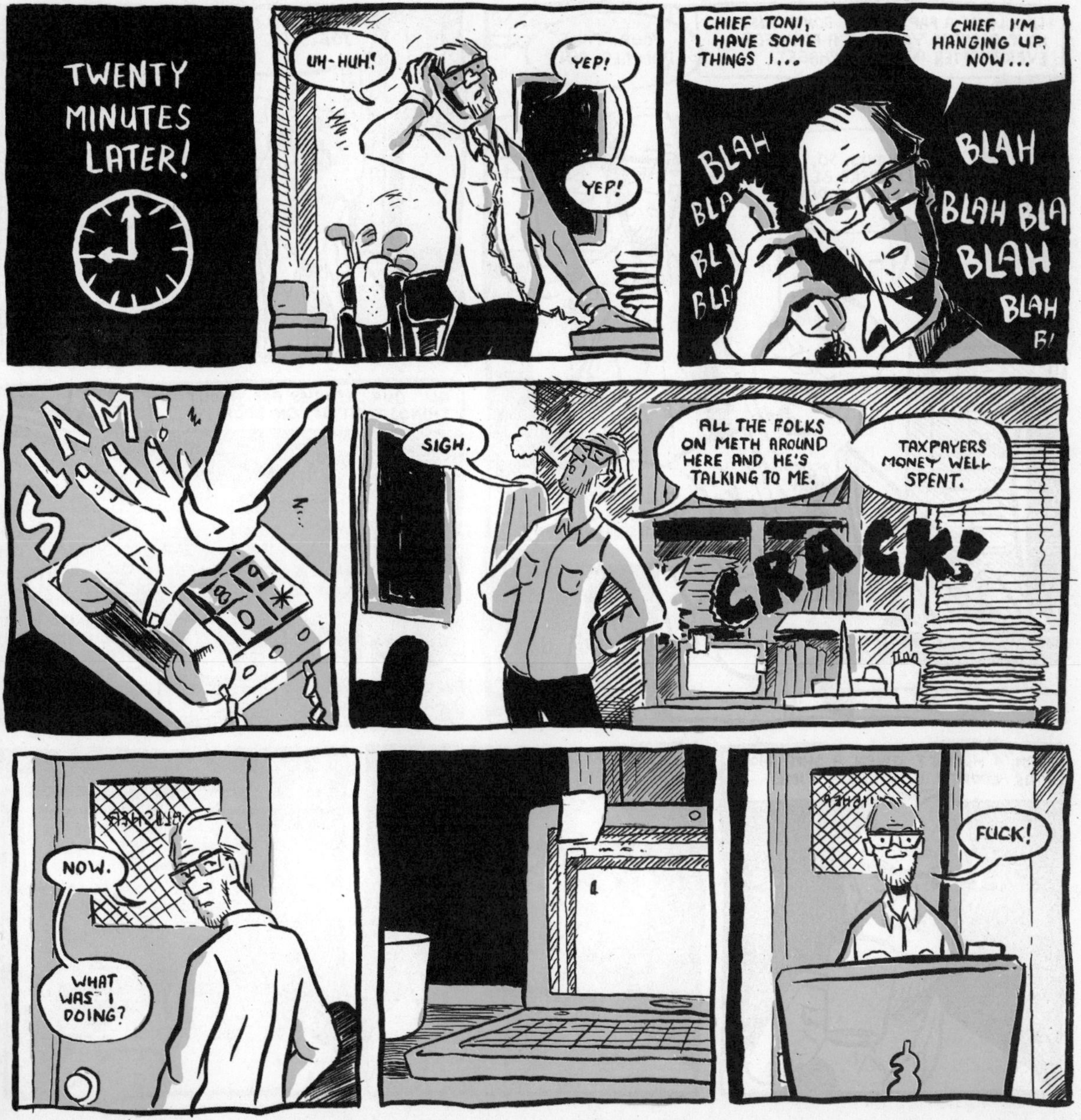
TWENTY MINUTES LATER!
UH-HUH!
YEP!
YEP!
CHIEF TONI, I HAVE SOME THINGS I...
CHIEF I'M HANGING UP NOW...
BLAH BLAH BL BLA
BLAH BLAH BLA BLAH BLAH BL
SLAM!
SIGH.
ALL THE FOLKS ON METH AROUND HERE AND HE'S TALKING TO ME.
TAXPAYERS MONEY WELL SPENT.
CRACK!
NOW.
WHAT WAS I DOING?
FUCK!

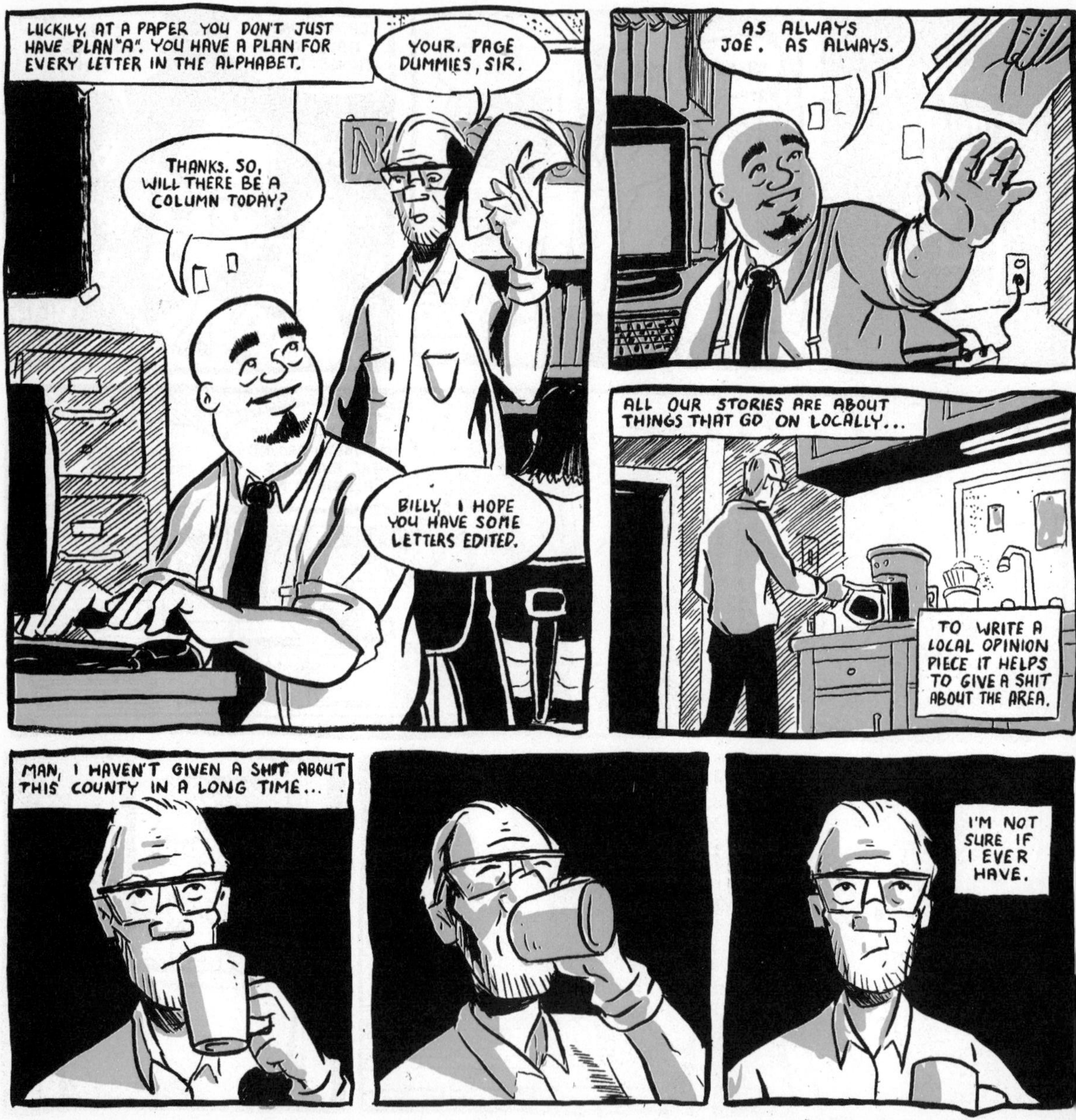
LUCKILY, AT A PAPER YOU DON'T JUST HAVE PLAN "A". YOU HAVE A PLAN FOR EVERY LETTER IN THE ALPHABET.
YOUR. PAGE DUMMIES, SIR.
THANKS. SO, WILL THERE BE A COLUMN TODAY?
BILLY, I HOPE YOU HAVE SOME LETTERS EDITED.
AS ALWAYS JOE. AS ALWAYS.
ALL OUR STORIES ARE ABOUT THINGS THAT GO ON LOCALLY...
TO WRITE A LOCAL OPINION PIECE IT HELPS TO GIVE A SHIT ABOUT THE AREA.
MAN, I HAVEN'T GIVEN A SHIT ABOUT THIS COUNTY IN A LONG TIME...
I'M NOT SURE IF I EVER HAVE.

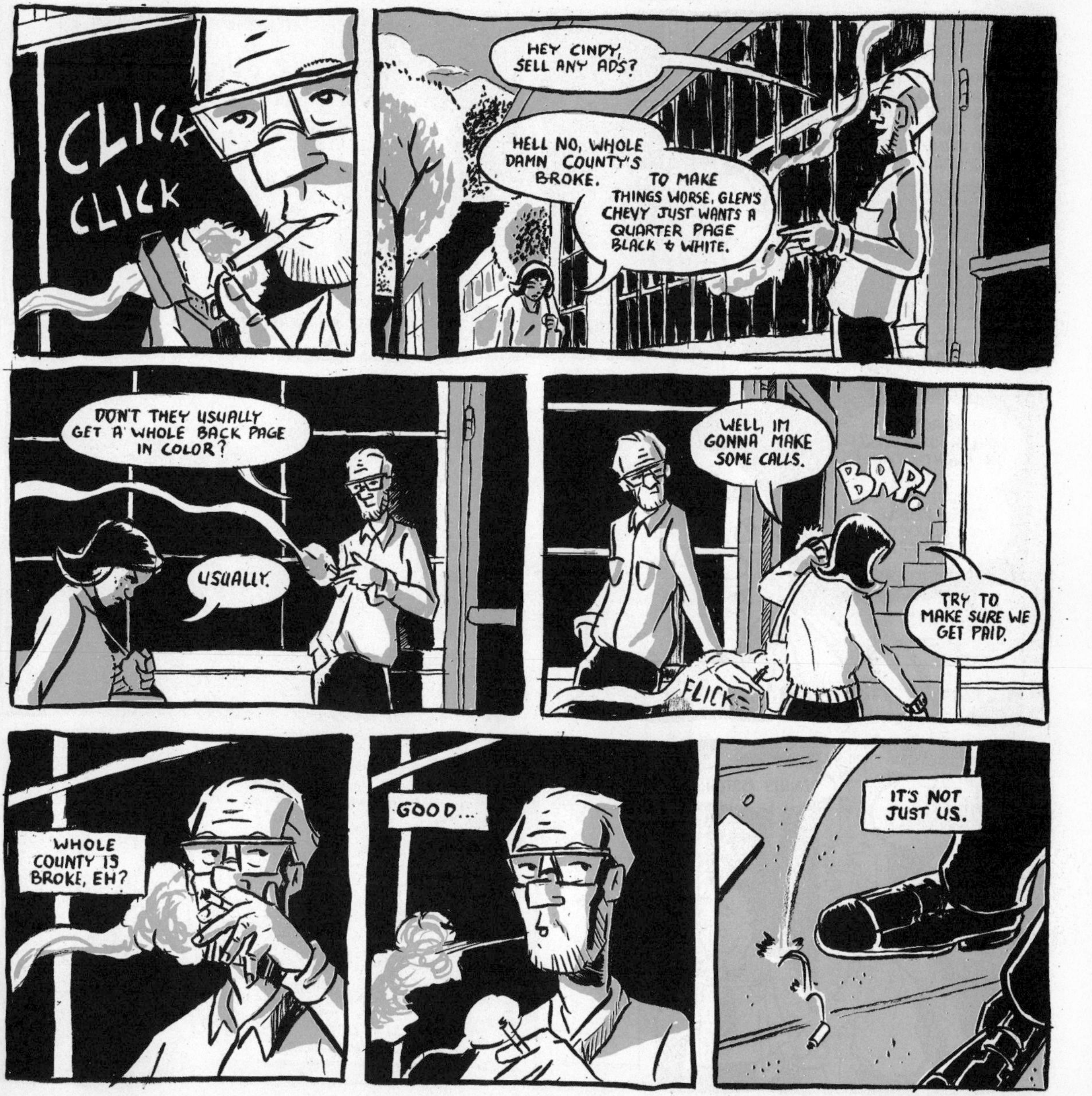
CLICK
CLICK
HEY CINDY, SELL ANY ADS?
HELL NO, WHOLE DAMN COUNTY'S BROKE.
TO MAKE THINGS WORSE, GLEN'S CHEVY JUST WANTS A QUARTER PAGE BLACK & WHITE.
DON'T THEY USUALLY GET A WHOLE BACK PAGE IN COLOR?
USUALLY.
WELL, IM GONNA MAKE SOME CALLS.
BAP!
TRY TO MAKE SURE WE GET PAID.
FLICK
WHOLE COUNTY IS BROKE, EH?
GOOD...
IT'S NOT JUST US.

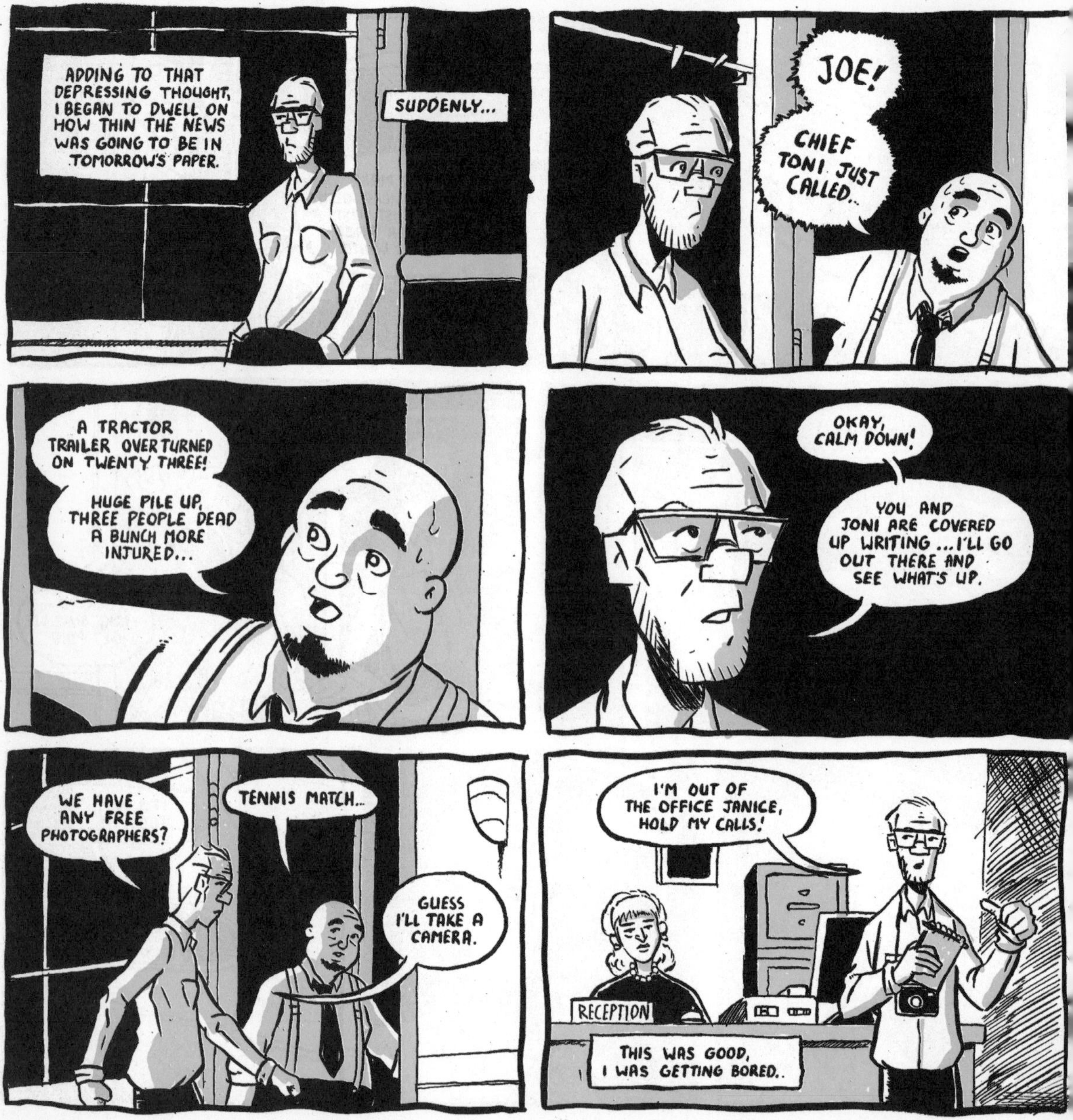
ADDING TO THAT DEPRESSING THOUGHT, I BEGAN TO DWELL ON HOW THIN THE NEWS WAS GOING TO BE IN TOMORROW'S PAPER.
SUDDENLY...
JOE!
CHIEF TONI JUST CALLED..
A TRACTOR TRAILER OVERTURNED ON TWENTY THREE!
HUGE PILE UP, THREE PEOPLE DEAD A BUNCH MORE INJURED...
OKAY, CALM DOWN!
YOU AND JONI ARE COVERED UP WRITING ... I'LL GO OUT THERE AND SEE WHAT'S UP.
WE HAVE ANY FREE PHOTOGRAPHERS?
TENNIS MATCH..
GUESS I'LL TAKE A CAMERA.
I'M OUT OF THE OFFICE JANICE, HOLD MY CALLS!
RECEPTION
THIS WAS GOOD, I WAS GETTING BORED..

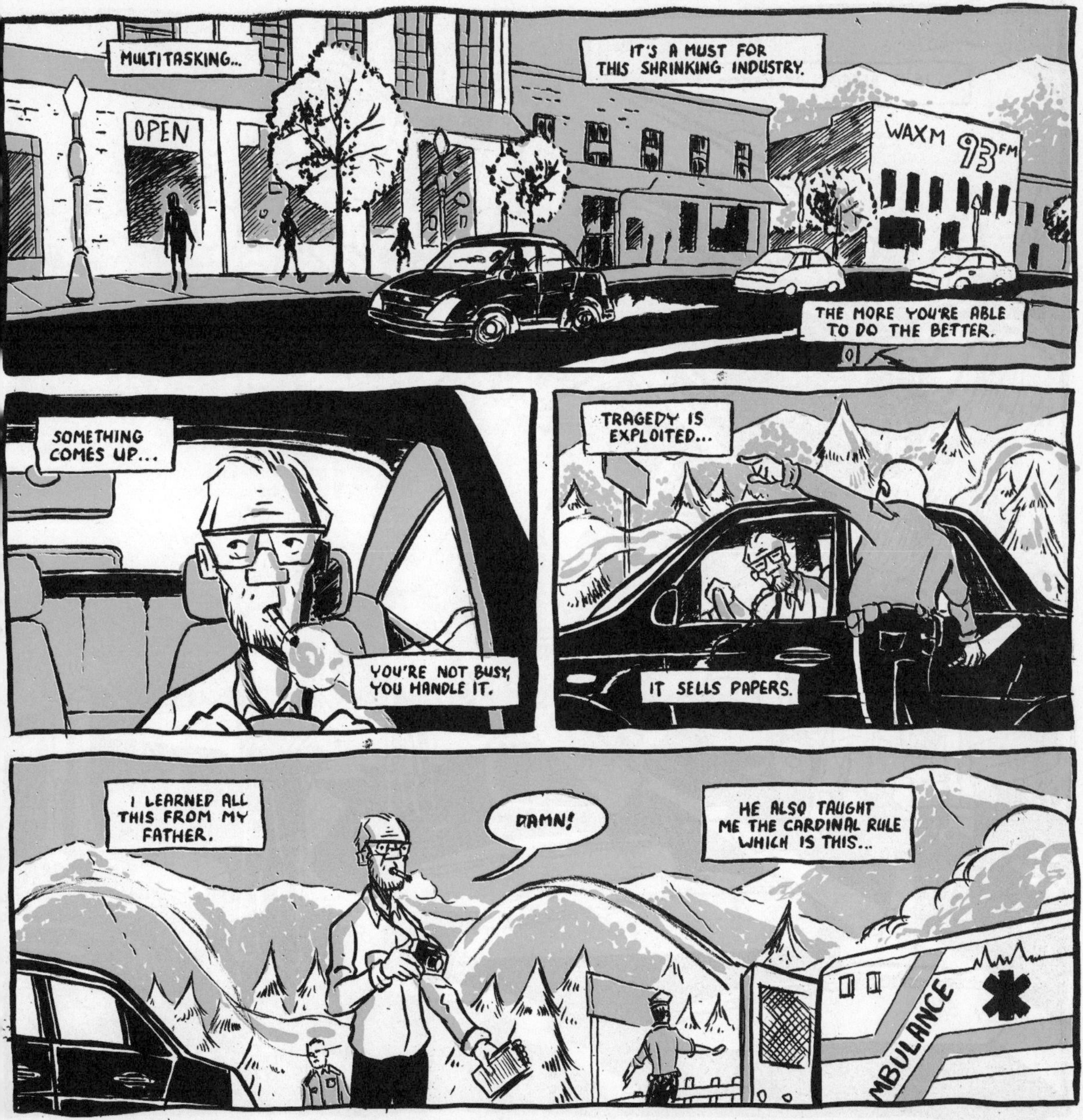
MULTITASKING...
IT'S A MUST FOR THIS SHRINKING INDUSTRY.
OPEN
WAXM 93FM
THE MORE YOU'RE ABLE TO DO THE BETTER.
SOMETHING COMES UP...
YOU'RE NOT BUSY, YOU HANDLE IT.
TRAGEDY IS EXPLOITED...
IT SELLS PAPERS.
I LEARNED ALL THIS FROM MY FATHER.
DAMN!
HE ALSO TAUGHT ME THE CARDINAL RULE WHICH IS THIS...
MBULANCE

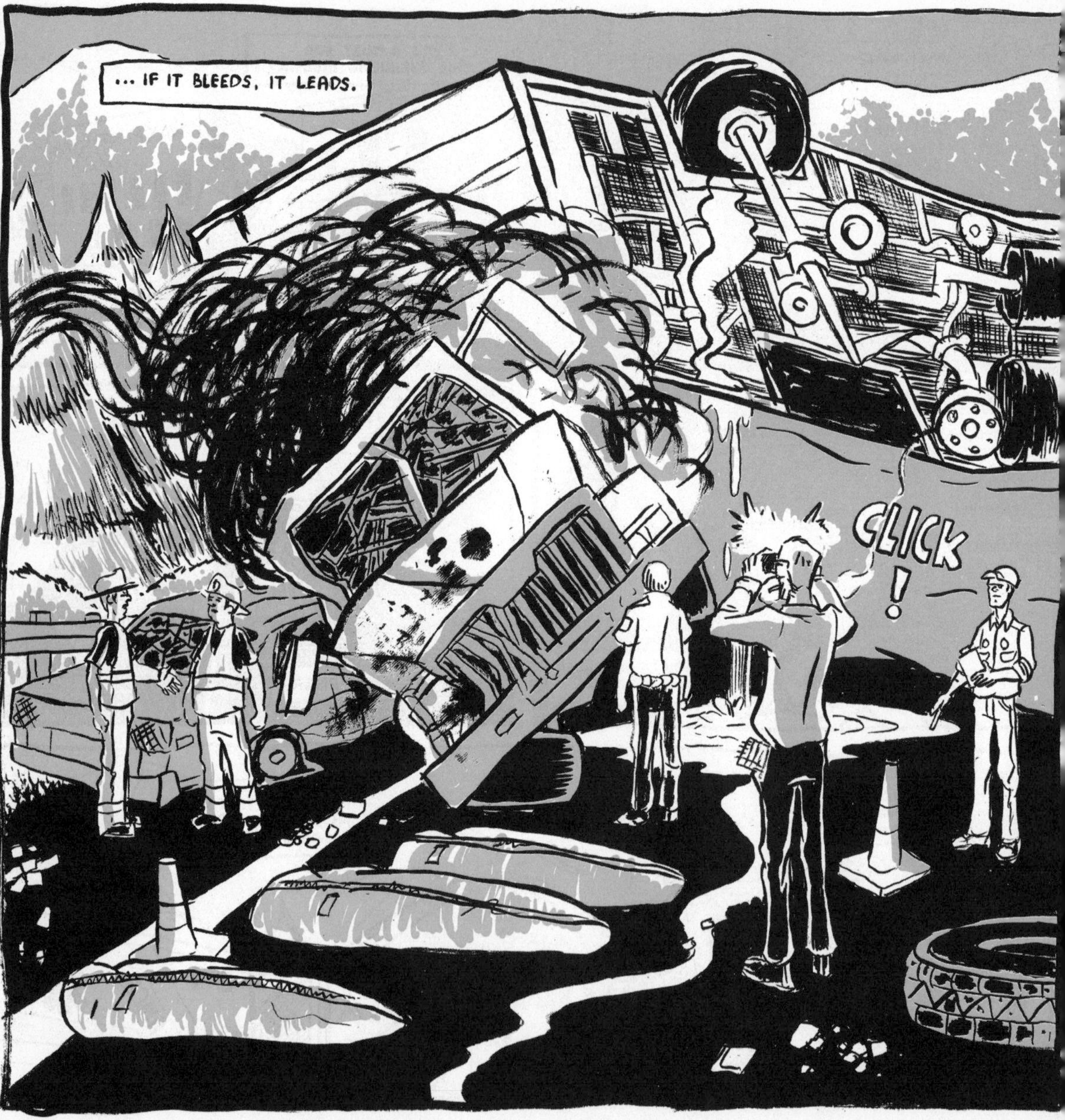
... IF IT BLEEDS, IT LEADS.
CLICK!

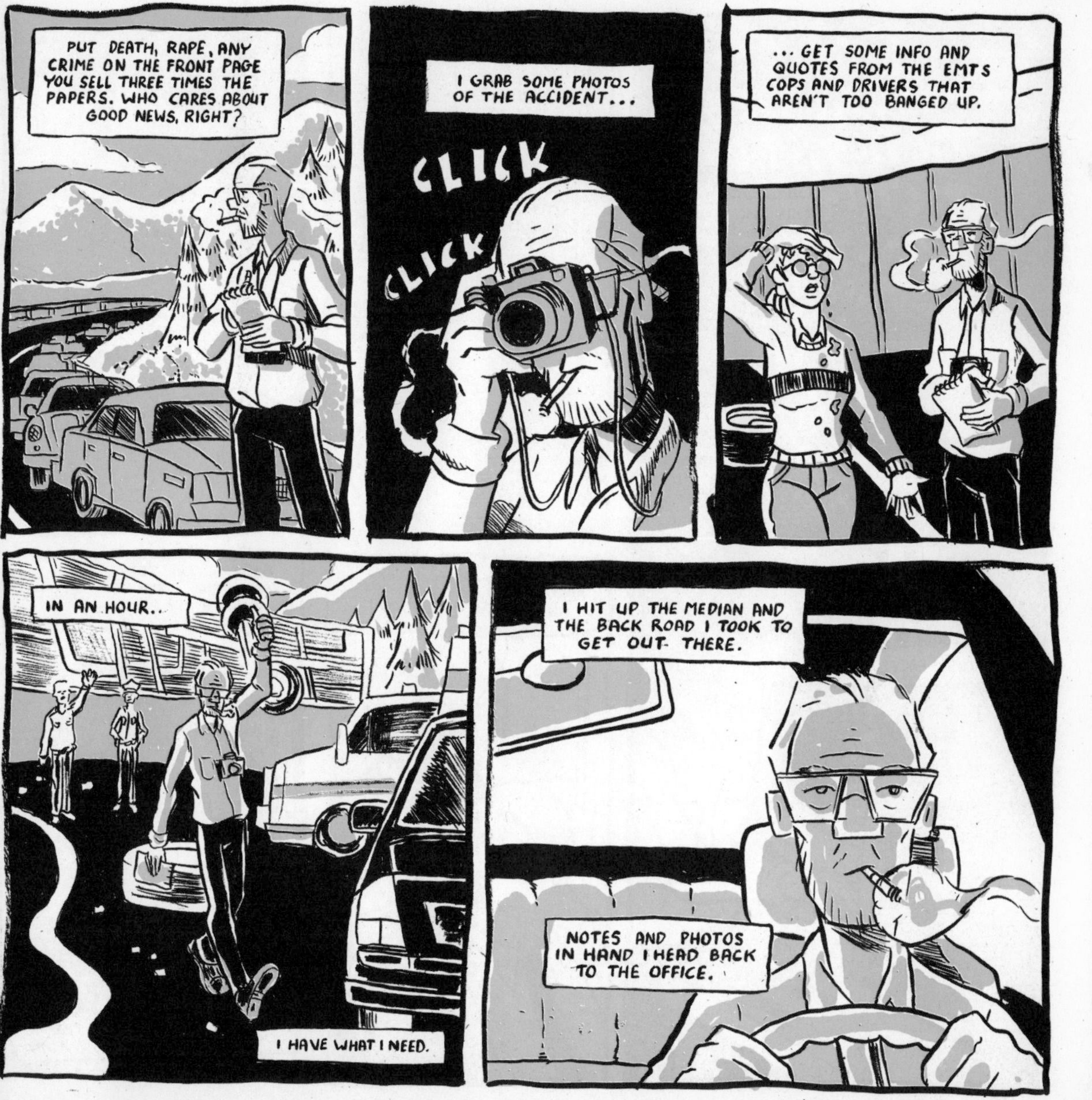
PUT DEATH, RAPE, ANY CRIME ON THE FRONT PAGE YOU SELL THREE TIMES THE PAPERS. WHO CARES ABOUT GOOD NEWS, RIGHT?
I GRAB SOME PHOTOS OF THE ACCIDENT...
CLICK
CLICK
... GET SOME INFO AND QUOTES FROM THE EMTS COPS AND DRIVERS THAT AREN'T TOO BANGED UP.
IN AN HOUR..
I HAVE WHAT I NEED.
I HIT UP THE MEDIAN AND THE BACK ROAD I TOOK TO GET OUT THERE.
NOTES AND PHOTOS IN HAND I HEAD BACK TO THE OFFICE.

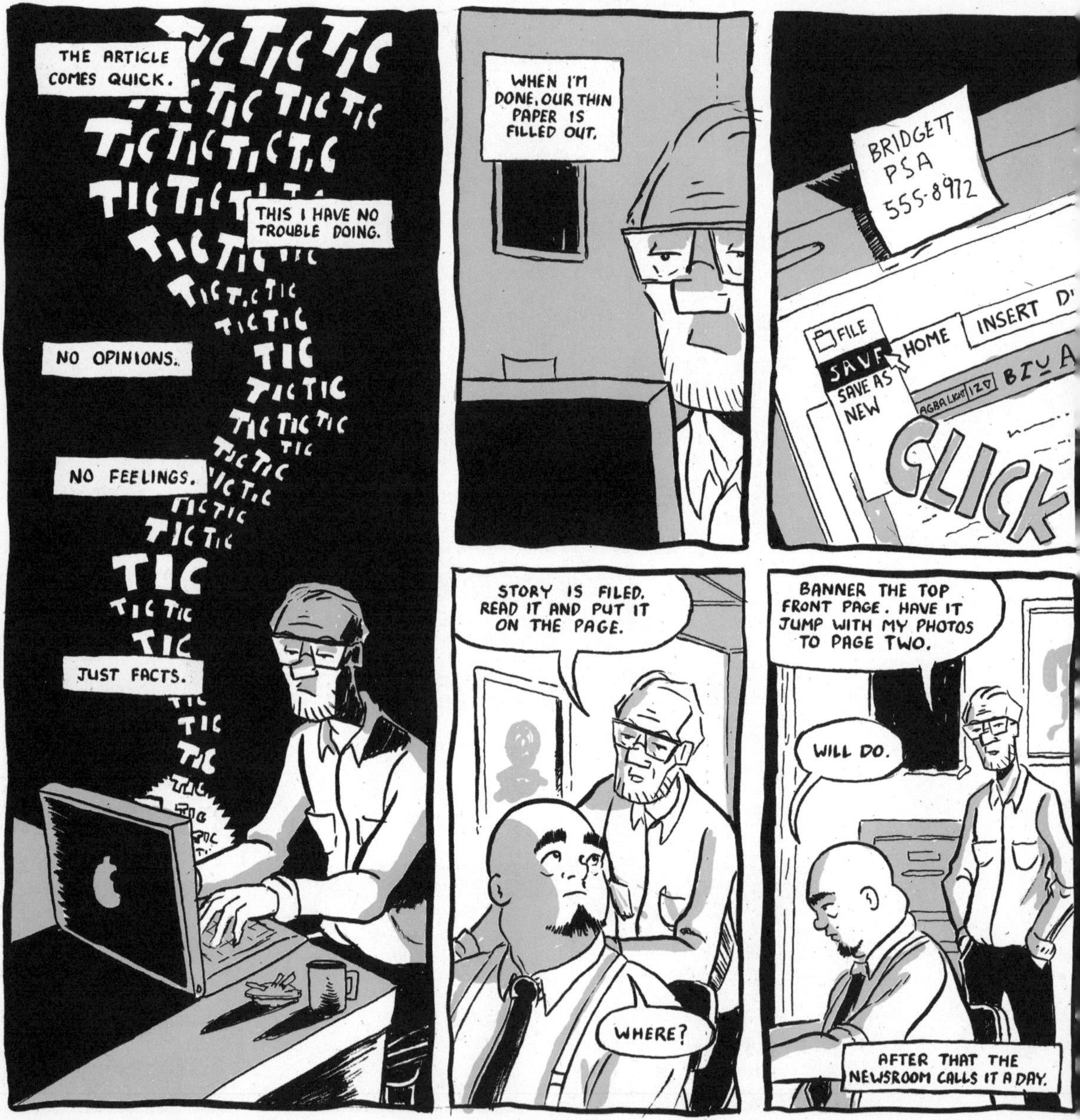

THE ARTICLE COMES QUICK.
TIC TIC TIC TIC
THIS I HAVE NO TROUBLE DOING.
NO OPINIONS.
NO FEELINGS.
JUST FACTS.
WHEN I'M DONE, OUR THIN PAPER IS FILLED OUT.
BRIDGETT PSA 555-8972
FILE
SAVE
SAVE AS NEW
HOME
INSERT
CLICK
STORY IS FILED. READ IT AND PUT IT ON THE PAGE.
WHERE?
BANNER THE TOP FRONT PAGE. HAVE IT JUMP WITH MY PHOTOS TO PAGE TWO.
WILL DO.
AFTER THAT THE NEWSROOM CALLS IT A DAY.

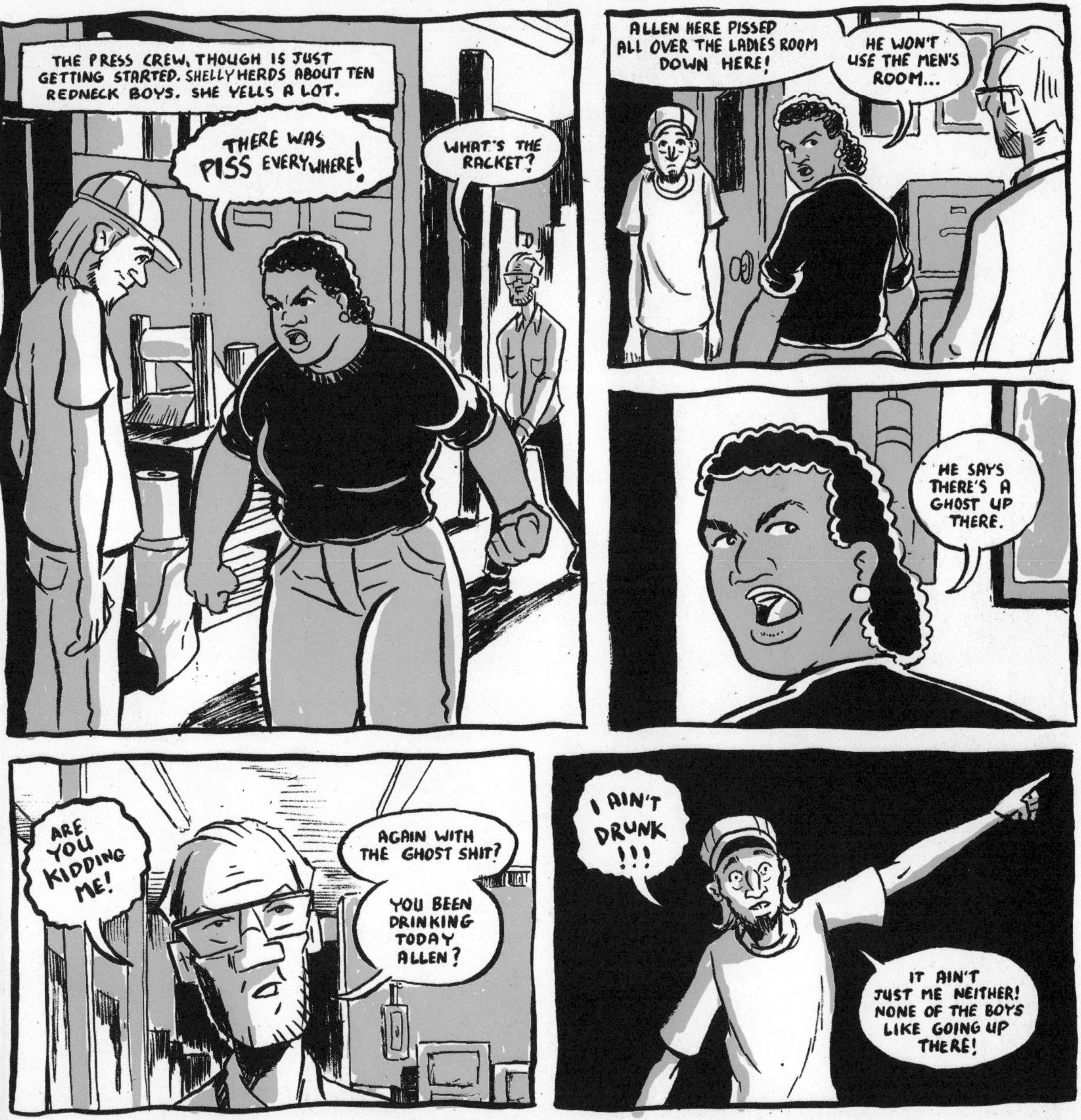
THE PRESS CREW, THOUGH IS JUST GETTING STARTED. SHELLY HERDS ABOUT TEN REDNECK BOYS. SHE YELLS A LOT.
THERE WAS PISS EVERYWHERE!
WHAT'S THE RACKET?
ALLEN HERE PISSED ALL OVER THE LADIES ROOM DOWN HERE!
HE WON'T USE THE MEN'S ROOM...
HE SAYS THERE'S A GHOST UP THERE.
ARE YOU KIDDING ME!
AGAIN WITH THE GHOST SHIT?
YOU BEEN DRINKING TODAY ALLEN?
I AIN'T DRUNK !!!
IT AIN'T JUST ME NEITHER! NONE OF THE BOYS LIKE GOING UP THERE!

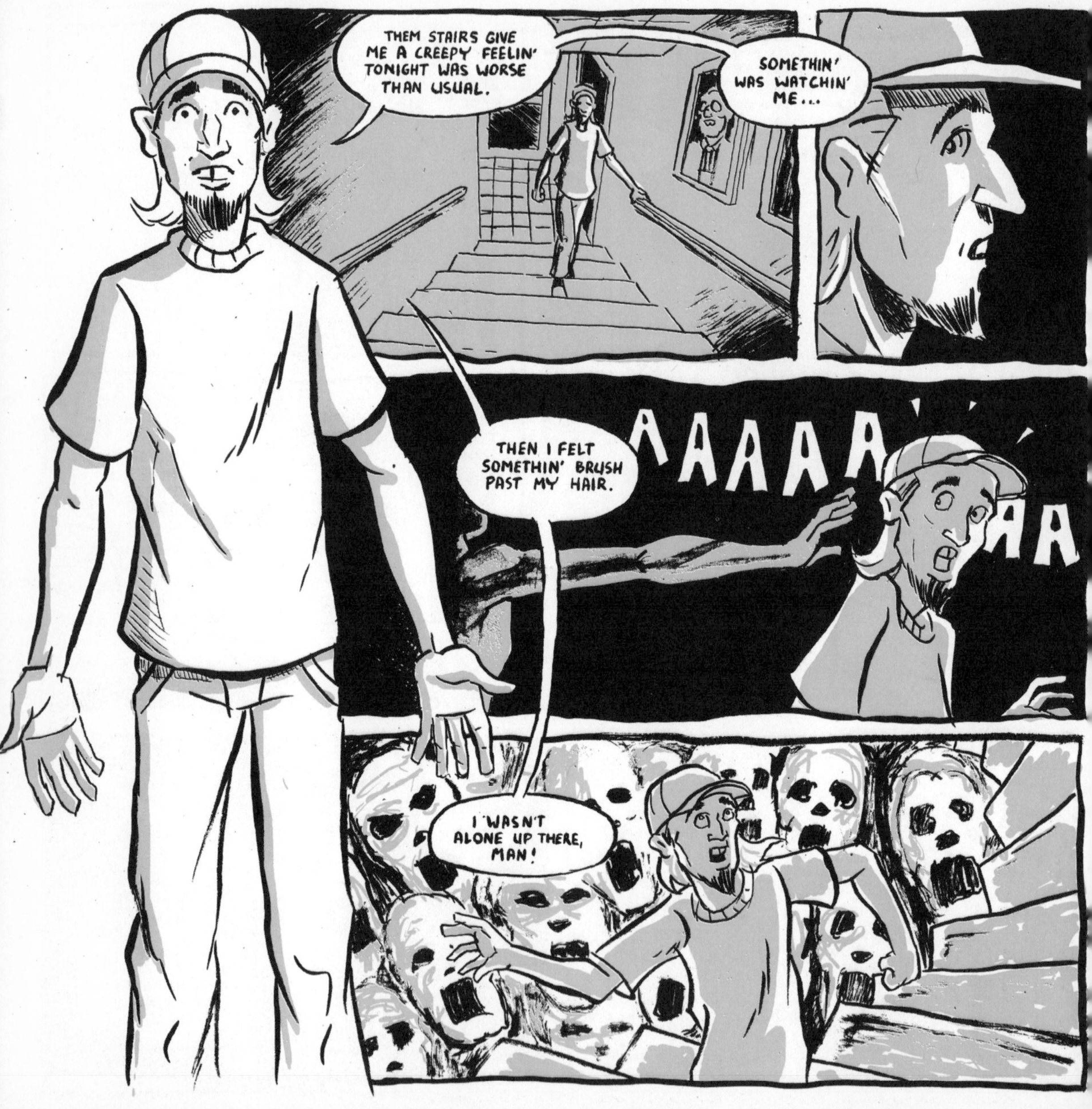
THEM STAIRS GIVE ME A CREEPY FEELIN' TONIGHT WAS WORSE THAN USUAL.
SOMETHIN' WAS WATCHIN' ME...
AAAAAAA
THEN I FELT SOMETHIN' BRUSH PAST MY HAIR.
I WASN'T ALONE UP THERE, MAN!

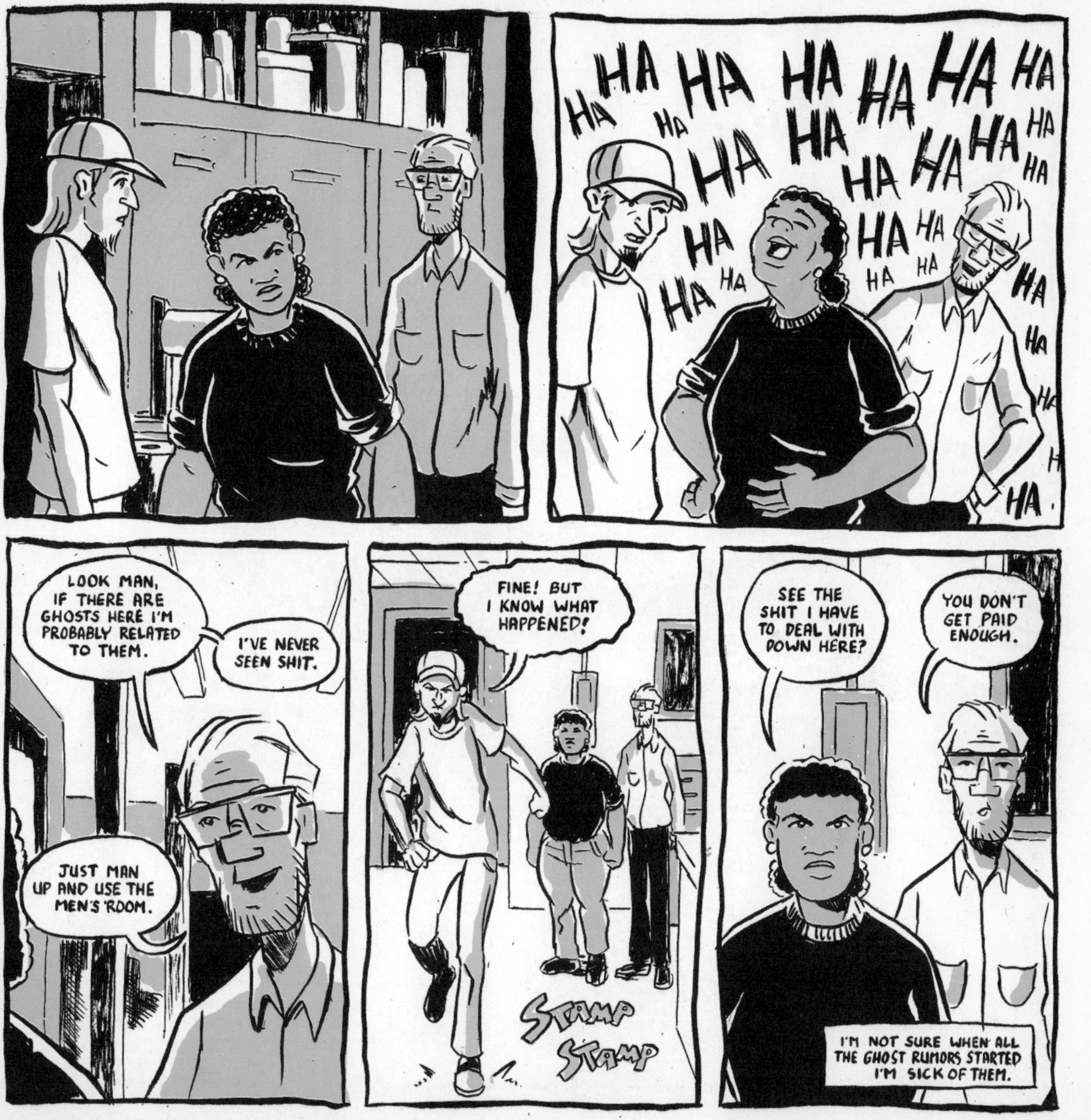
HA HA HA HA HA HA HA HA HA HA HA HA HA HA HA HA HA HA HA HA HA HA HA HA HA HA HA HA HA.
LOOK MAN, IF THERE ARE GHOSTS HERE I'M PROBABLY RELATED TO THEM.
I'VE NEVER SEEN SHIT.
JUST MAN UP AND USE THE MEN'S ROOM.
FINE! BUT I KNOW WHAT HAPPENED!
STAMP
STAMP
SEE THE SHIT I HAVE TO DEAL WITH DOWN HERE?
YOU DON'T GET PAID ENOUGH.
I'M NOT SURE WHEN ALL THE GHOST RUMORS STARTED I'M SICK OF THEM.

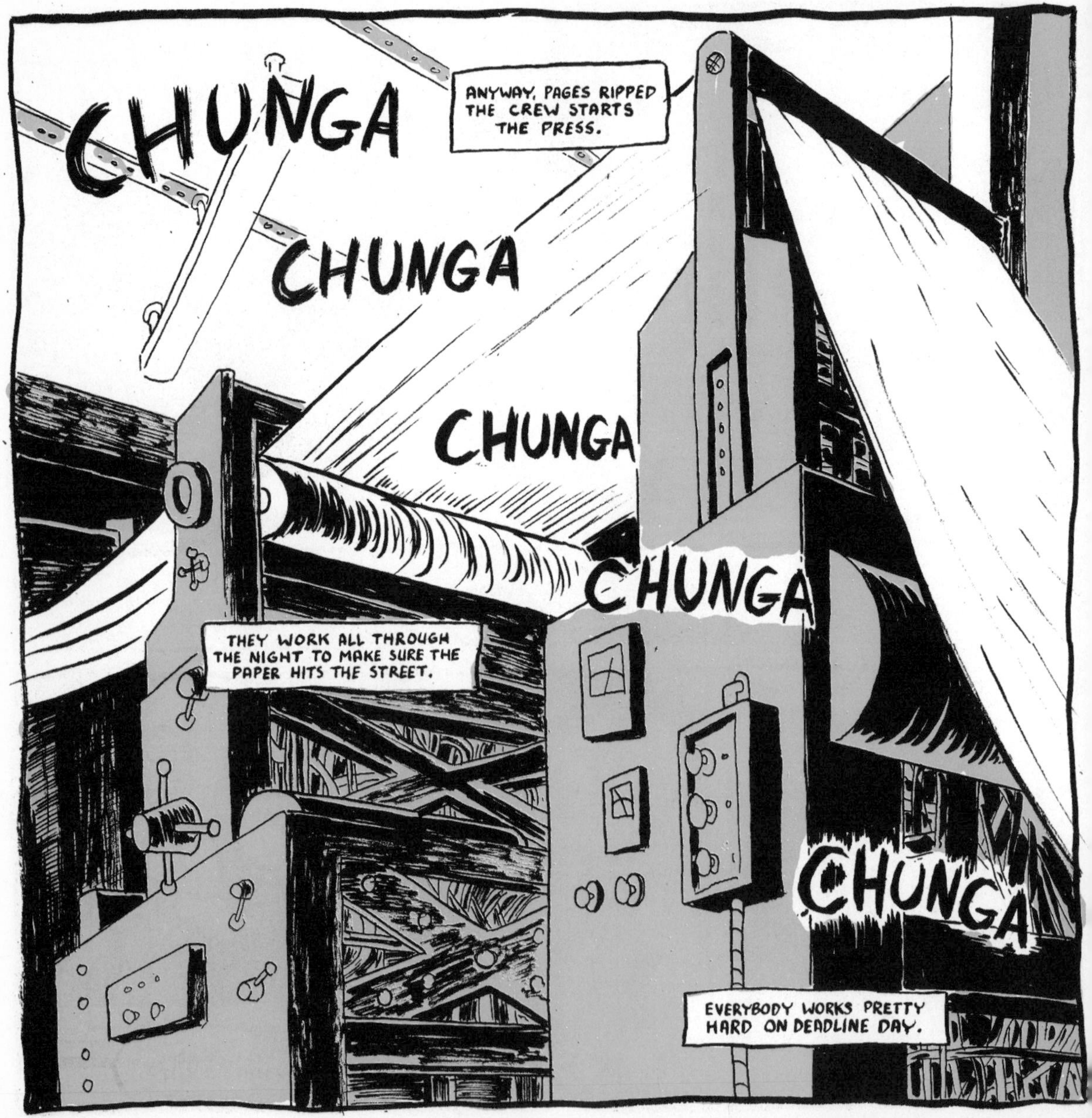
CHUNGA
ANYWAY, PAGES RIPPED THE CREW STARTS THE PRESS.
CHUNGA
CHUNGA
CHUNGA
THEY WORK ALL THROUGH THE NIGHT TO MAKE SURE THE PAPER HITS THE STREET.
CHUNGA
EVERYBODY WORKS PRETTY HARD ON DEADLINE DAY.

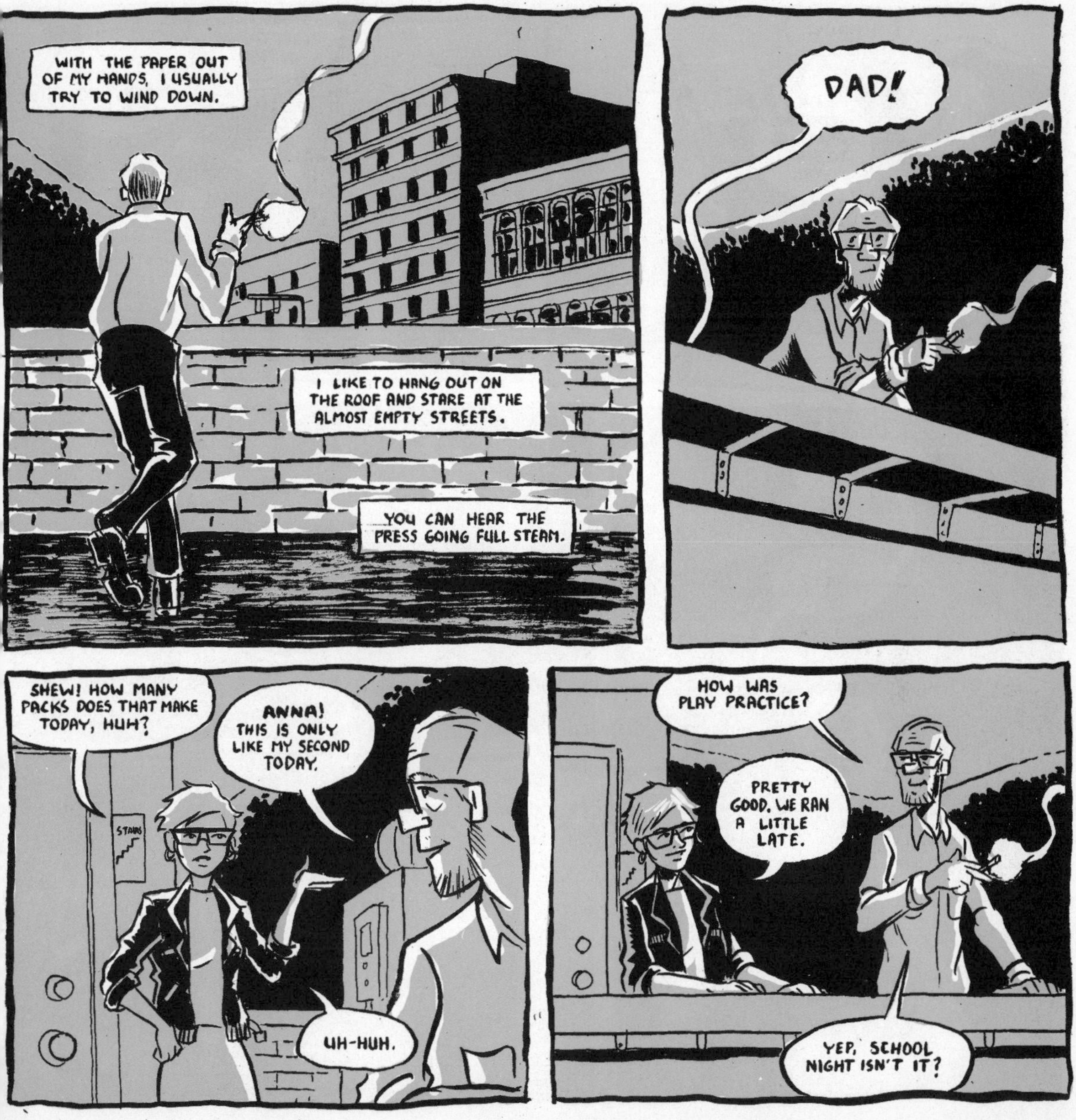
WITH THE PAPER OUT OF MY HANDS, I USUALLY TRY TO WIND DOWN.
I LIKE TO HANG OUT ON THE ROOF AND STARE AT THE ALMOST EMPTY STREETS.
YOU CAN HEAR THE PRESS GOING FULL STEAM.
DAD!
SHEW! HOW MANY PACKS DOES THAT MAKE TODAY, HUH?
ANNA! THIS IS ONLY LIKE MY SECOND TODAY.
STAIRS
UH-HUH.
HOW WAS PLAY PRACTICE?
PRETTY GOOD. WE RAN A LITTLE LATE.
YEP, SCHOOL NIGHT ISN'T IT?

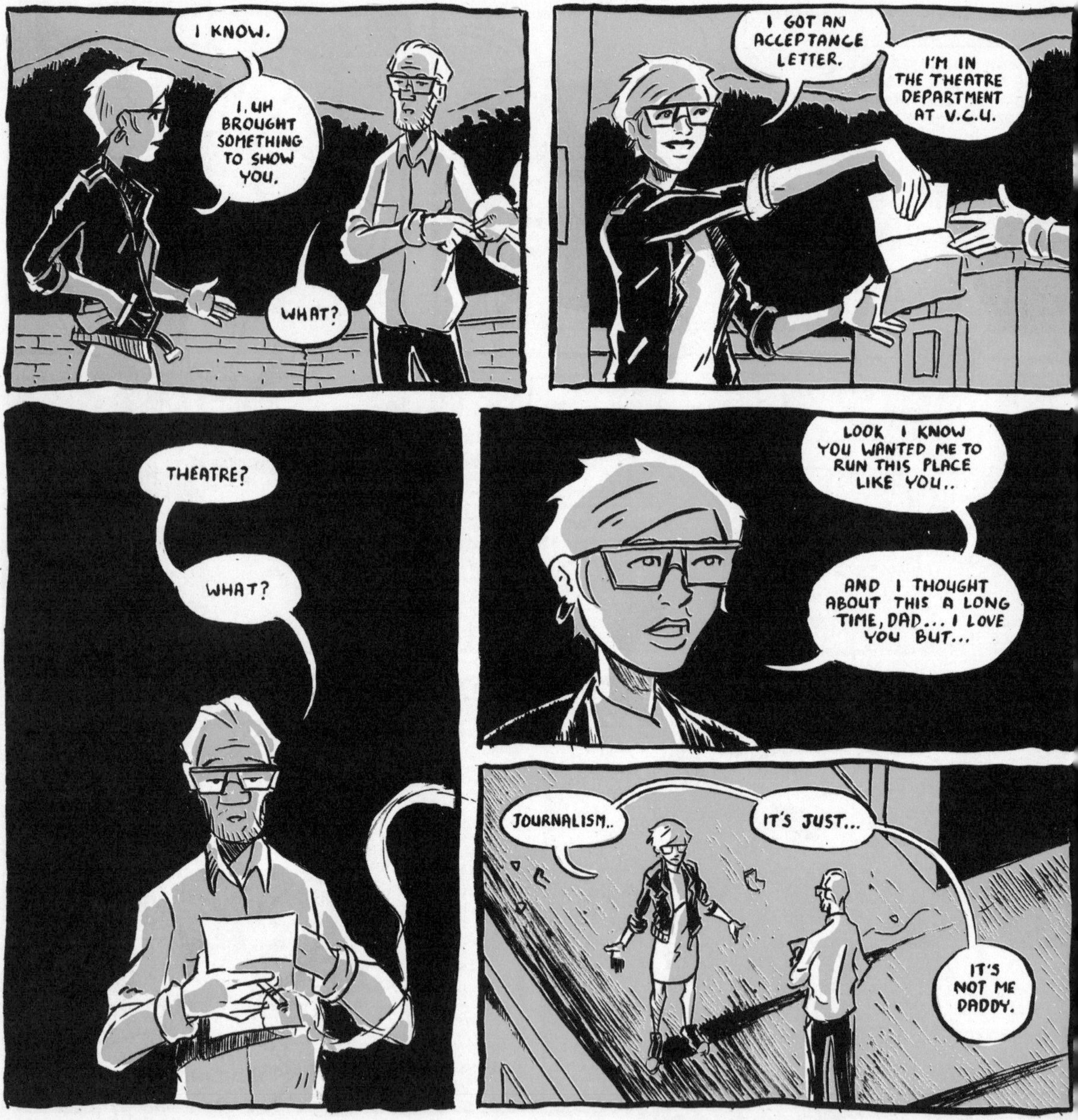
I KNOW.
I, UH BROUGHT SOMETHING TO SHOW YOU.
WHAT?
I GOT AN ACCEPTANCE LETTER.
I'M IN THE THEATRE DEPARTMENT AT V.C.U.
THEATRE?
WHAT?
LOOK I KNOW YOU WANTED ME TO RUN THIS PLACE LIKE YOU..
AND I THOUGHT ABOUT THIS A LONG TIME, DAD... I LOVE YOU BUT...
JOURNALISM..
IT'S JUST...
IT'S NOT ME DADDY.

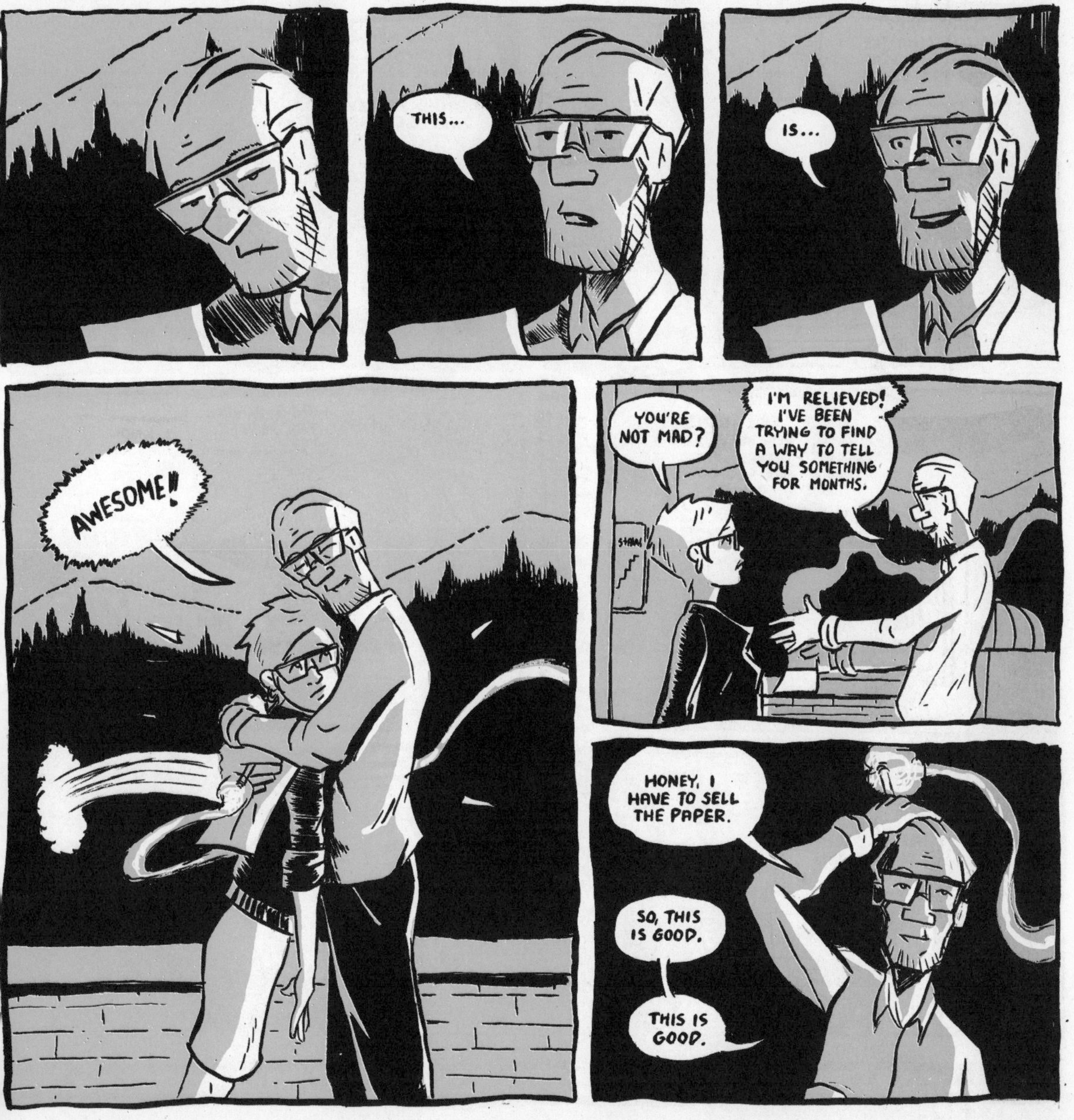
THIS...
IS...
AWESOME!!
YOU'RE NOT MAD?
I'M RELIEVED! I'VE BEEN TRYING TO FIND A WAY TO TELL YOU SOMETHING FOR MONTHS.
HONEY, I HAVE TO SELL THE PAPER.
SO, THIS IS GOOD.
THIS IS GOOD.

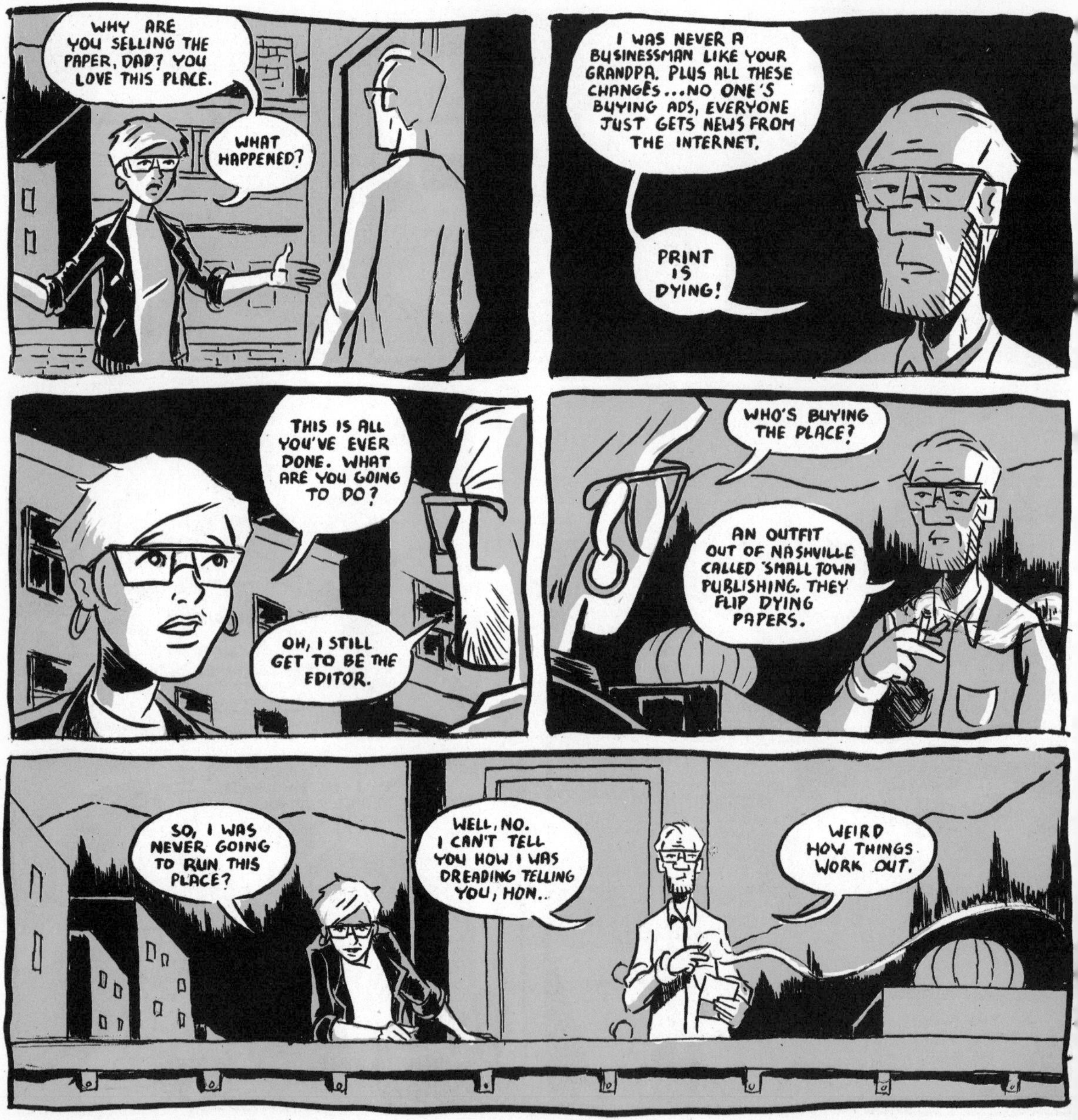
WHY ARE YOU SELLING THE PAPER, DAD? YOU LOVE THIS PLACE.
WHAT HAPPENED?
I WAS NEVER A BUSINESSMAN LIKE YOUR GRANDPA. PLUS ALL THESE CHANGES...NO ONE'S BUYING ADS, EVERYONE JUST GETS NEWS FROM THE INTERNET.
PRINT IS DYING!
THIS IS ALL YOU'VE EVER DONE. WHAT ARE YOU GOING TO DO?
OH, I STILL GET TO BE THE EDITOR.
WHO'S BUYING THE PLACE?
AN OUTFIT OUT OF NASHVILLE CALLED 'SMALL TOWN PUBLISHING. THEY FLIP DYING PAPERS.
SO, I WAS NEVER GOING TO RUN THIS PLACE?
WELL, NO. I CAN'T TELL YOU HOW I WAS DREADING TELLING YOU, HON..
WEIRD HOW THINGS WORK OUT.

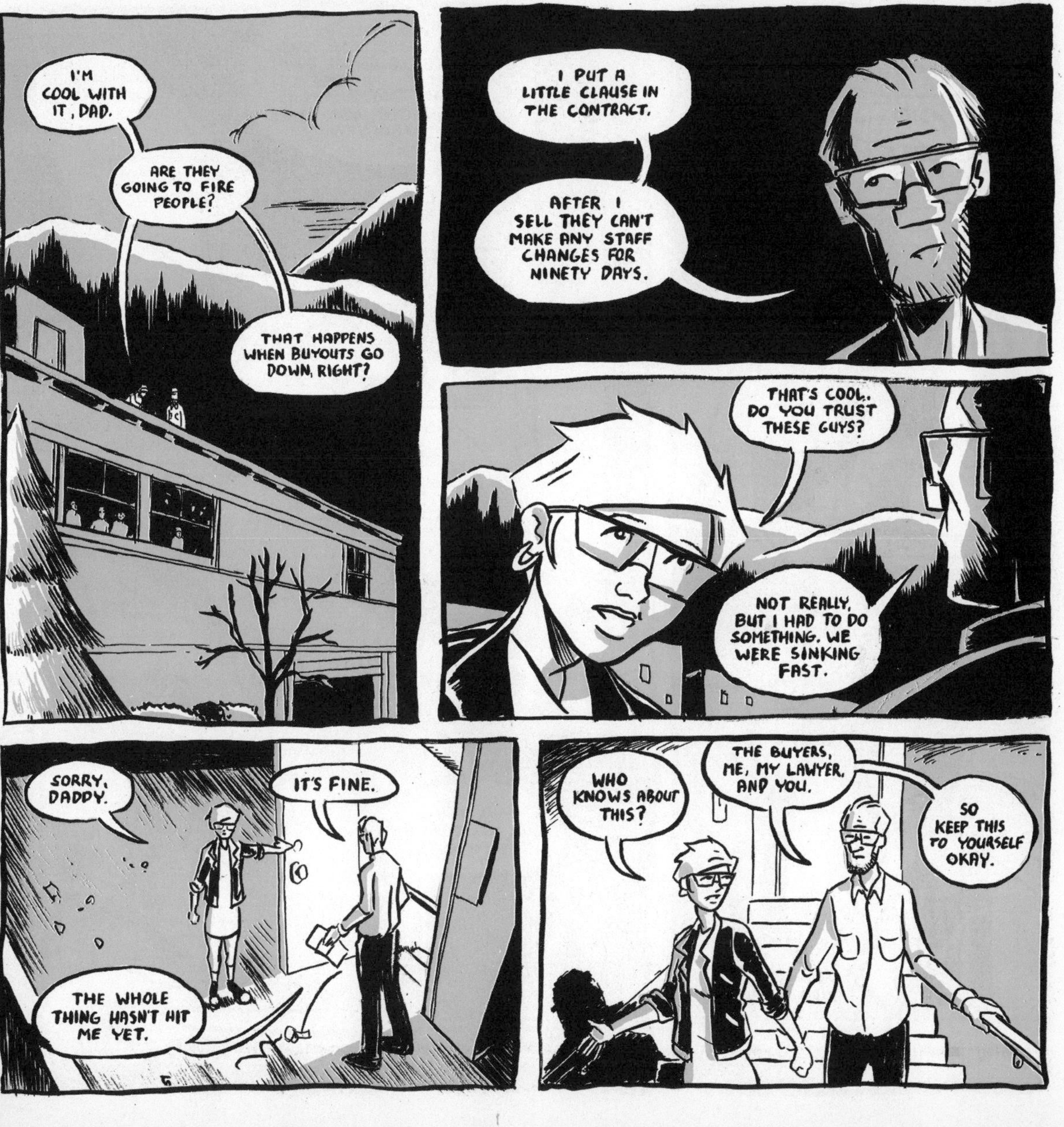
I'M COOL WITH IT, DAD.
ARE THEY GOING TO FIRE PEOPLE?
THAT HAPPENS WHEN BUYOUTS GO DOWN, RIGHT?
I PUT A LITTLE CLAUSE IN THE CONTRACT.
AFTER I SELL THEY CAN'T MAKE ANY STAFF CHANGES FOR NINETY DAYS.
THAT'S COOL. DO YOU TRUST THESE GUYS?
NOT REALLY, BUT I HAD TO DO SOMETHING. WE WERE SINKING FAST.
SORRY, DADDY.
IT'S FINE.
THE WHOLE THING HASN'T HIT ME YET.
WHO KNOWS ABOUT THIS?
THE BUYERS, ME, MY LAWYER, AND YOU.
SO KEEP THIS TO YOURSELF OKAY.

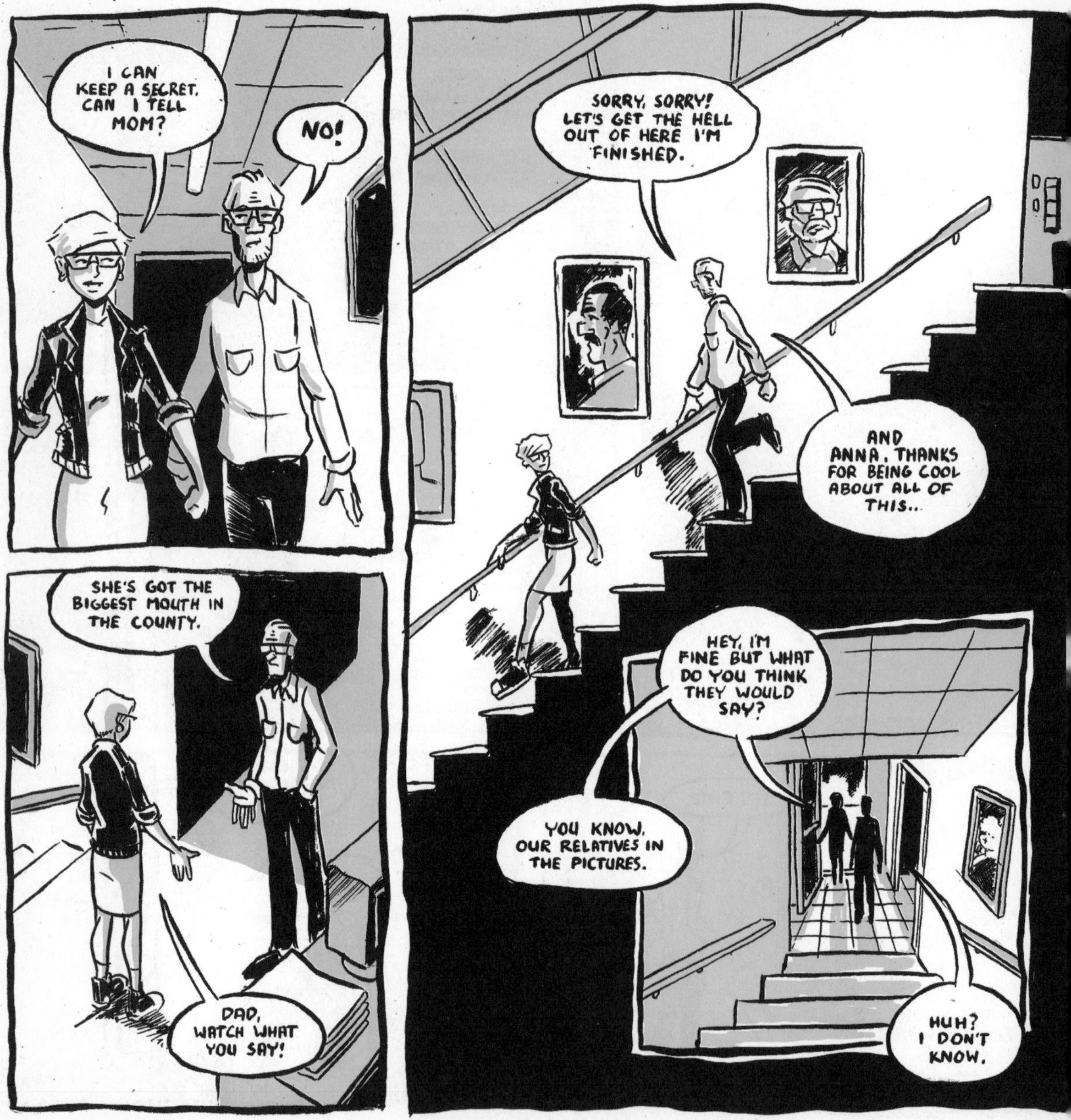
I CAN KEEP A SECRET. CAN I TELL MOM?
NO!
SHE'S GOT THE BIGGEST MOUTH IN THE COUNTY.
DAD, WATCH WHAT YOU SAY!
SORRY, SORRY! LET'S GET THE HELL OUT OF HERE I'M FINISHED.
AND ANNA, THANKS FOR BEING COOL ABOUT ALL OF THIS...
HEY, I'M FINE BUT WHAT DO YOU THINK THEY WOULD SAY?
YOU KNOW, OUR RELATIVES IN THE PICTURES.
HUH? I DON'T KNOW.

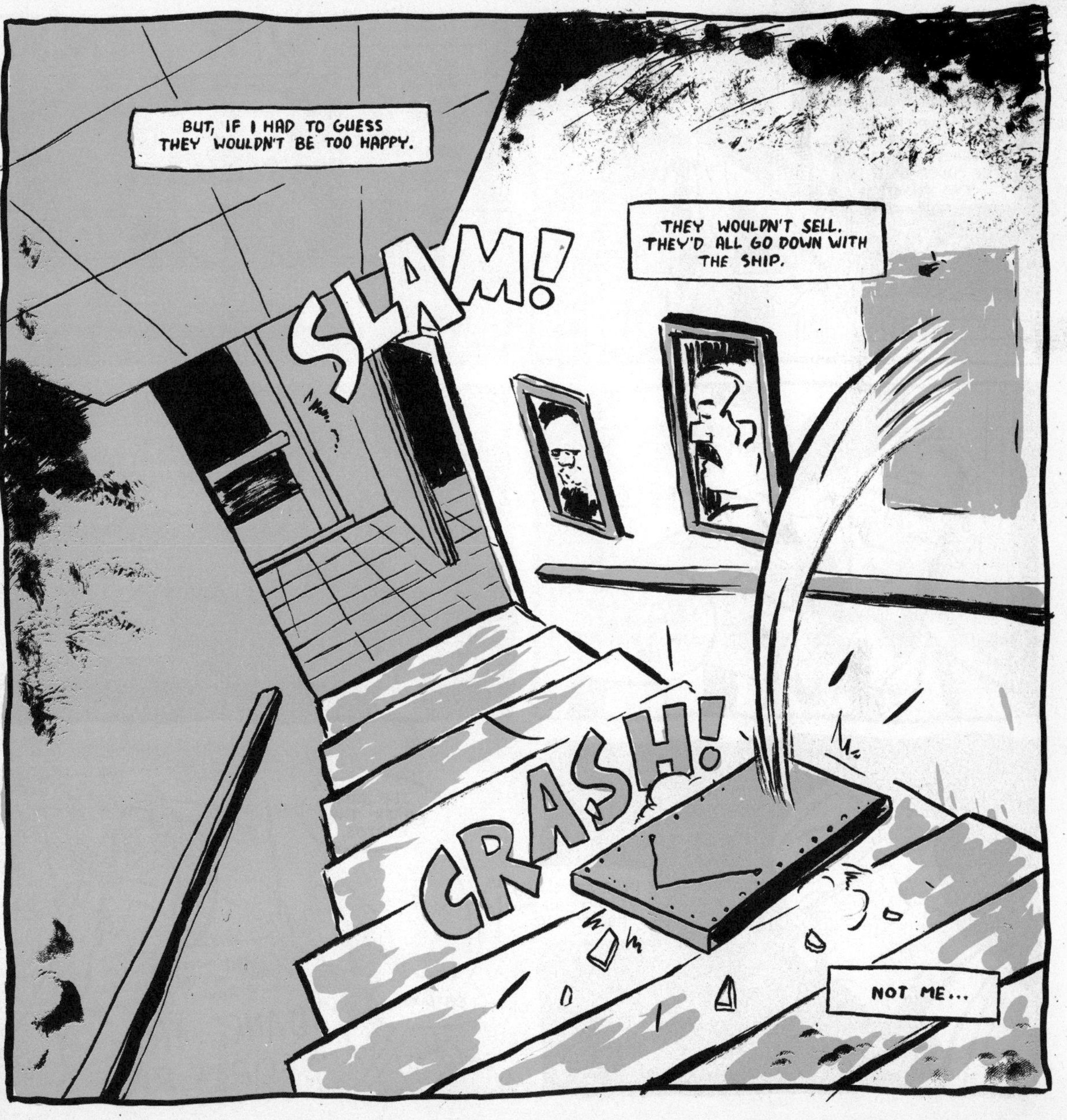
BUT, IF I HAD TO GUESS THEY WOULDN'T BE TOO HAPPY.
THEY WOULDN'T SELL. THEY'D ALL GO DOWN WITH THE SHIP.
SLAM!
CRASH!
NOT ME...

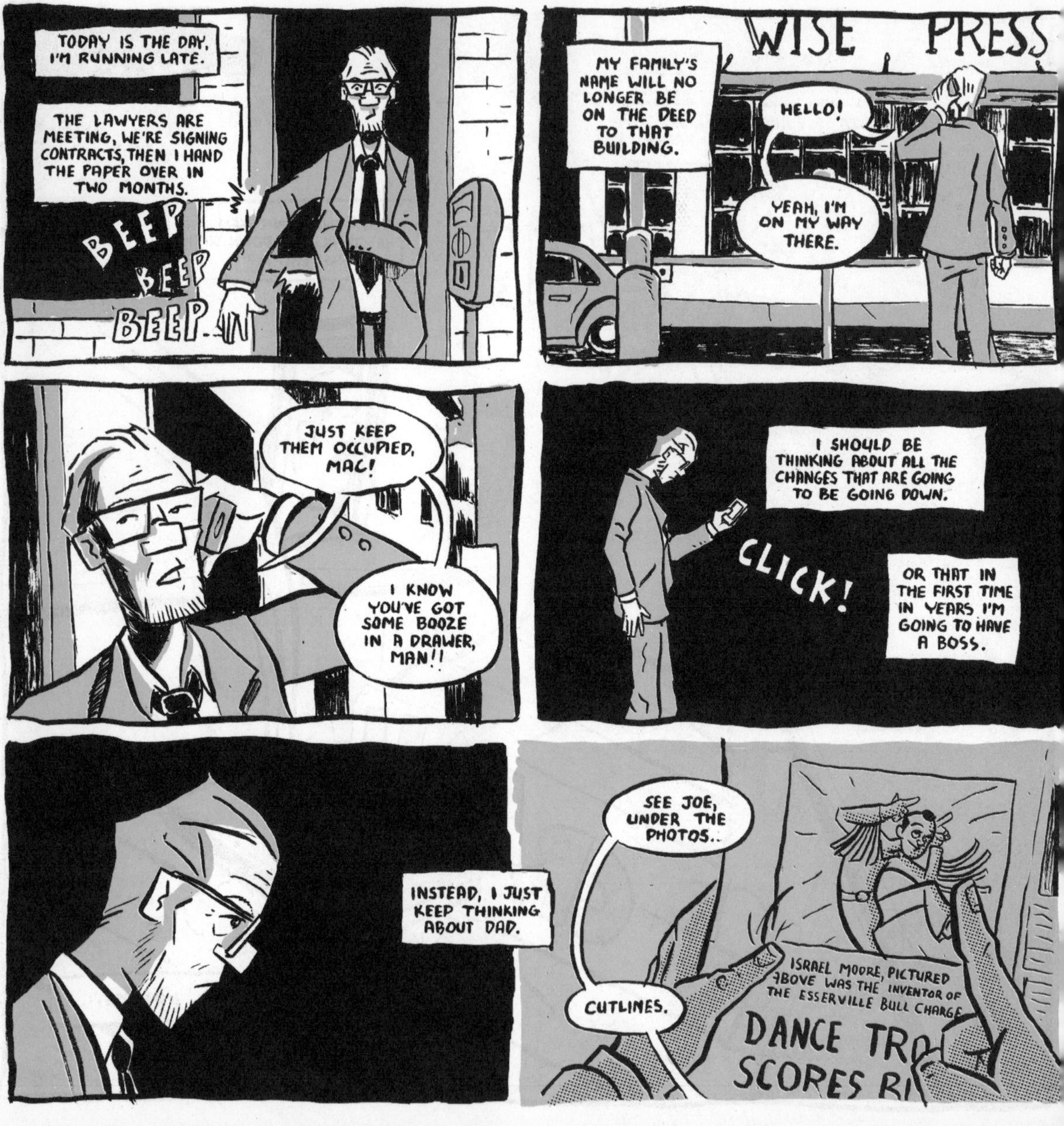
TODAY IS THE DAY, I'M RUNNING LATE.
THE LAWYERS ARE MEETING, WE'RE SIGNING CONTRACTS, THEN I HAND THE PAPER OVER IN TWO MONTHS.
BEEP BEEP BEEP
WISE PRESS
MY FAMILY'S NAME WILL NO LONGER BE ON THE DEED TO THAT BUILDING.
HELLO!
YEAH, I'M ON MY WAY THERE.
JUST KEEP THEM OCCUPIED, MAC!
I KNOW YOU'VE GOT SOME BOOZE IN A DRAWER, MAN!!
I SHOULD BE THINKING ABOUT ALL THE CHANGES THAT ARE GOING TO BE GOING DOWN.
CLICK!
OR THAT IN THE FIRST TIME IN YEARS I'M GOING TO HAVE A BOSS.
INSTEAD, I JUST KEEP THINKING ABOUT DAD.
SEE JOE, UNDER THE PHOTOS..
CUTLINES.
ISRAEL MOORE, PICTURED ABOVE WAS THE INVENTOR OF THE ESSERVILLE BULL CHARGE
DANCE TR
SCORES R

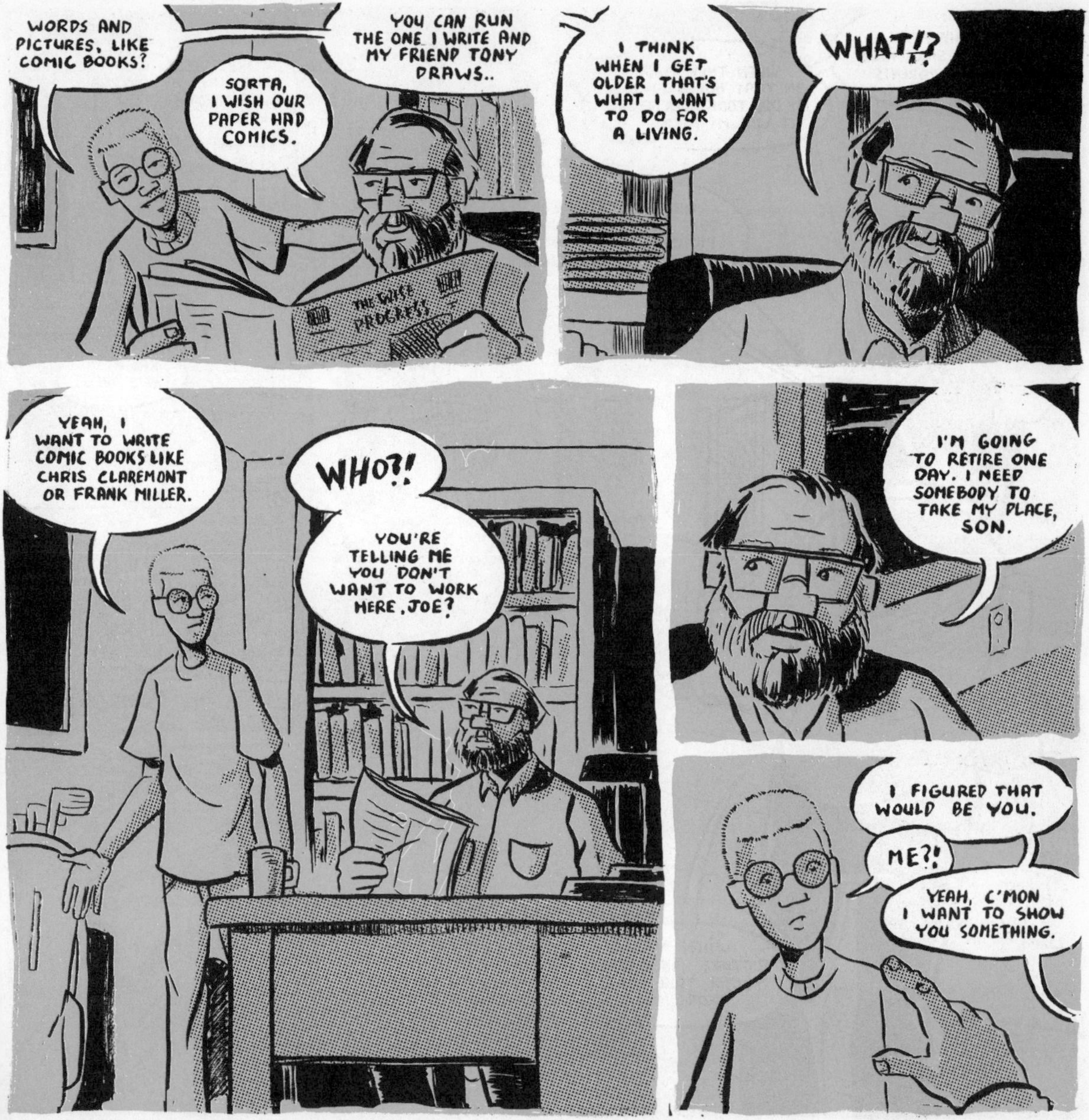
WORDS AND PICTURES, LIKE COMIC BOOKS?
SORTA, I WISH OUR PAPER HAD COMICS.
YOU CAN RUN THE ONE I WRITE AND MY FRIEND TONY DRAWS..
THE WISE PROGRESS
I THINK WHEN I GET OLDER THAT'S WHAT I WANT TO DO FOR A LIVING.
WHAT!?
YEAH, I WANT TO WRITE COMIC BOOKS LIKE CHRIS CLAREMONT OR FRANK MILLER.
WHO?!
YOU'RE TELLING ME YOU DON'T WANT TO WORK HERE, JOE?
I'M GOING TO RETIRE ONE DAY. I NEED SOMEBODY TO TAKE MY PLACE, SON.
I FIGURED THAT WOULD BE YOU.
ME?!
YEAH, C'MON I WANT TO SHOW YOU SOMETHING.

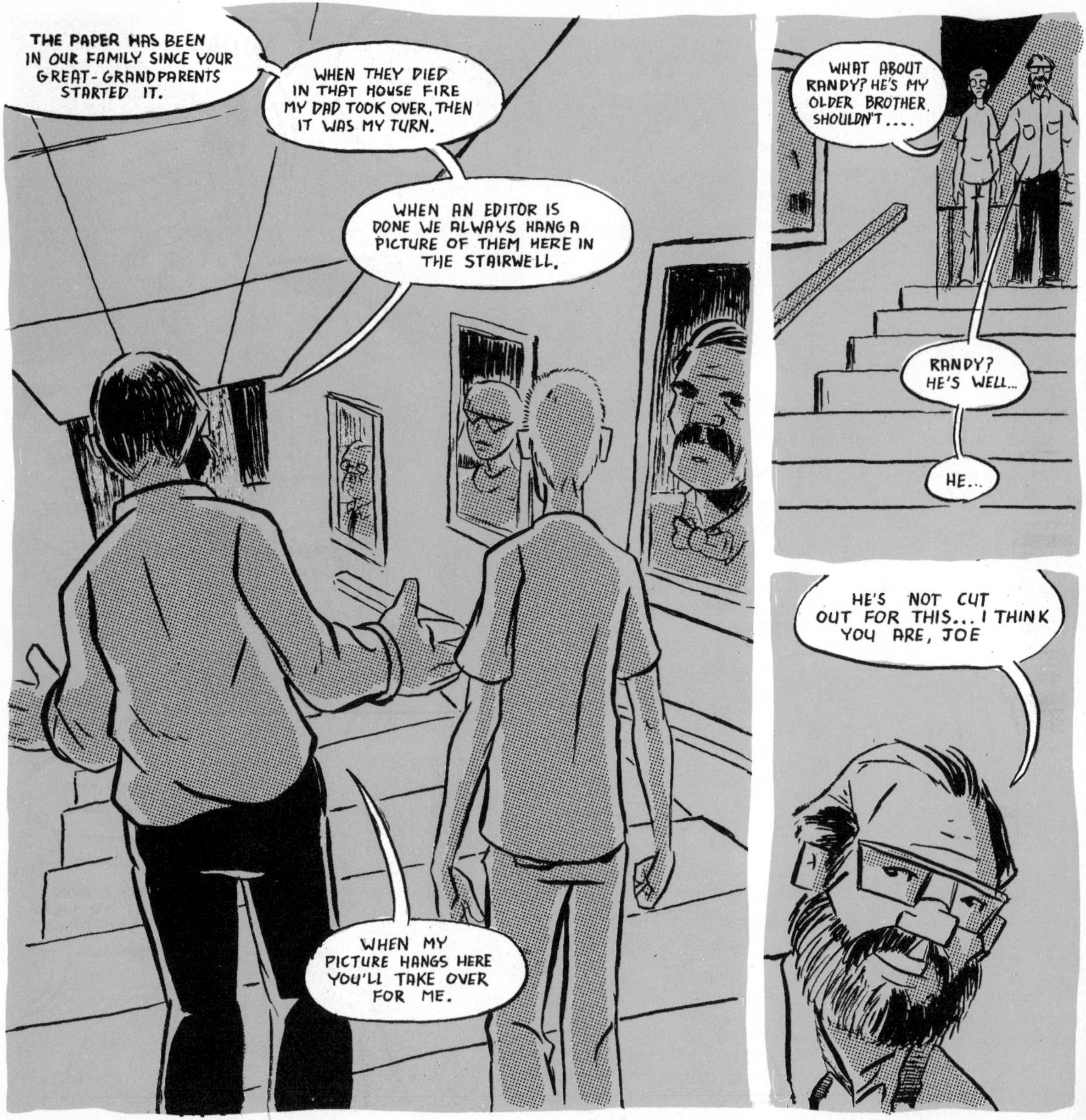
THE PAPER HAS BEEN IN OUR FAMILY SINCE YOUR GREAT-GRANDPARENTS STARTED IT.
WHEN THEY DIED IN THAT HOUSE FIRE MY DAD TOOK OVER, THEN IT WAS MY TURN.
WHEN AN EDITOR IS DONE WE ALWAYS HANG A PICTURE OF THEM HERE IN THE STAIRWELL.
WHEN MY PICTURE HANGS HERE YOU'LL TAKE OVER FOR ME.
WHAT ABOUT RANDY? HE'S MY OLDER BROTHER. SHOULDN'T....
RANDY? HE'S WELL...
HE...
HE'S NOT CUT OUT FOR THIS... I THINK YOU ARE, JOE

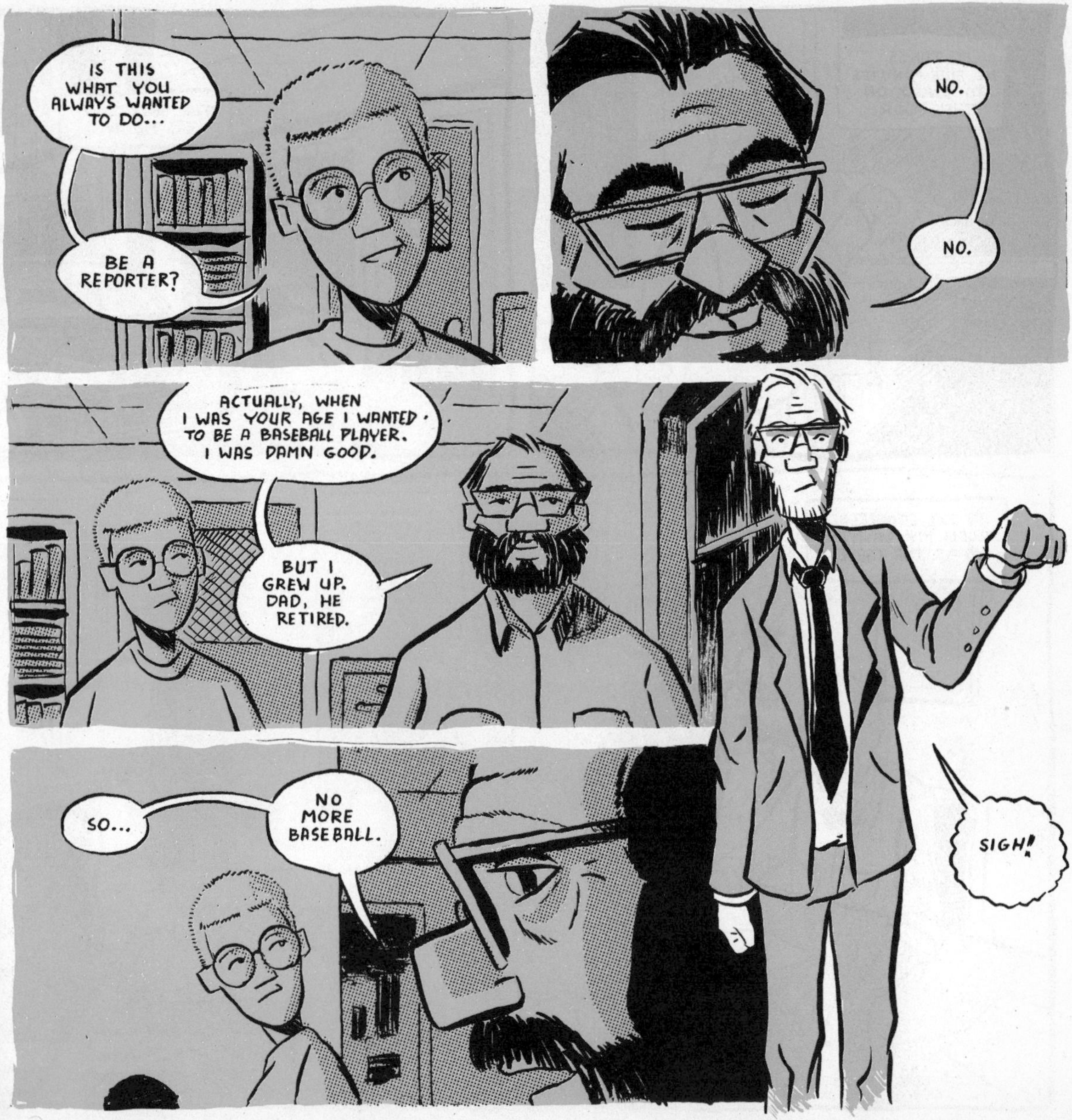
IS THIS WHAT YOU ALWAYS WANTED TO DO...
BE A REPORTER?
NO.
NO.
ACTUALLY, WHEN I WAS YOUR AGE I WANTED TO BE A BASEBALL PLAYER. I WAS DAMN GOOD.
BUT I GREW UP. DAD, HE RETIRED.
SO...
NO MORE BASEBALL.
SIGH!

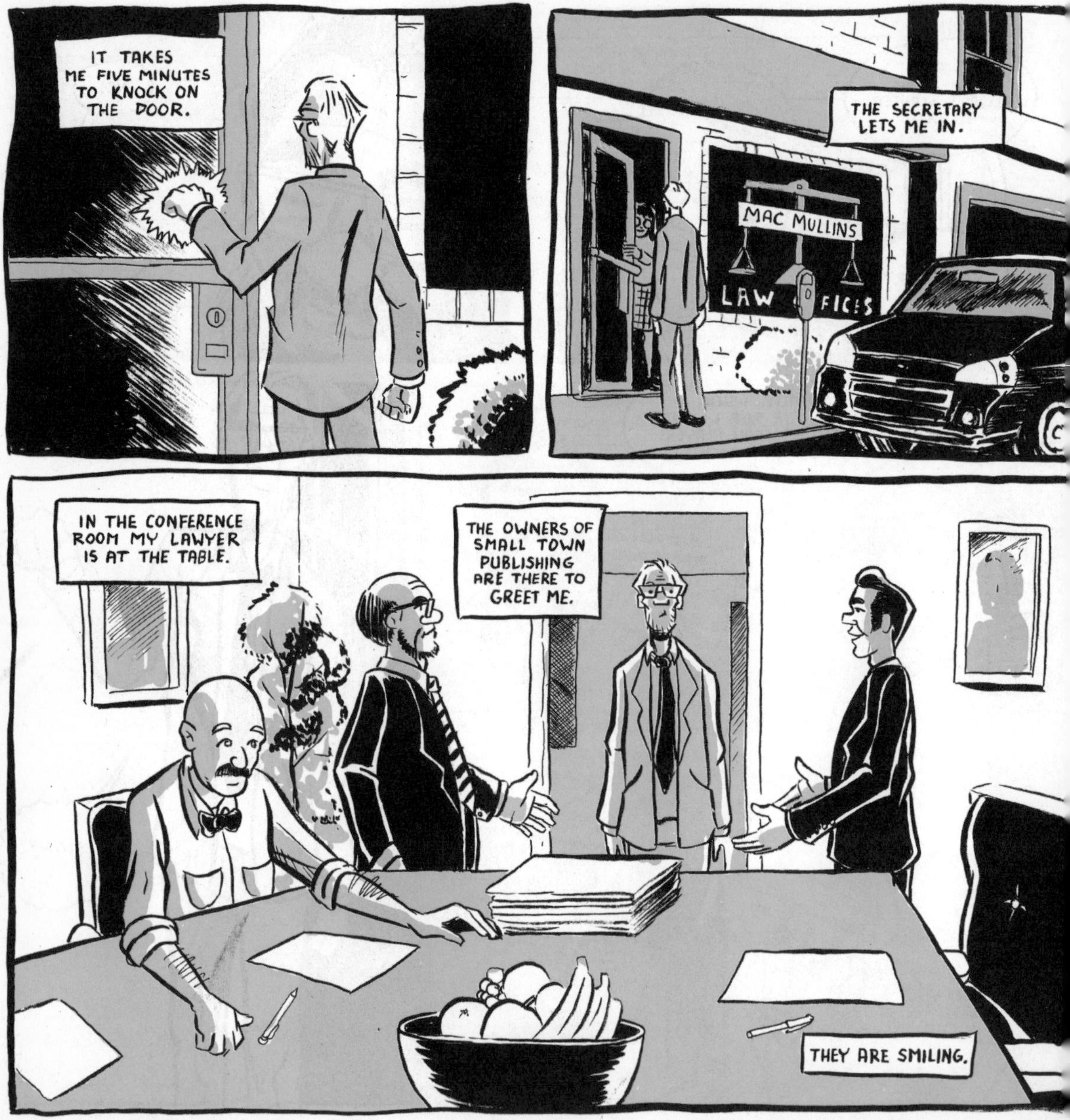
IT TAKES ME FIVE MINUTES TO KNOCK ON THE DOOR.
THE SECRETARY LETS ME IN.
MAC MULLINS
LAW
FICES
IN THE CONFERENCE ROOM MY LAWYER IS AT THE TABLE.
THE OWNERS OF SMALL TOWN PUBLISHING ARE THERE TO GREET ME.
THEY ARE SMILING.

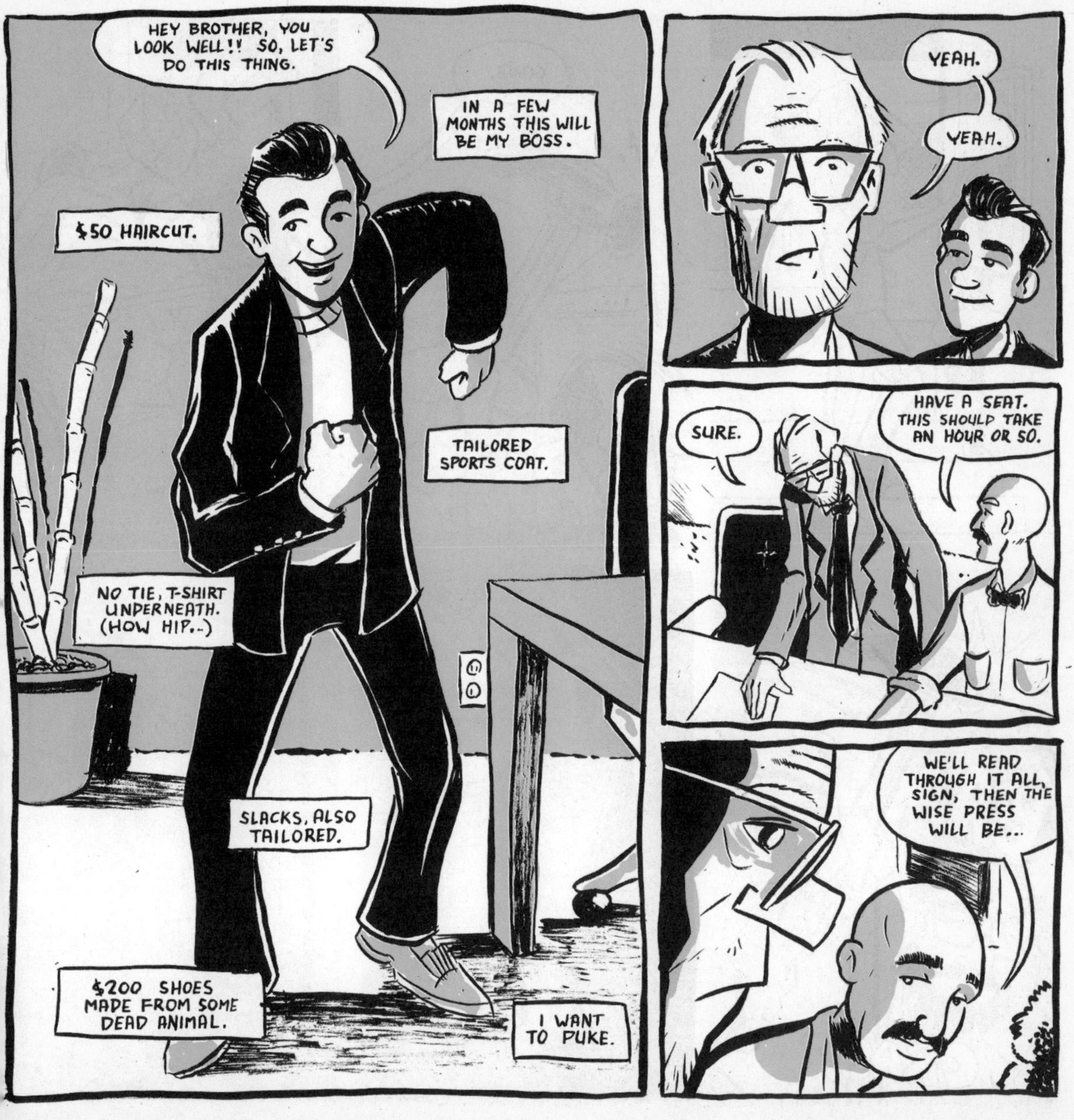
HEY BROTHER, YOU LOOK WELL!! SO, LET'S DO THIS THING.
IN A FEW MONTHS THIS WILL BE MY BOSS.
$50 HAIRCUT.
TAILORED SPORTS COAT.
NO TIE, T-SHIRT UNDERNEATH. (HOW HIP..)
SLACKS, ALSO TAILORED.
$200 SHOES MADE FROM SOME DEAD ANIMAL.
I WANT TO PUKE.
YEAH.
YEAH.
HAVE A SEAT. THIS SHOULD TAKE AN HOUR OR SO.
SURE.
WE'LL READ THROUGH IT ALL, SIGN, THEN THE WISE PRESS WILL BE...

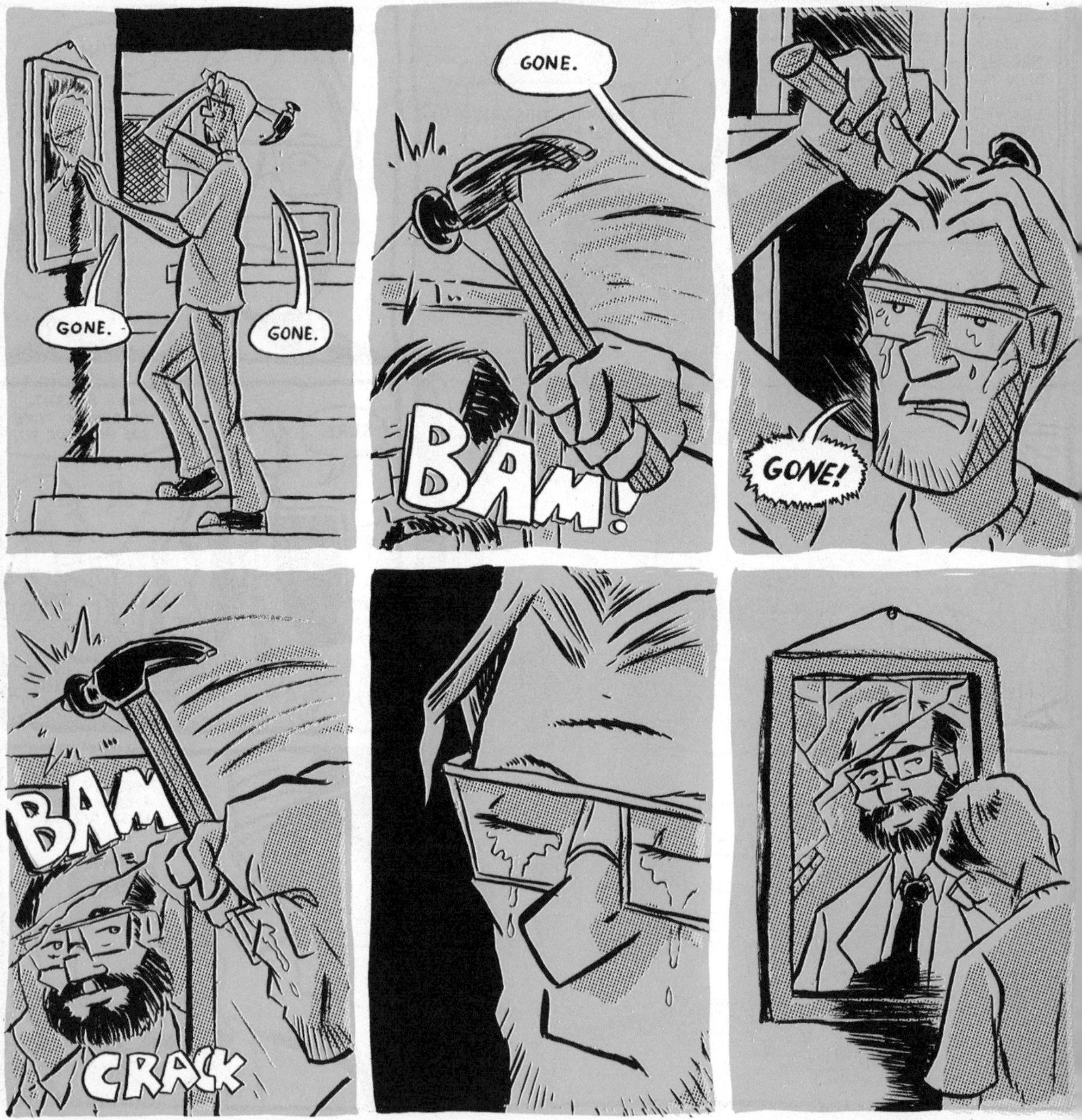
GONE.
GONE.
GONE.
BAM!
GONE!
BAM
CRACK

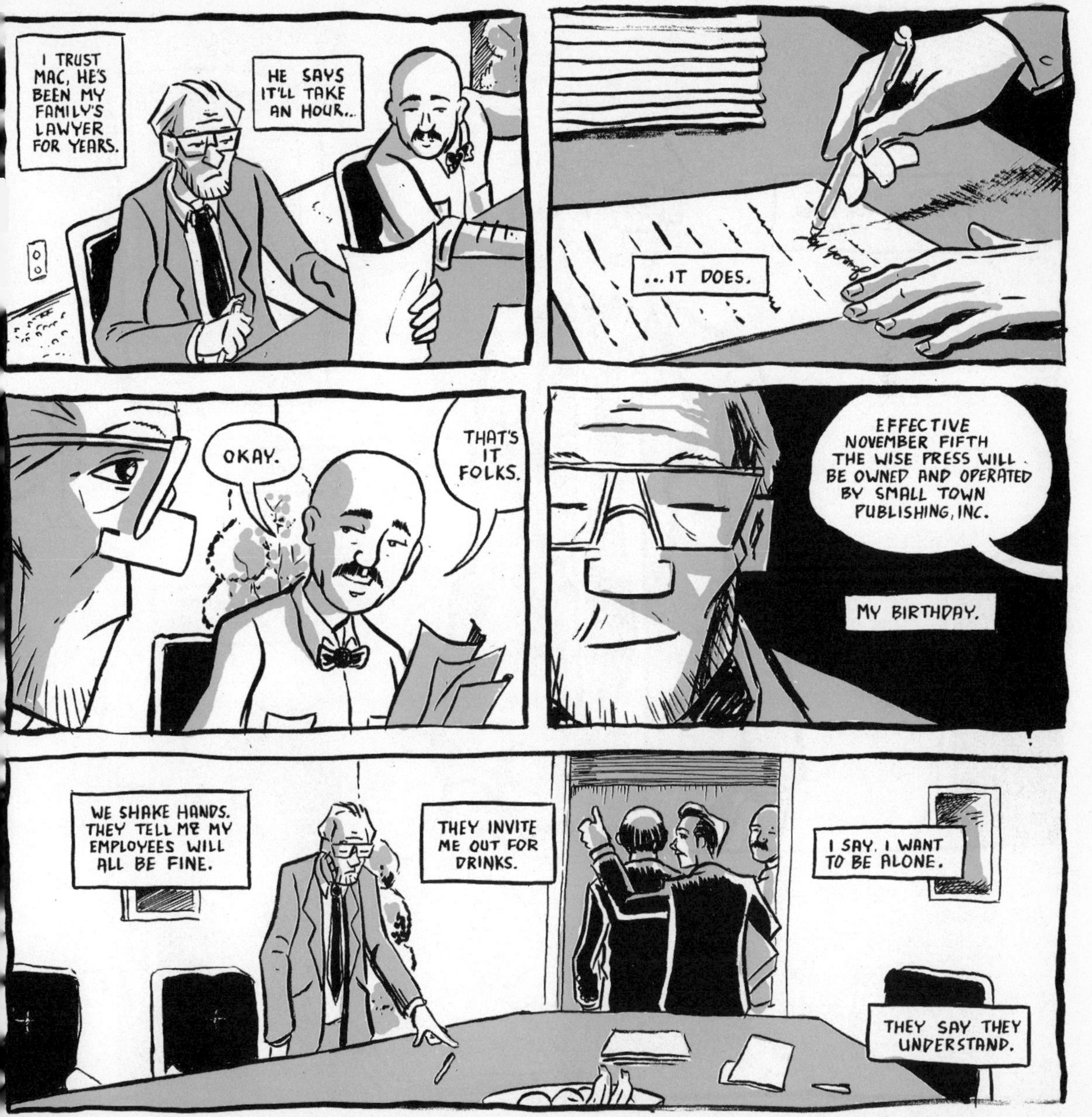
I TRUST MAC, HE'S BEEN MY FAMILY'S LAWYER FOR YEARS.
HE SAYS IT'LL TAKE AN HOUR...
...IT DOES.
OKAY.
THAT'S IT FOLKS.
EFFECTIVE NOVEMBER FIFTH THE WISE PRESS WILL BE OWNED AND OPERATED BY SMALL TOWN PUBLISHING, INC.
MY BIRTHDAY.
WE SHAKE HANDS. THEY TELL ME MY EMPLOYEES WILL ALL BE FINE.
THEY INVITE ME OUT FOR DRINKS.
I SAY, I WANT TO BE ALONE.
THEY SAY THEY UNDERSTAND.

MY FAMILY'S BUSINESS FOR OVER SIXTY YEARS...
GONE...
IN A MERE FUCKING HOUR.
TAP TAP TAP
TAP TAP

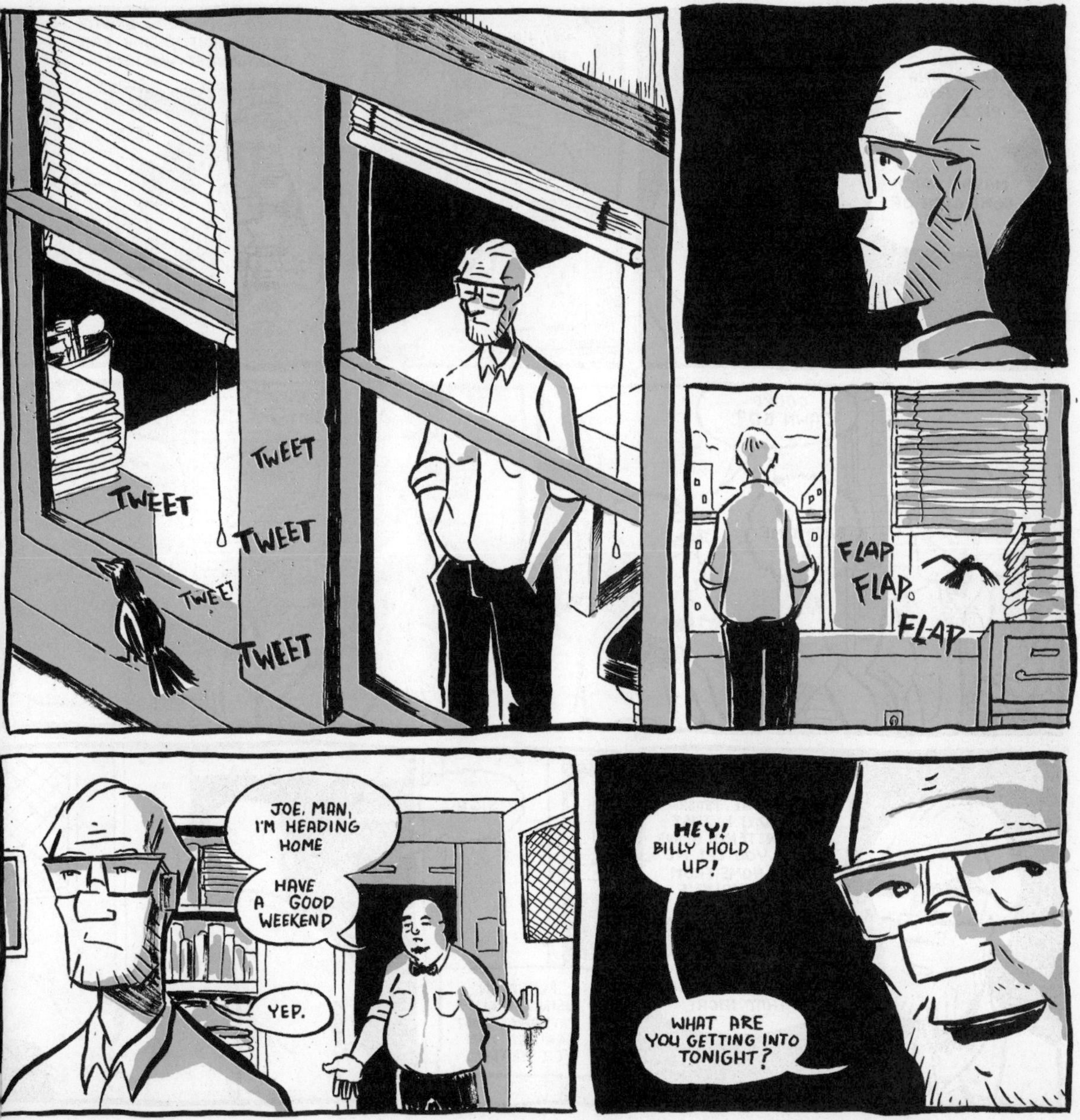
TWEET
TWEET
TWEET
TWEET
TWEET
FLAP
FLAP.
FLAP
JOE, MAN, I'M HEADING HOME
HAVE A GOOD WEEKEND
YEP.
HEY! BILLY HOLD UP!
WHAT ARE YOU GETTING INTO TONIGHT?

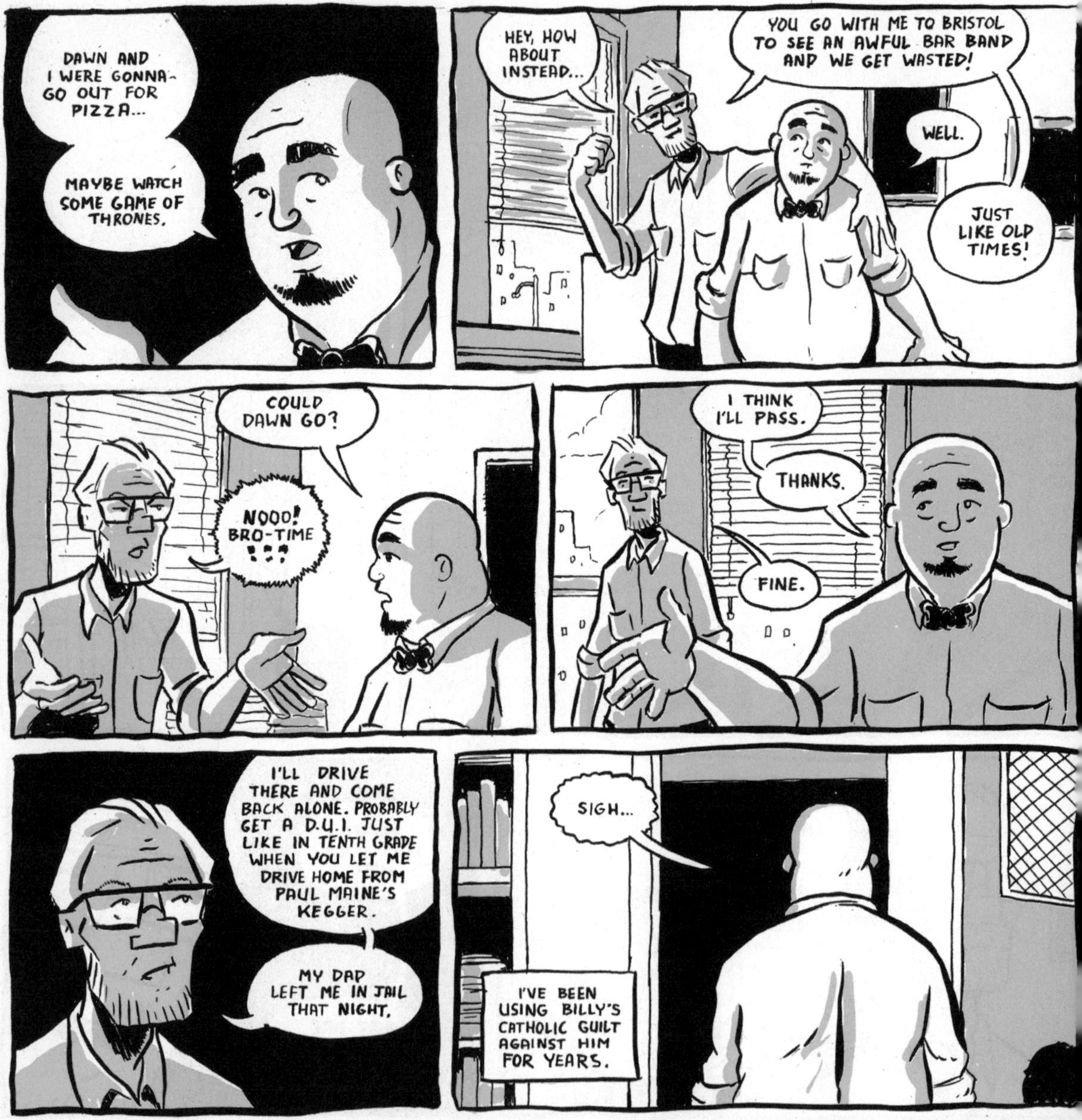
DAWN AND I WERE GONNA GO OUT FOR PIZZA...
MAYBE WATCH SOME GAME OF THRONES.
HEY, HOW ABOUT INSTEAD...
YOU GO WITH ME TO BRISTOL TO SEE AN AWFUL BAR BAND AND WE GET WASTED!
WELL.
JUST LIKE OLD TIMES!
COULD DAWN GO?
NOOO! BRO-TIME!!!
I THINK I'LL PASS.
THANKS.
FINE.
I'LL DRIVE THERE AND COME BACK ALONE. PROBABLY GET A D.U.I. JUST LIKE IN TENTH GRADE WHEN YOU LET ME DRIVE HOME FROM PAUL MAINE'S KEGGER.
MY DAD LEFT ME IN JAIL THAT NIGHT.
SIGH...
I'VE BEEN USING BILLY'S CATHOLIC GUILT AGAINST HIM FOR YEARS.

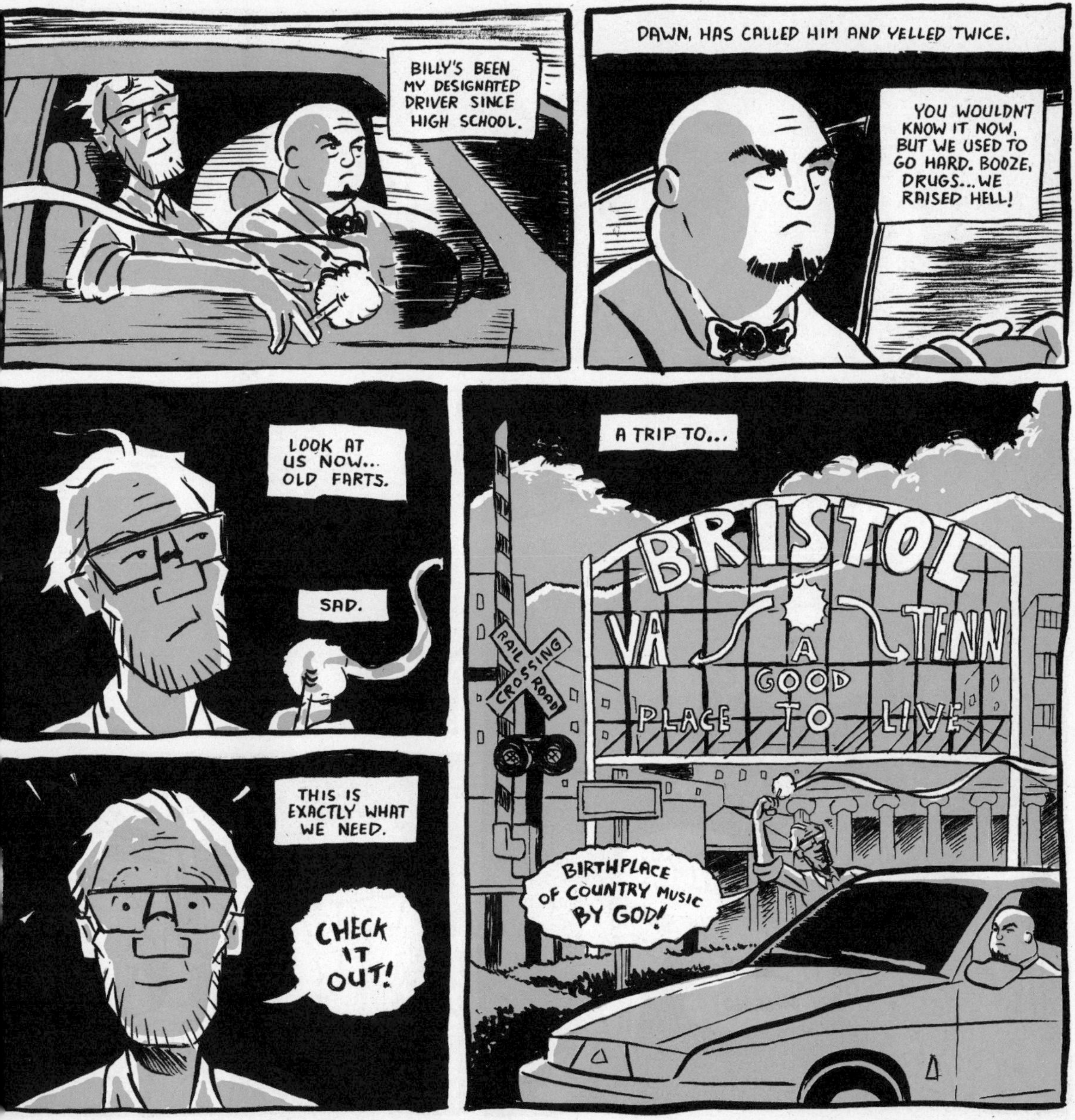
BILLY'S BEEN MY DESIGNATED DRIVER SINCE HIGH SCHOOL.
DAWN, HAS CALLED HIM AND YELLED TWICE.
YOU WOULDN'T KNOW IT NOW, BUT WE USED TO GO HARD. BOOZE, DRUGS... WE RAISED HELL!
LOOK AT US NOW... OLD FARTS.
SAD.
THIS IS EXACTLY WHAT WE NEED.
CHECK IT OUT!
A TRIP TO...
BRISTOL
VA
TENN
A GOOD PLACE TO LIVE
RAIL ROAD CROSSING
BIRTHPLACE OF COUNTRY MUSIC BY GOD!

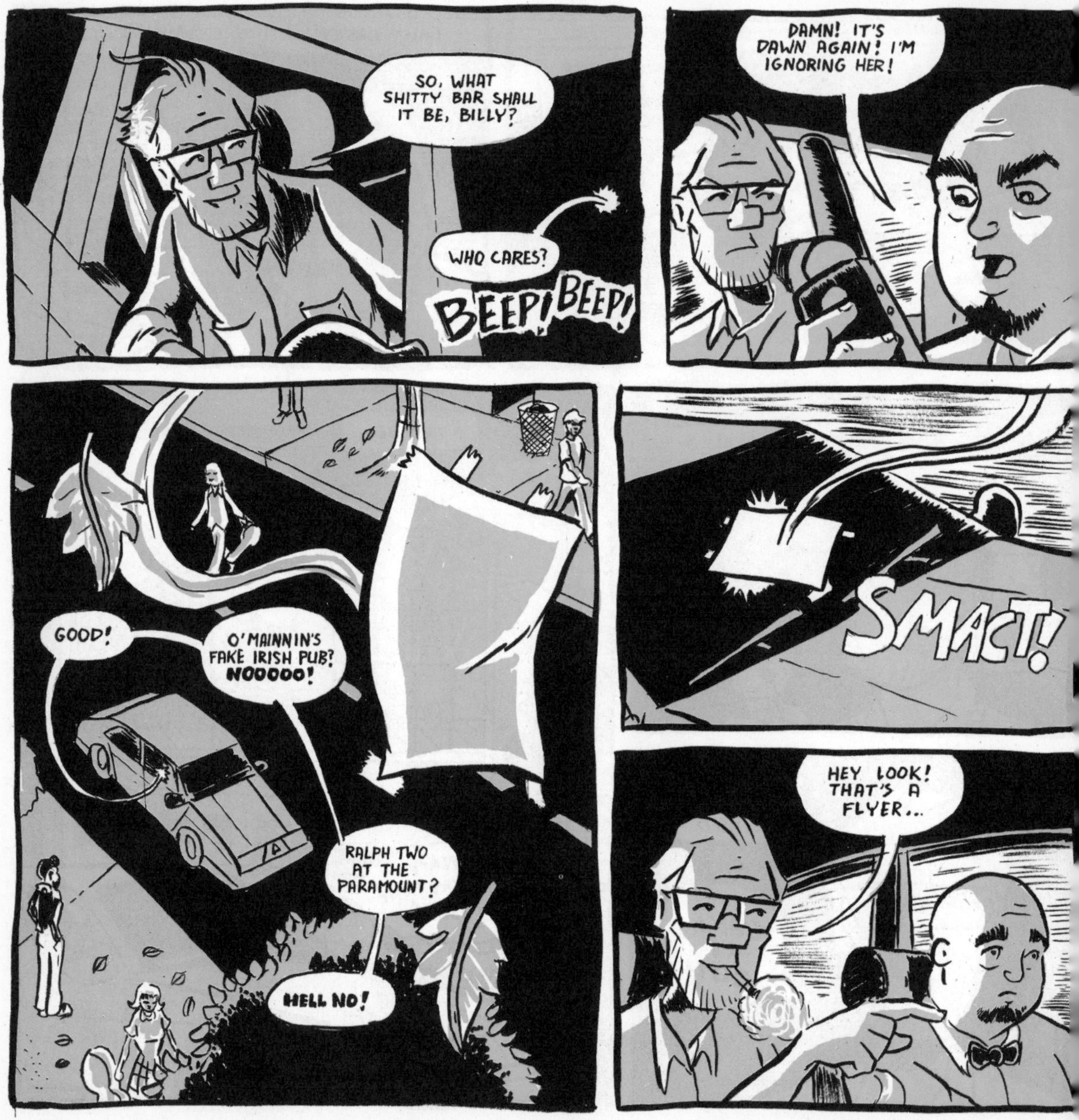
SO, WHAT SHITTY BAR SHALL IT BE, BILLY?
WHO CARES?
BEEP! BEEP!
DAMN! IT'S DAWN AGAIN! I'M IGNORING HER!
GOOD!
O'MAINNIN'S FAKE IRISH PUB? NOOOOO!
RALPH TWO AT THE PARAMOUNT?
HELL NO!
SMACT!
HEY LOOK! THAT'S A FLYER...

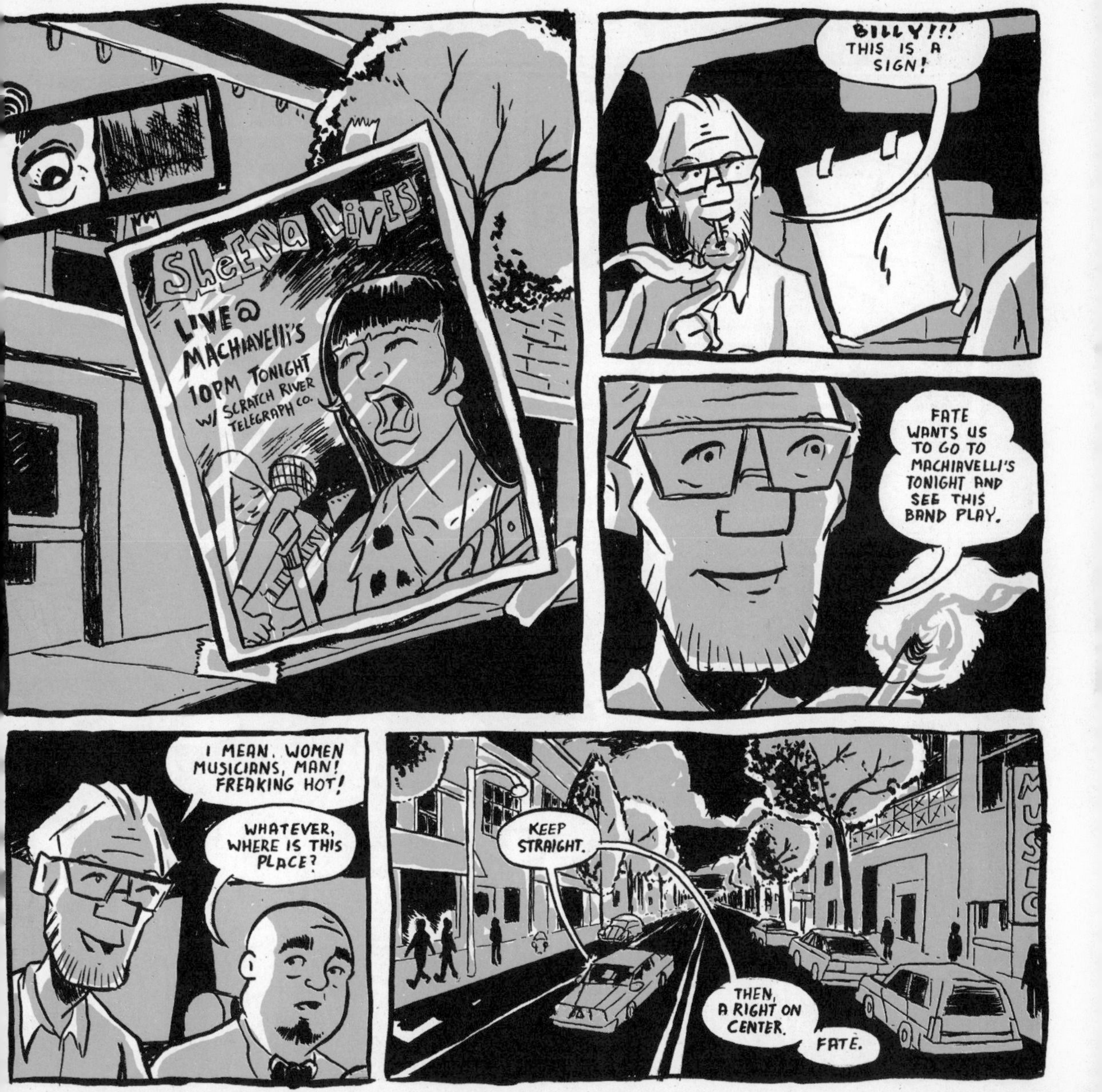
SHEENA LIVES
LIVE @ MACHIAVELLI'S
10PM TONIGHT
W/ SCRATCH RIVER TELEGRAPH CO.
BILLY!!! THIS IS A SIGN!
FATE WANTS US TO GO TO MACHIAVELLI'S TONIGHT AND SEE THIS BAND PLAY.
I MEAN, WOMEN MUSICIANS, MAN! FREAKING HOT!
WHATEVER, WHERE IS THIS PLACE?
KEEP STRAIGHT.
THEN, A RIGHT ON CENTER.
FATE.
MUSIC

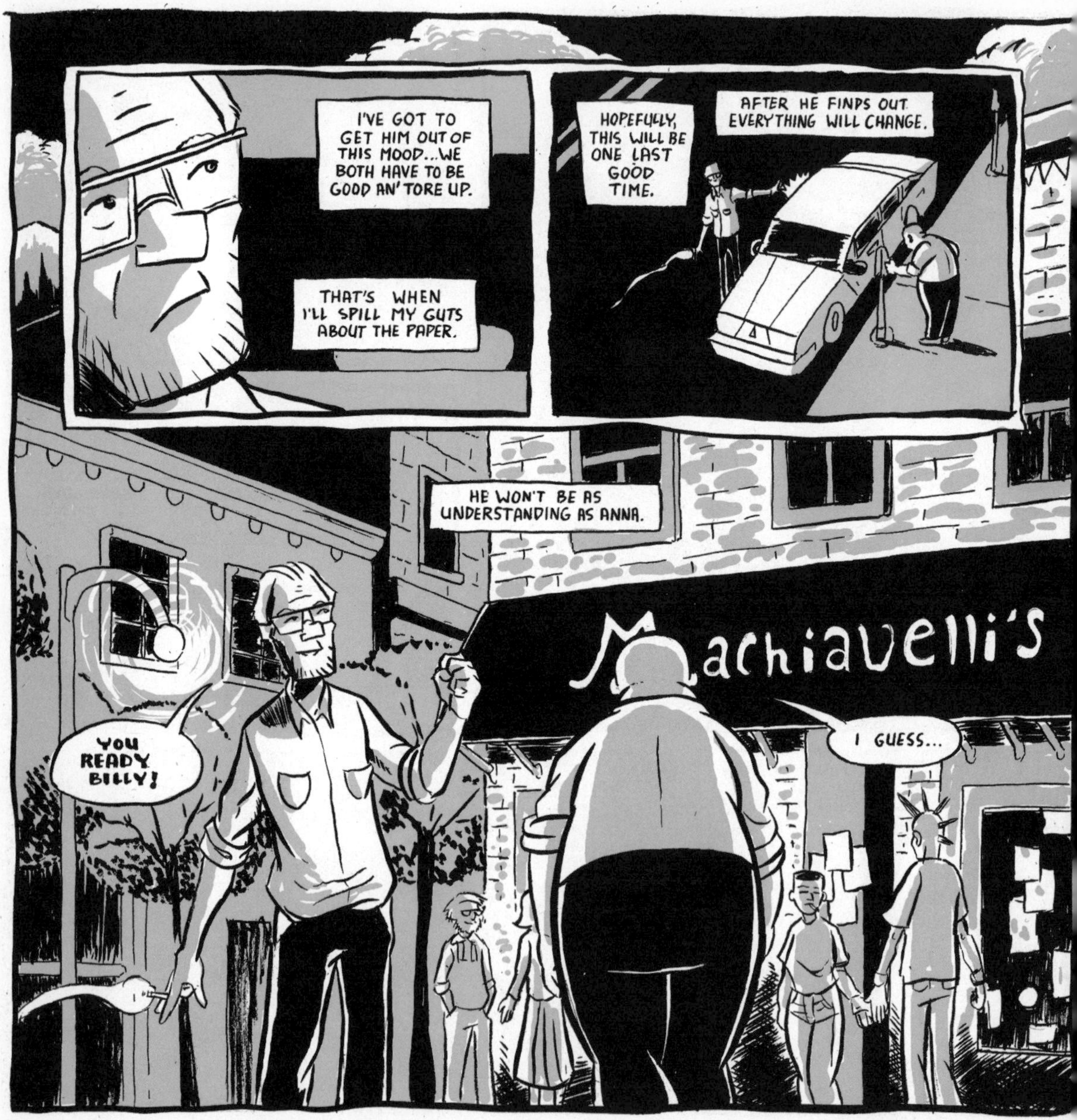
I'VE GOT TO GET HIM OUT OF THIS MOOD...WE BOTH HAVE TO BE GOOD AN' TORE UP.
THAT'S WHEN I'LL SPILL MY GUTS ABOUT THE PAPER.
HOPEFULLY, THIS WILL BE ONE LAST GOOD TIME.
AFTER HE FINDS OUT EVERYTHING WILL CHANGE.
HE WON'T BE AS UNDERSTANDING AS ANNA.
Machiavelli's
YOU READY BILLY!
I GUESS...

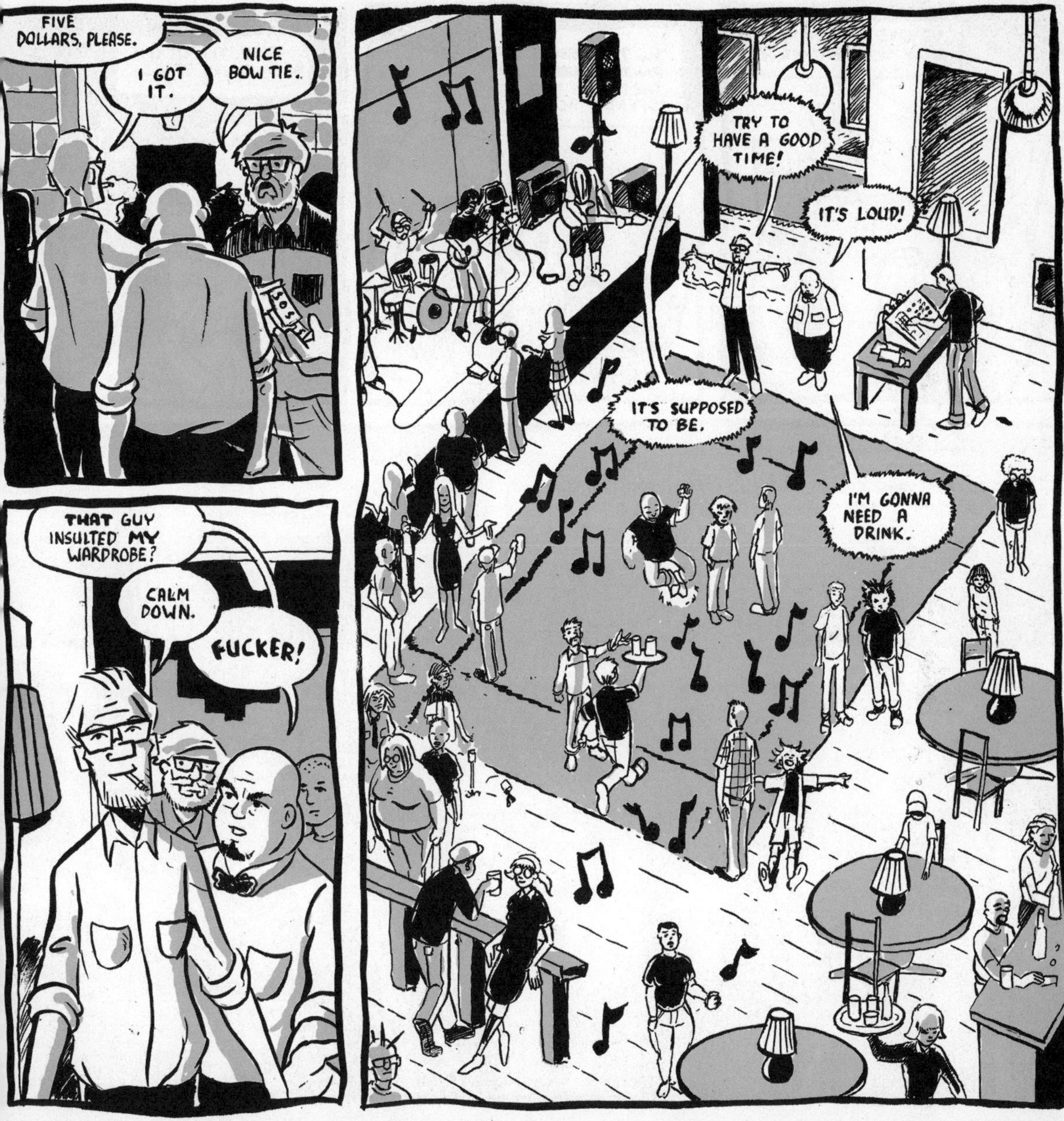
FIVE DOLLARS, PLEASE.
I GOT IT.
NICE BOW TIE..
THAT GUY INSULTED MY WARDROBE?
CALM DOWN.
FUCKER!
TRY TO HAVE A GOOD TIME!
IT'S LOUD!
IT'S SUPPOSED TO BE.
I'M GONNA NEED A DRINK.

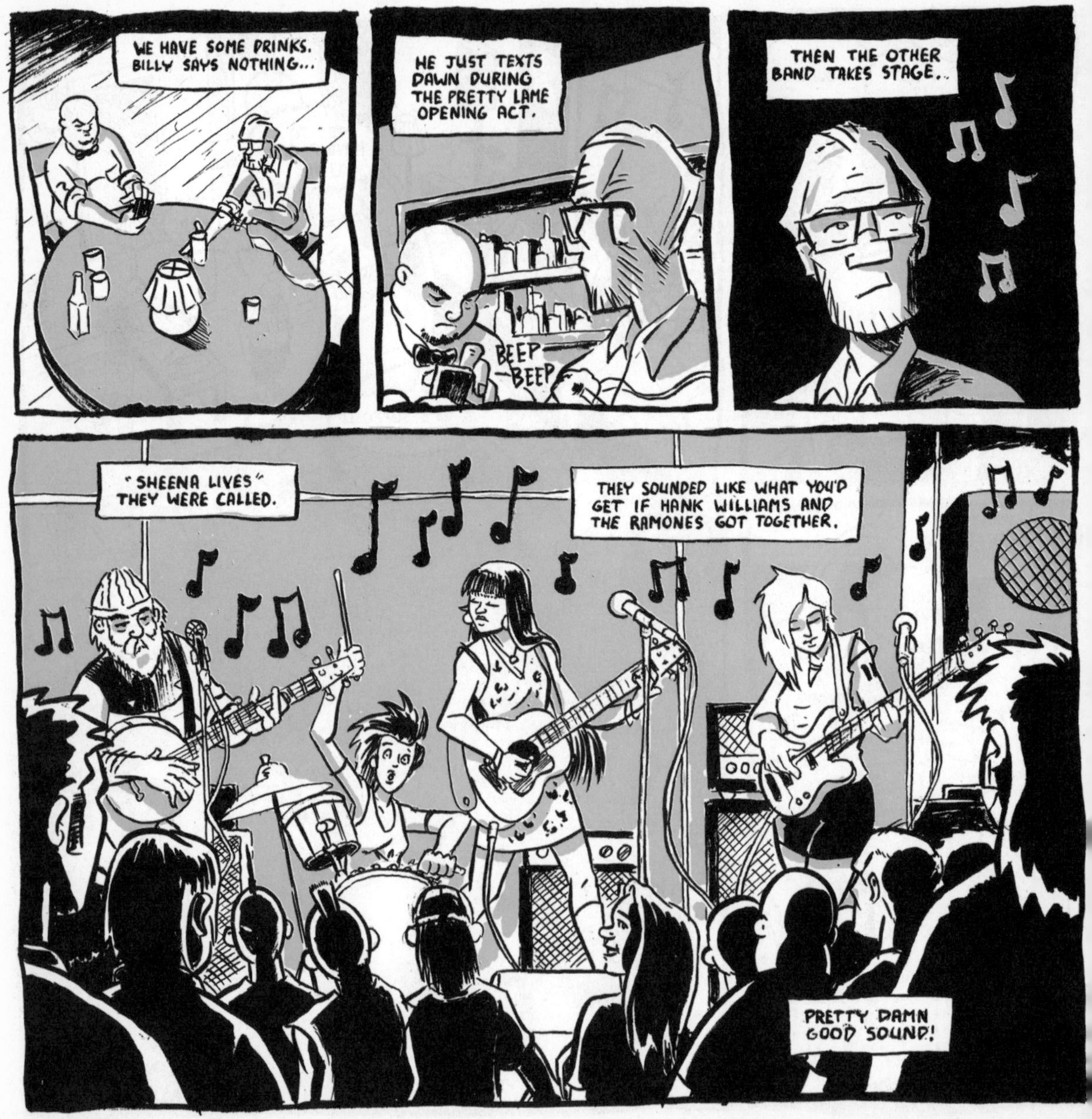
WE HAVE SOME DRINKS. BILLY SAYS NOTHING...
HE JUST TEXTS DAWN DURING THE PRETTY LAME OPENING ACT.
BEEP BEEP
THEN THE OTHER BAND TAKES STAGE...
"SHEENA LIVES" THEY WERE CALLED.
THEY SOUNDED LIKE WHAT YOU'D GET IF HANK WILLIAMS AND THE RAMONES GOT TOGETHER.
PRETTY DAMN GOOD SOUND!

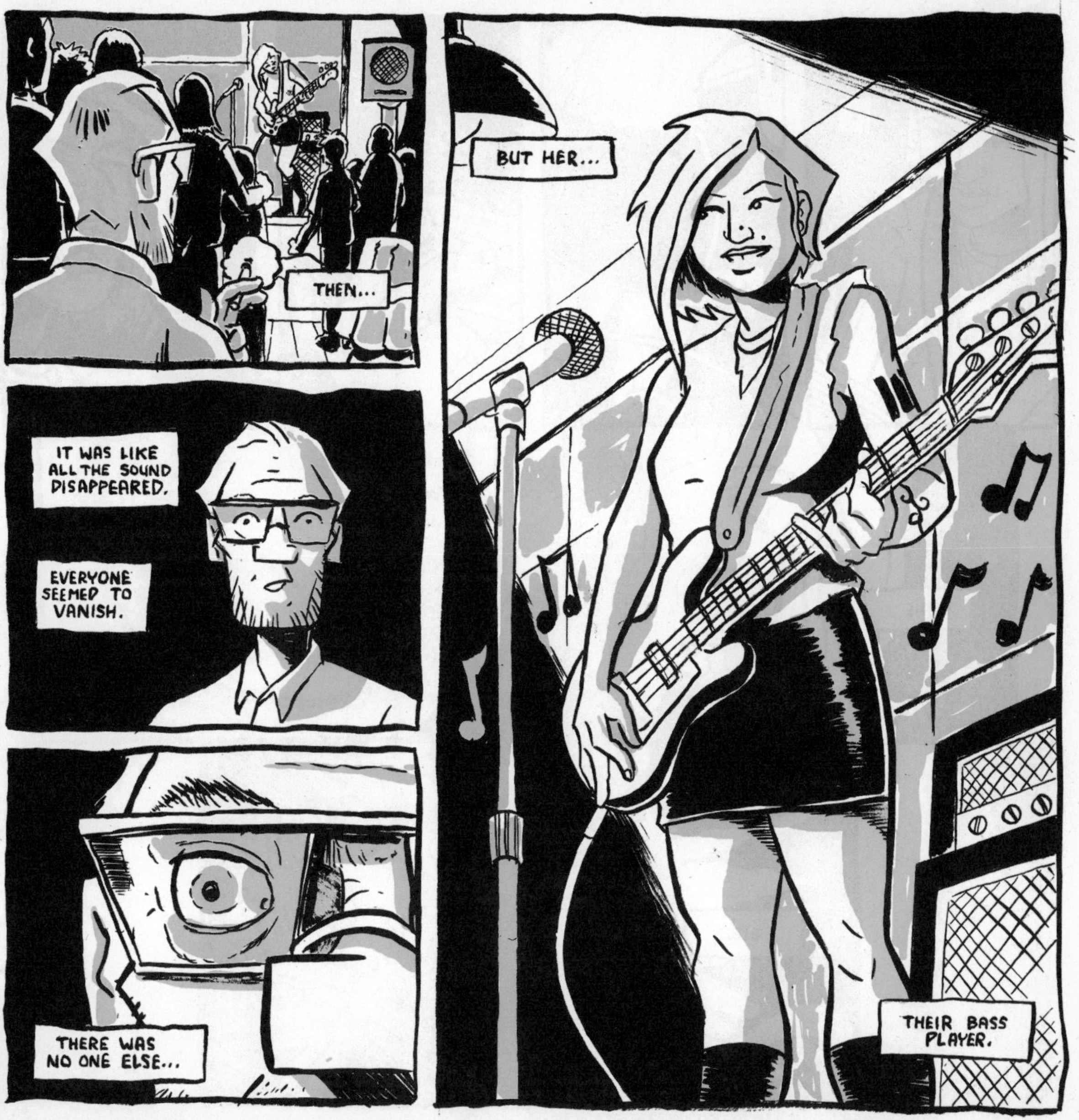
THEN...
IT WAS LIKE ALL THE SOUND DISAPPEARED.
EVERYONE SEEMED TO VANISH.
THERE WAS NO ONE ELSE...
BUT HER...
THEIR BASS PLAYER.

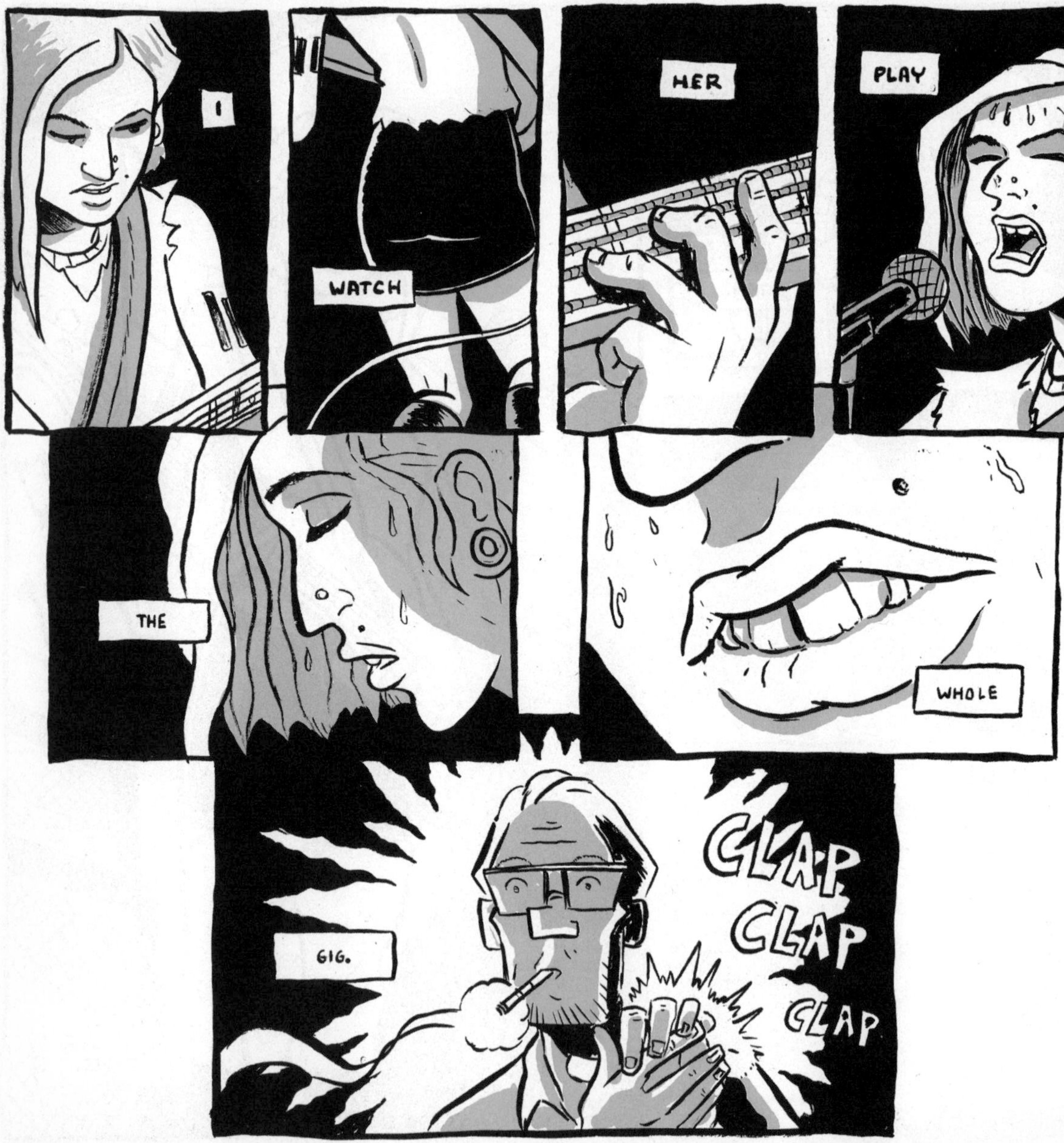
I
WATCH
HER
PLAY
THE
WHOLE
GIG.
CLAP
CLAP
CLAP

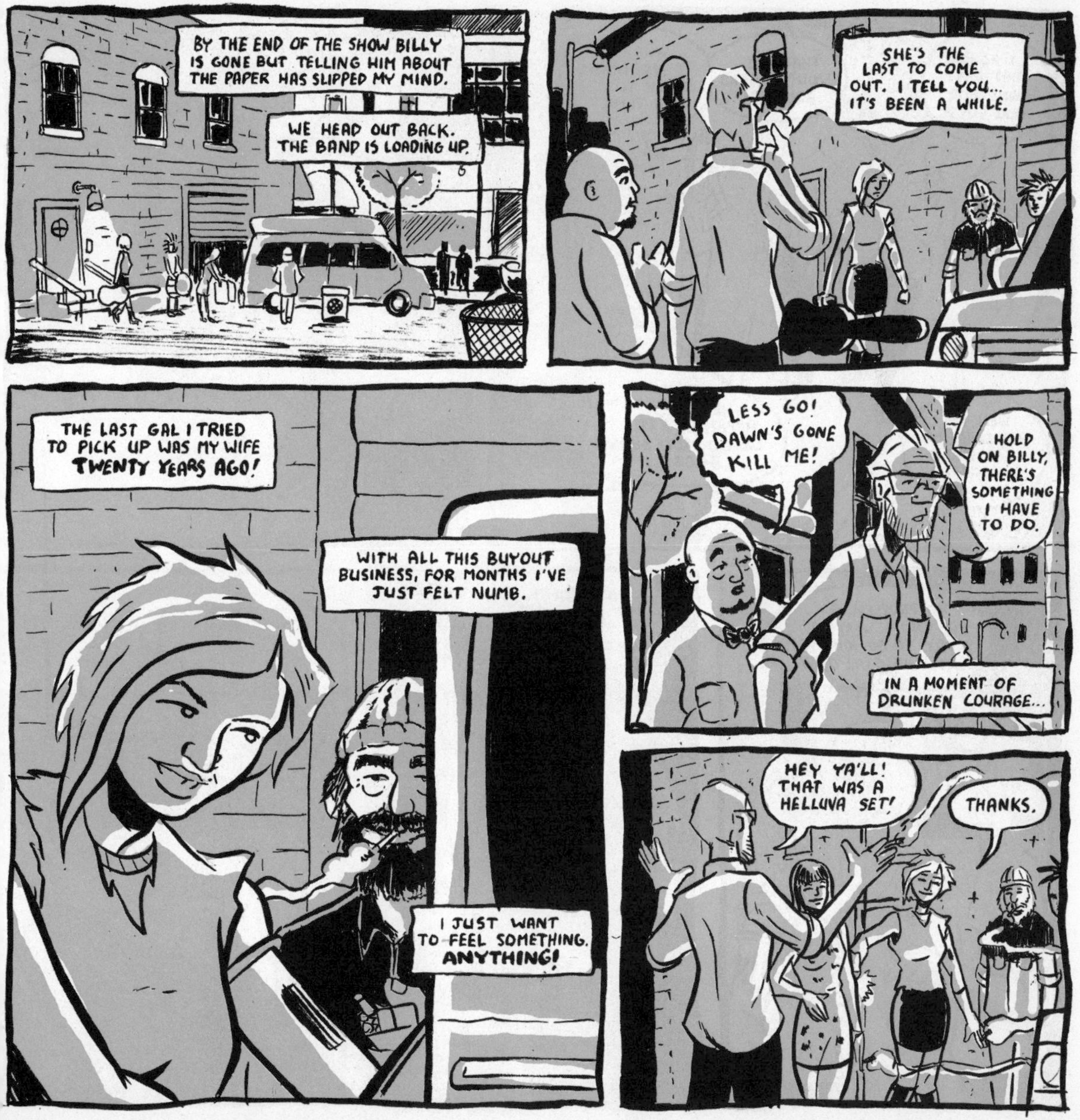
BY THE END OF THE SHOW BILLY IS GONE BUT TELLING HIM ABOUT THE PAPER HAS SLIPPED MY MIND.
WE HEAD OUT BACK. THE BAND IS LOADING UP.
SHE'S THE LAST TO COME OUT. I TELL YOU... IT'S BEEN A WHILE.
THE LAST GAL I TRIED TO PICK UP WAS MY WIFE TWENTY YEARS AGO!
WITH ALL THIS BUYOUT BUSINESS, FOR MONTHS I'VE JUST FELT NUMB.
I JUST WANT TO FEEL SOMETHING. ANYTHING!
LESS GO! DAWN'S GONE KILL ME!
HOLD ON BILLY, THERE'S SOMETHING I HAVE TO DO.
IN A MOMENT OF DRUNKEN COURAGE...
HEY YA'LL! THAT WAS A HELLUVA SET!
THANKS.

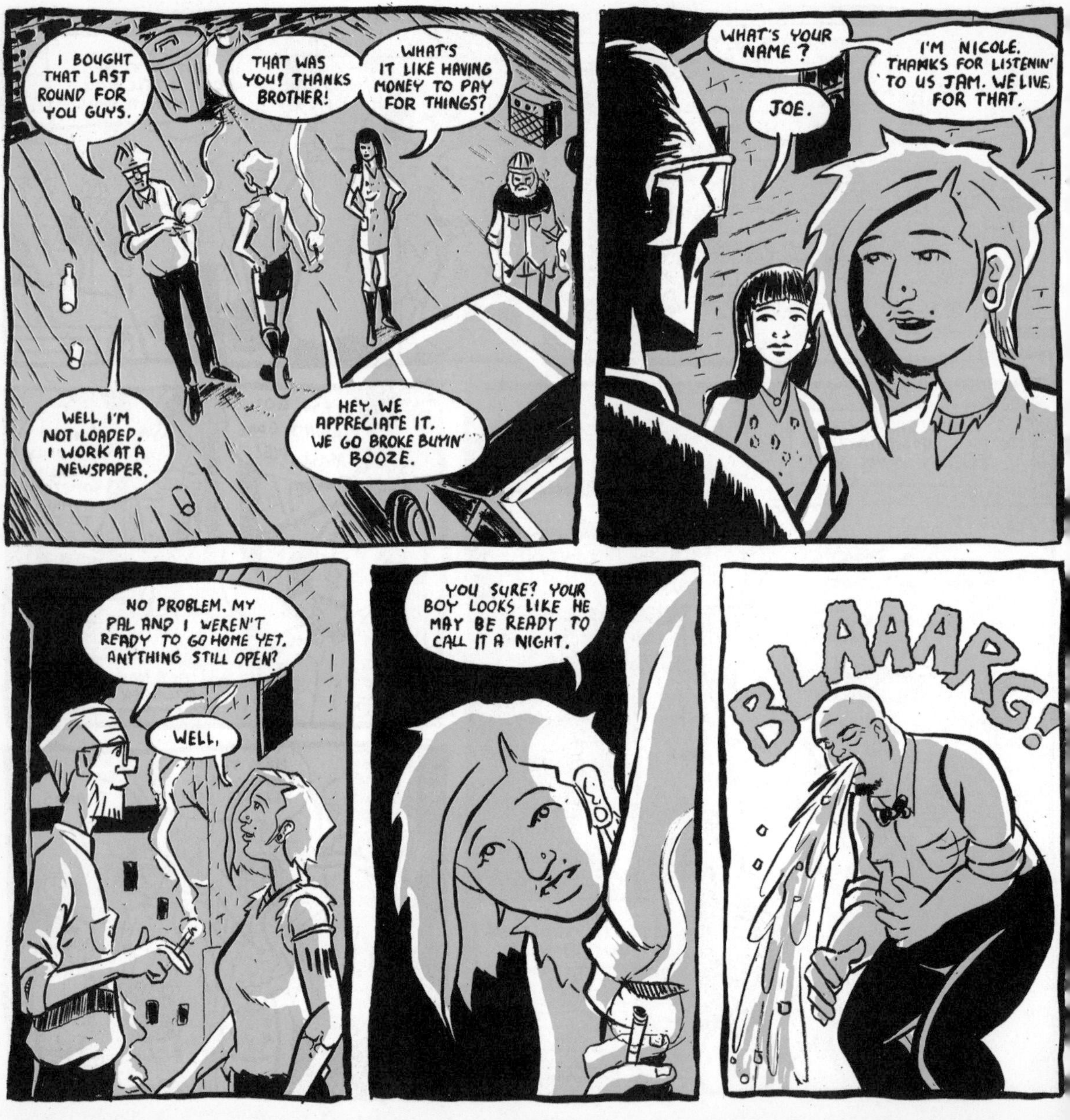
I BOUGHT THAT LAST ROUND FOR YOU GUYS.
THAT WAS YOU! THANKS BROTHER!
WHAT'S IT LIKE HAVING MONEY TO PAY FOR THINGS?
WELL, I'M NOT LOADED. I WORK AT A NEWSPAPER.
HEY, WE APPRECIATE IT. WE GO BROKE BUYIN' BOOZE.
WHAT'S YOUR NAME?
JOE.
I'M NICOLE. THANKS FOR LISTENIN' TO US JAM. WE LIVE FOR THAT.
NO PROBLEM. MY PAL AND I WEREN'T READY TO GO HOME YET. ANYTHING STILL OPEN?
WELL,
YOU SURE? YOUR BOY LOOKS LIKE HE MAY BE READY TO CALL IT A NIGHT.
BLAAARG!

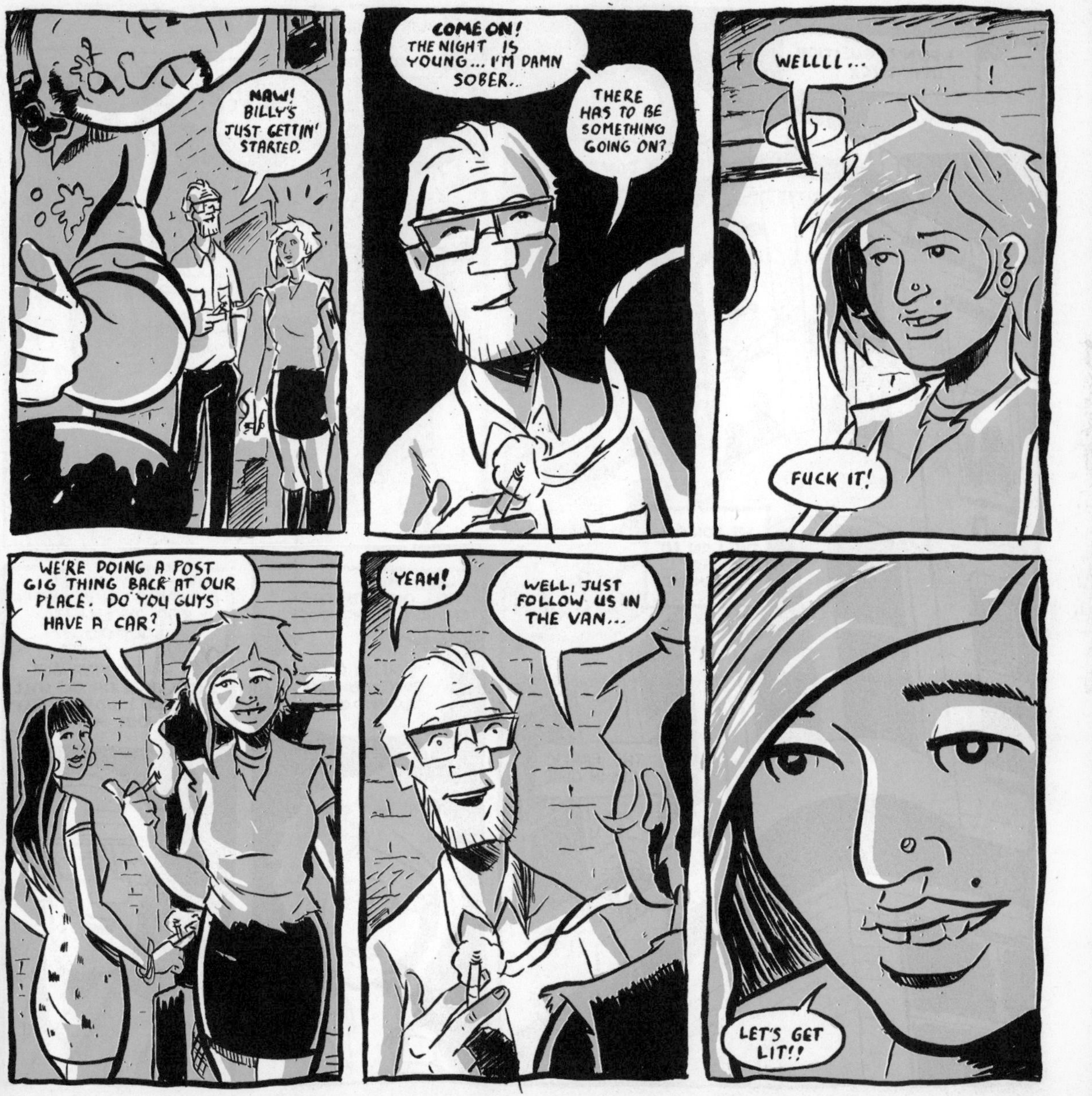
NAW! BILLY'S JUST GETTIN' STARTED.
COME ON! THE NIGHT IS YOUNG... I'M DAMN SOBER..
THERE HAS TO BE SOMETHING GOING ON?
WELLLL...
FUCK IT!
WE'RE DOING A POST GIG THING BACK AT OUR PLACE. DO YOU GUYS HAVE A CAR?
YEAH!
WELL, JUST FOLLOW US IN THE VAN...
LET'S GET LIT!!

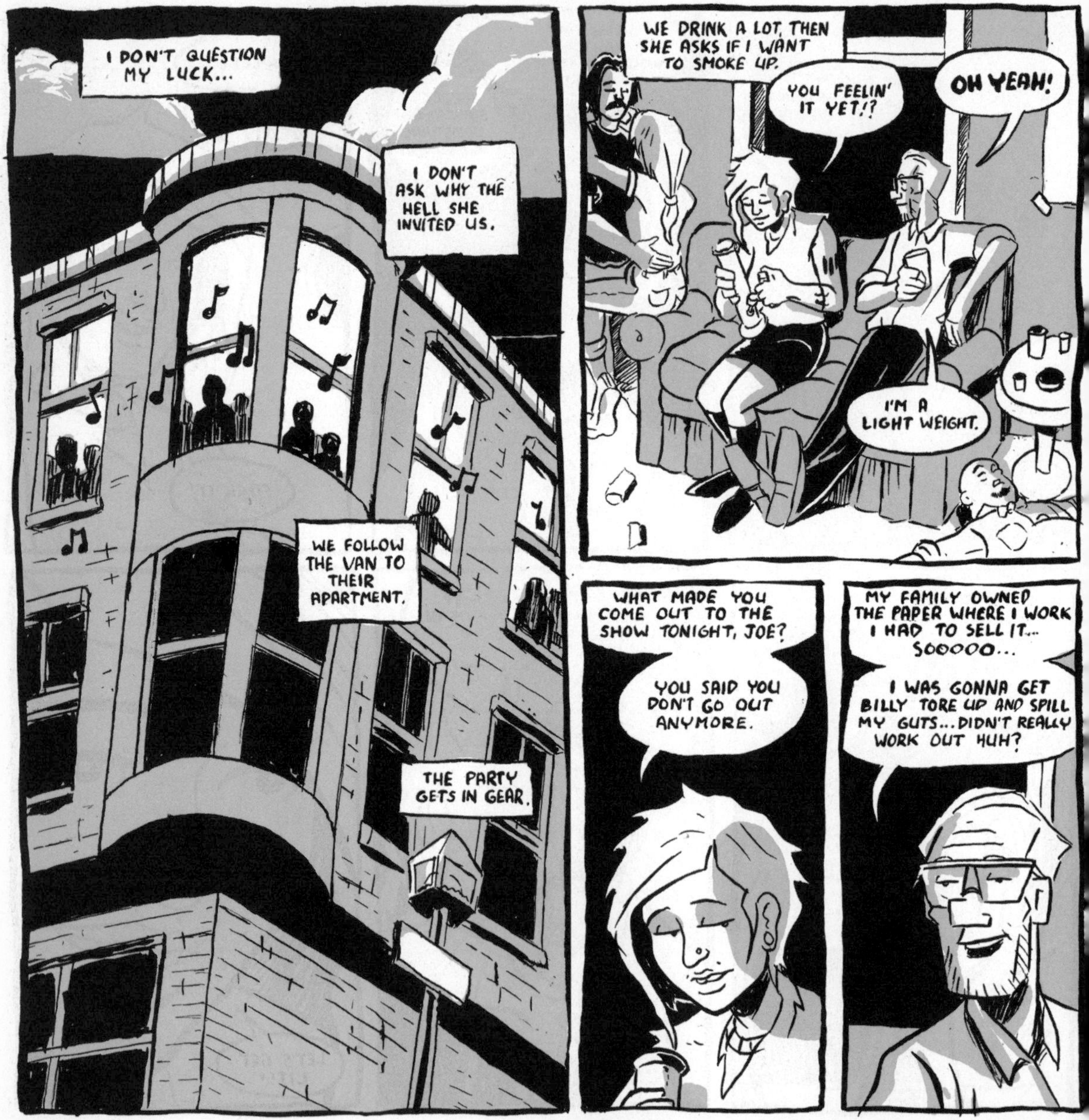
I DON'T QUESTION MY LUCK...
I DON'T ASK WHY THE HELL SHE INVITED US.
WE FOLLOW THE VAN TO THEIR APARTMENT.
THE PARTY GETS IN GEAR.
WE DRINK A LOT, THEN SHE ASKS IF I WANT TO SMOKE UP.
YOU FEELIN' IT YET!?
OH YEAH!
I'M A LIGHT WEIGHT.
WHAT MADE YOU COME OUT TO THE SHOW TONIGHT, JOE?
YOU SAID YOU DON'T GO OUT ANYMORE.
MY FAMILY OWNED THE PAPER WHERE I WORK I HAD TO SELL IT... SOOOOO...
I WAS GONNA GET BILLY TORE UP AND SPILL MY GUTS... DIDN'T REALLY WORK OUT HUH?

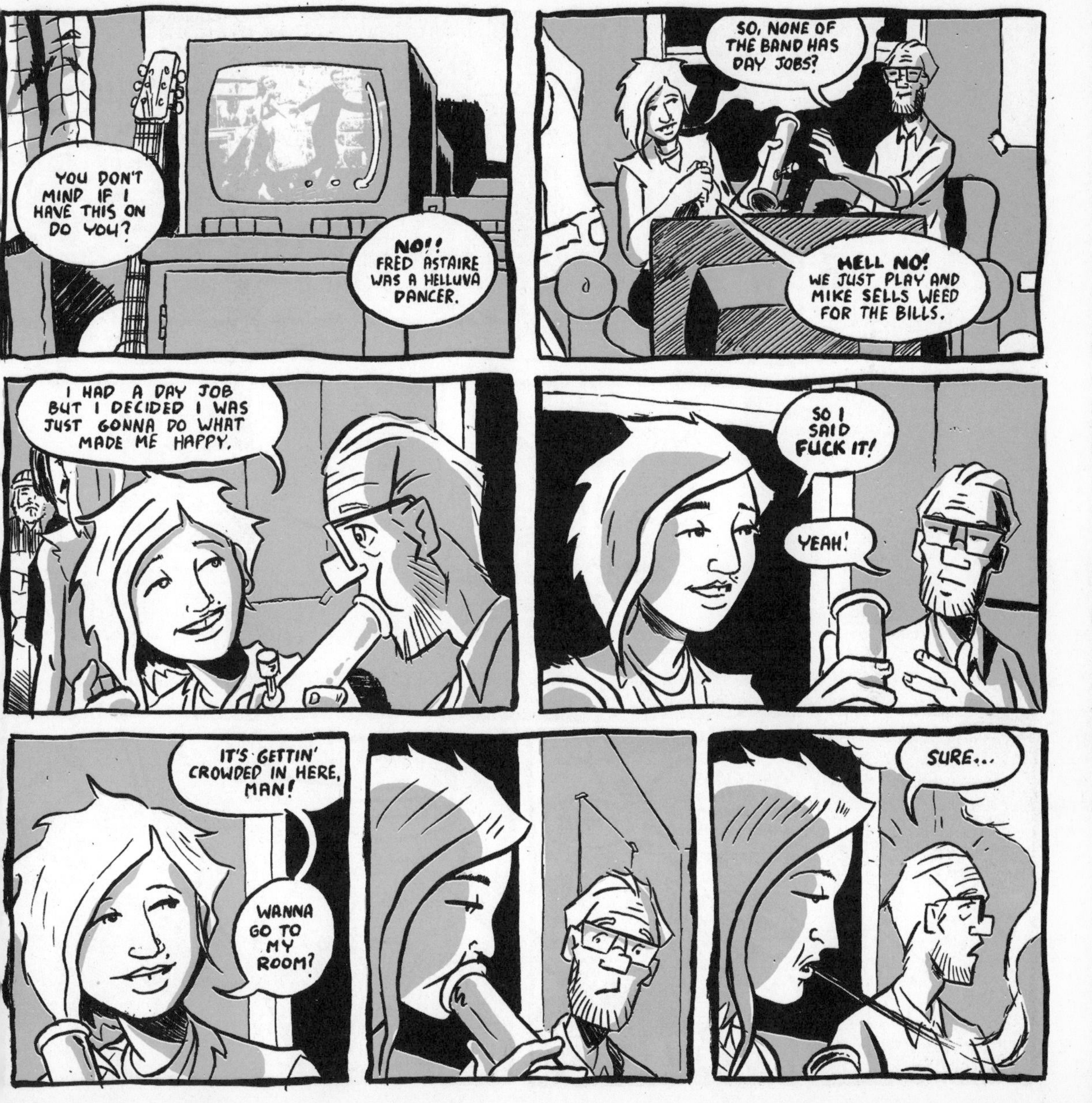
YOU DON'T MIND IF I HAVE THIS ON DO YOU?
NO!! FRED ASTAIRE WAS A HELLUVA DANCER.
SO, NONE OF THE BAND HAS DAY JOBS?
HELL NO! WE JUST PLAY AND MIKE SELLS WEED FOR THE BILLS.
I HAD A DAY JOB BUT I DECIDED I WAS JUST GONNA DO WHAT MADE ME HAPPY.
SO I SAID FUCK IT!
YEAH!
IT'S GETTIN' CROWDED IN HERE, MAN!
WANNA GO TO MY ROOM?
SURE...

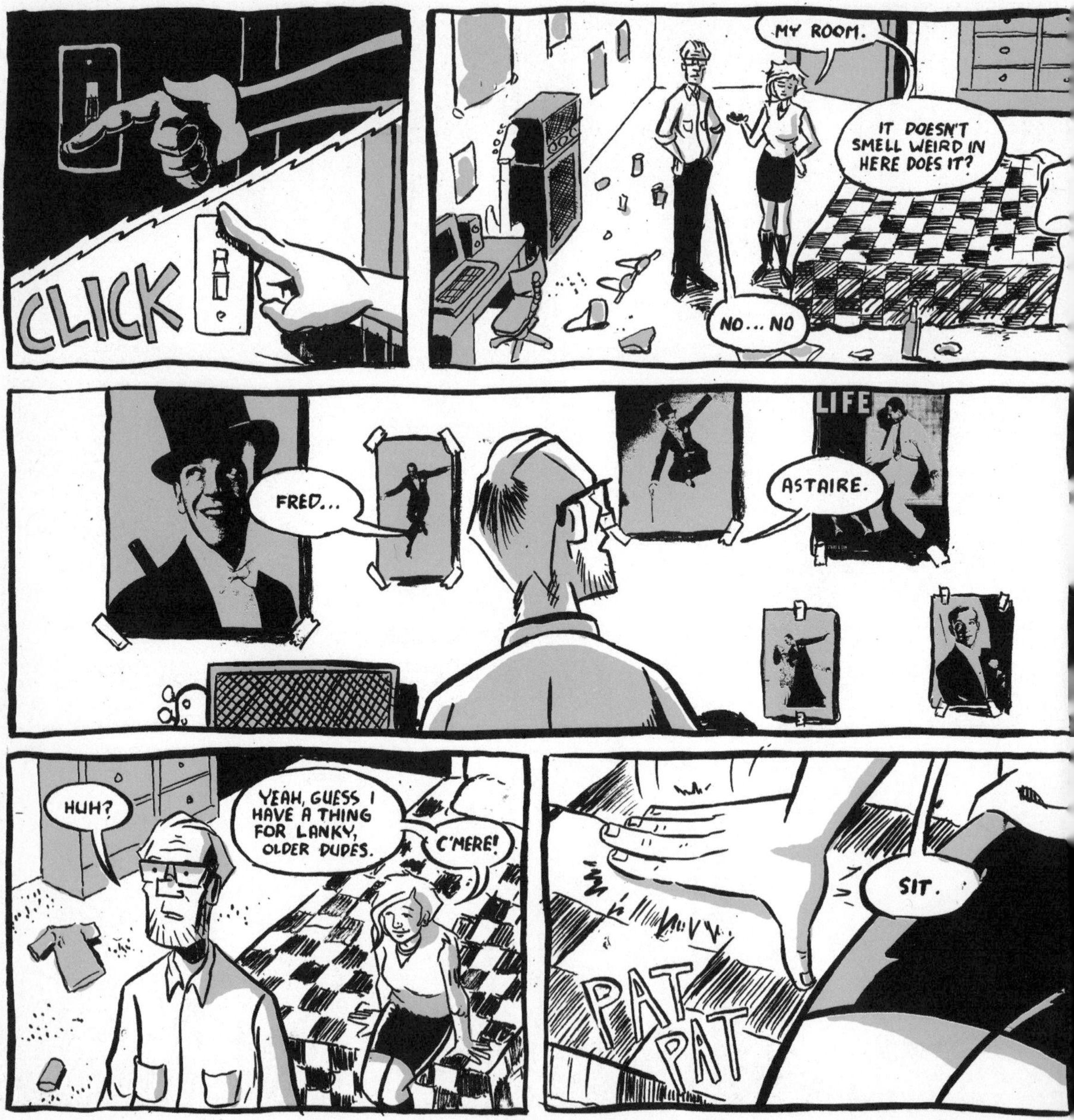
CLICK
MY ROOM.
IT DOESN'T SMELL WEIRD IN HERE DOES IT?
NO... NO
FRED...
ASTAIRE.
LIFE
HUH?
YEAH, GUESS I HAVE A THING FOR LANKY, OLDER DUDES.
C'MERE!
SIT.
PAT PAT

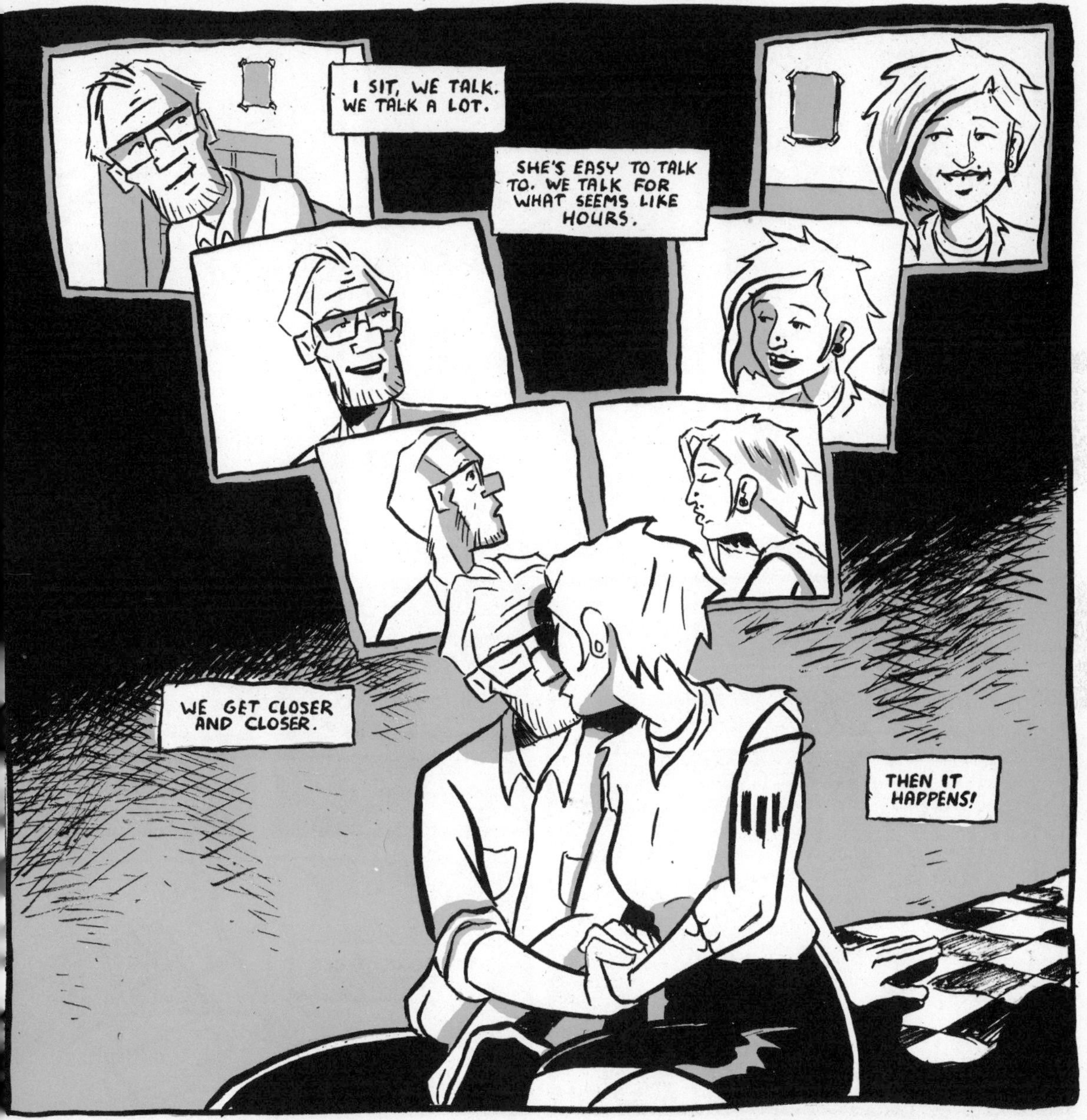
I SIT, WE TALK. WE TALK A LOT.
SHE'S EASY TO TALK TO. WE TALK FOR WHAT SEEMS LIKE HOURS.
WE GET CLOSER AND CLOSER.
THEN IT HAPPENS!

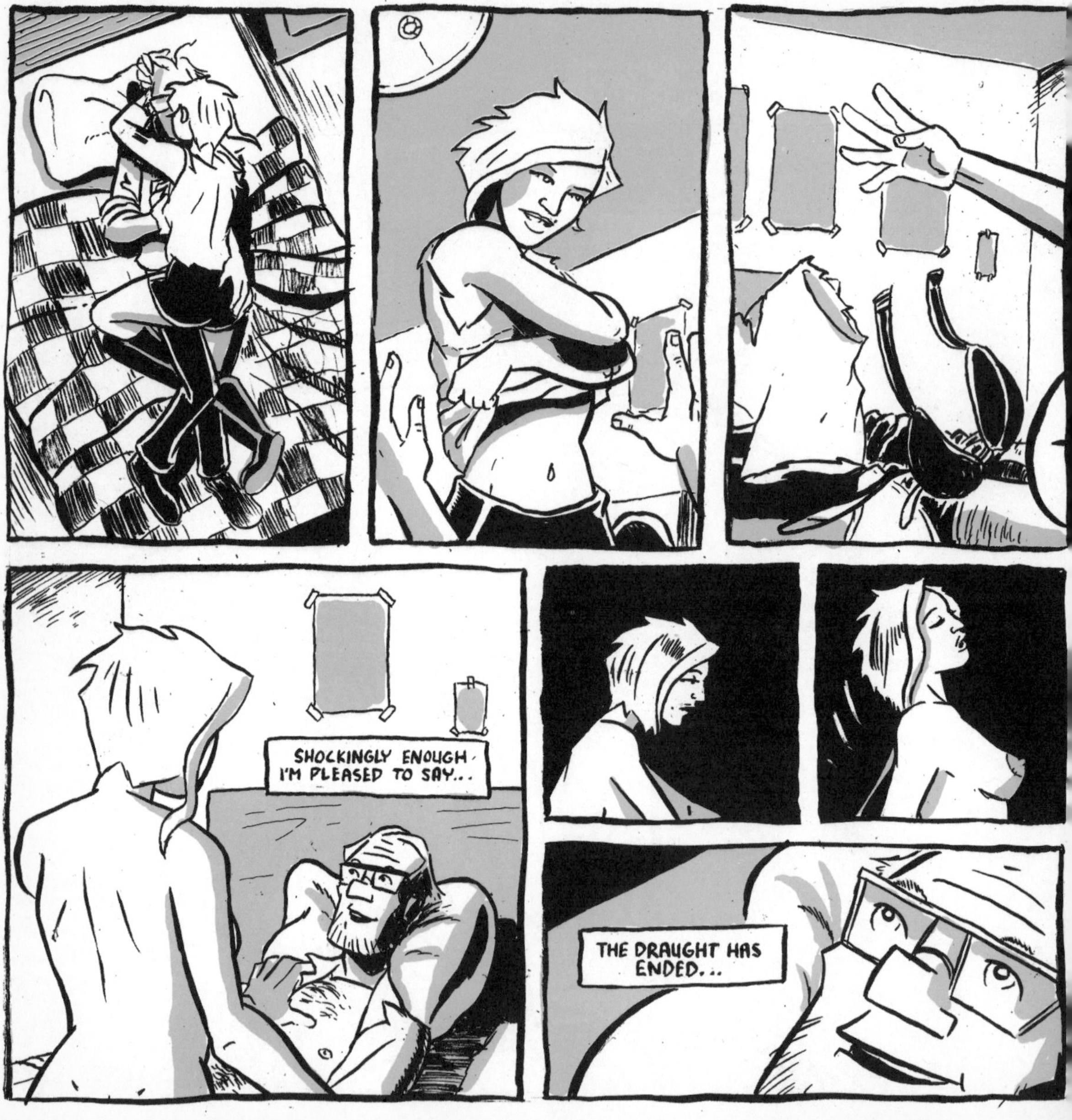
SHOCKINGLY ENOUGH I'M PLEASED TO SAY...
THE DRAUGHT HAS ENDED...

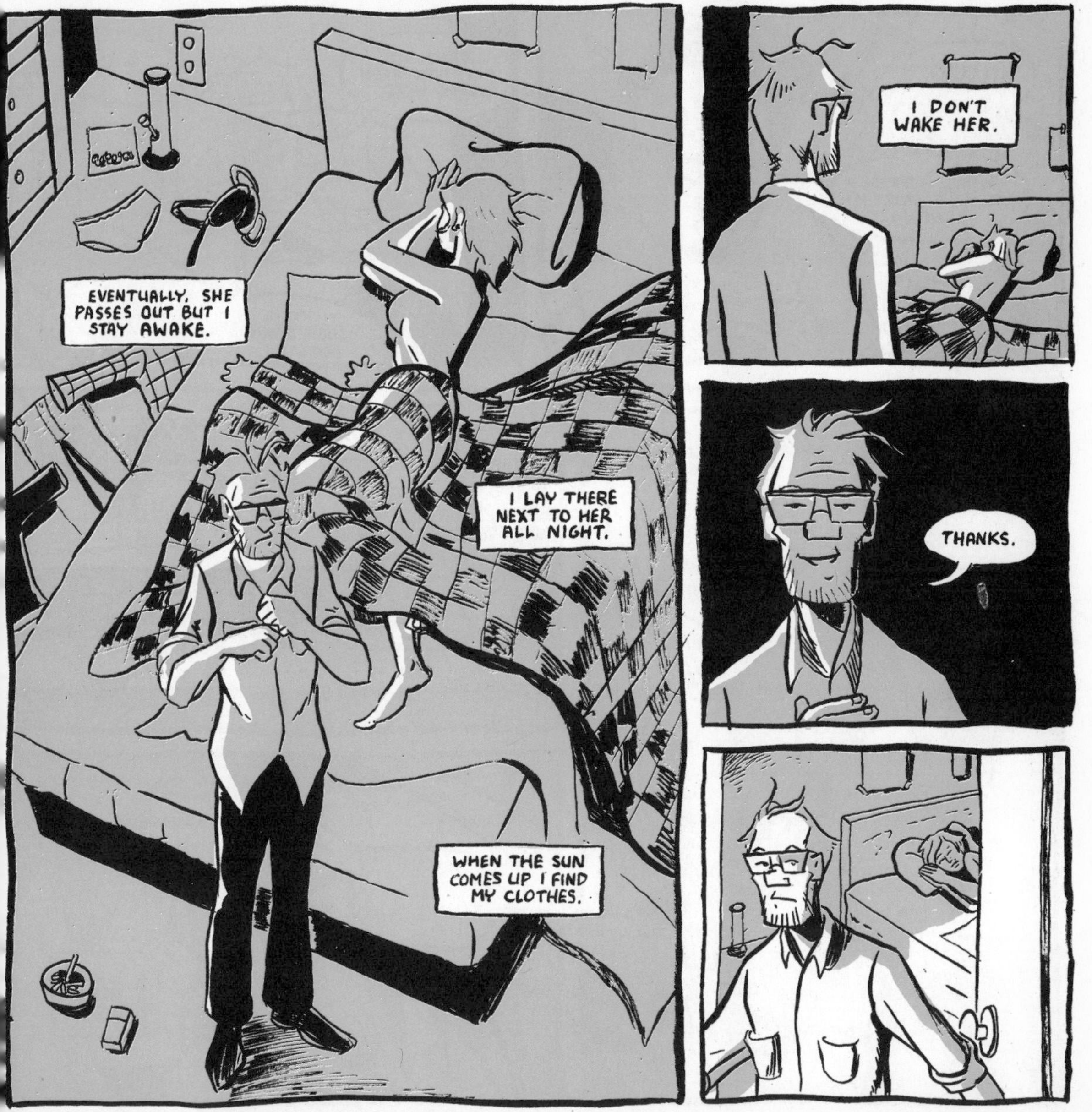
EVENTUALLY, SHE PASSES OUT BUT I STAY AWAKE.
I LAY THERE NEXT TO HER ALL NIGHT.
WHEN THE SUN COMES UP I FIND MY CLOTHES.
I DON'T WAKE HER.
THANKS.

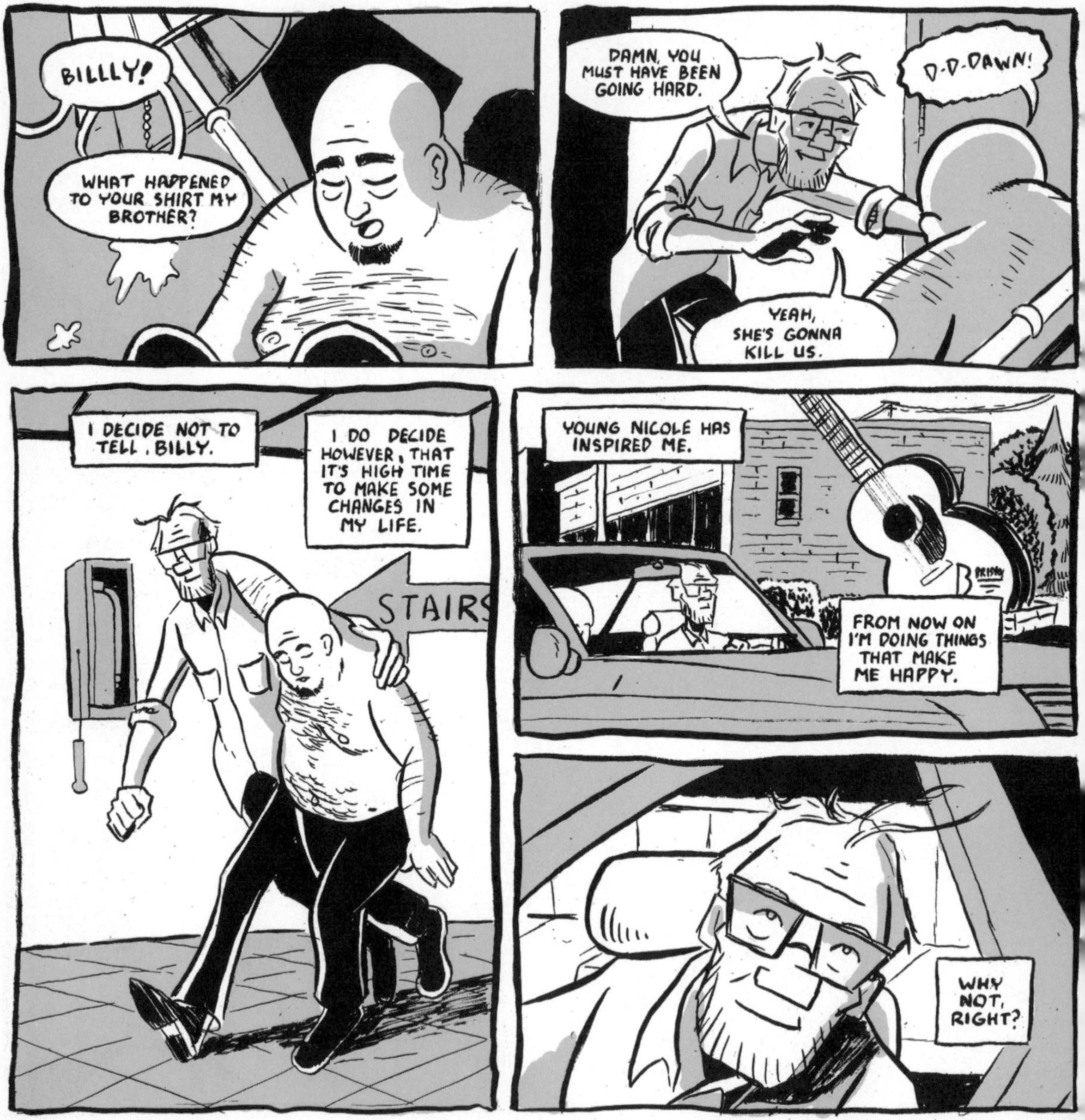
BILLLY!
WHAT HAPPENED TO YOUR SHIRT MY BROTHER?
DAMN, YOU MUST HAVE BEEN GOING HARD.
D-D-DAWN!
YEAH, SHE'S GONNA KILL US.
I DECIDE NOT TO TELL BILLY.
I DO DECIDE HOWEVER, THAT IT'S HIGH TIME TO MAKE SOME CHANGES IN MY LIFE.
STAIRS
YOUNG NICOLE HAS INSPIRED ME.
FROM NOW ON I'M DOING THINGS THAT MAKE ME HAPPY.
WHY NOT, RIGHT?

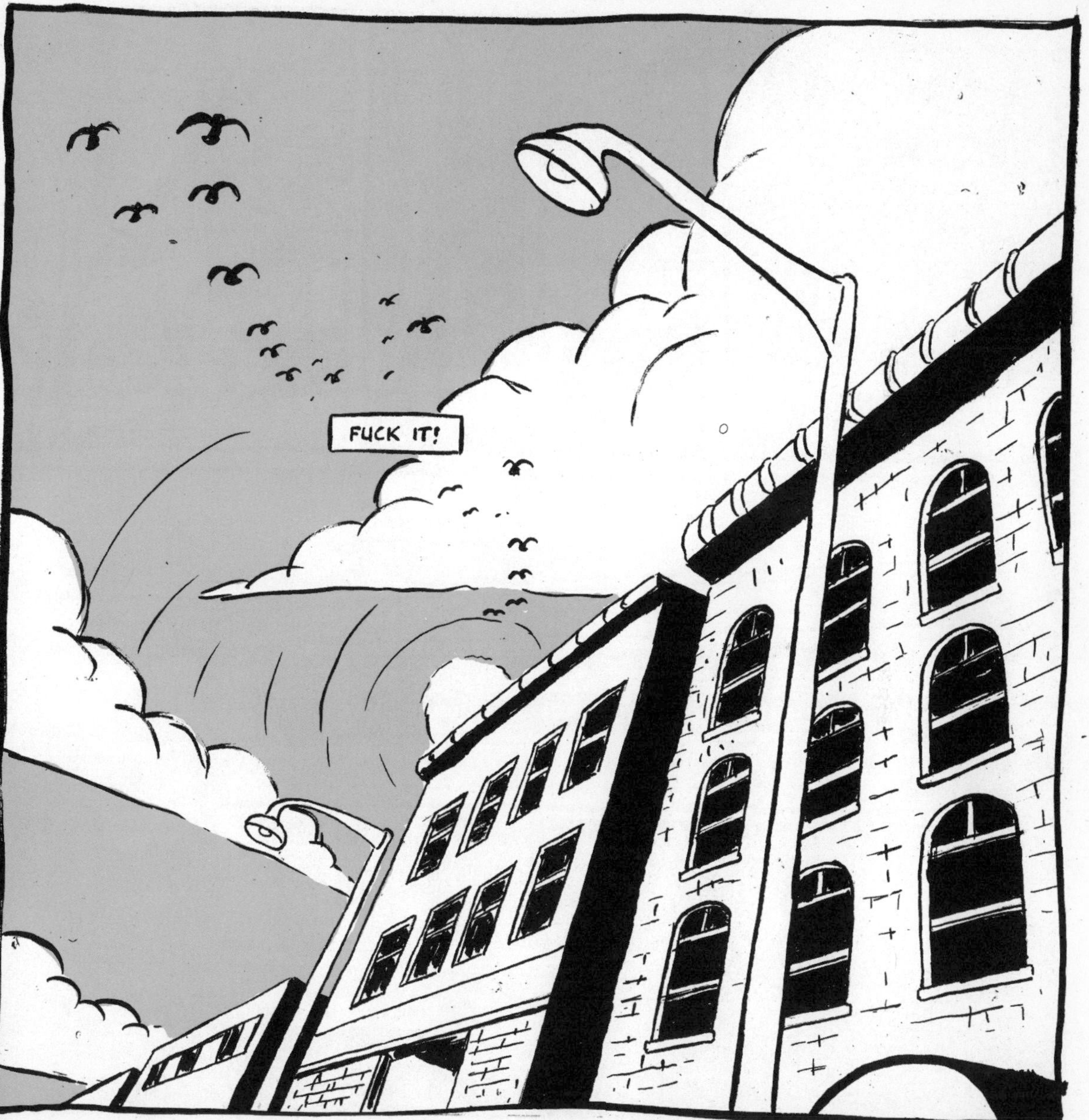
FUCK IT!

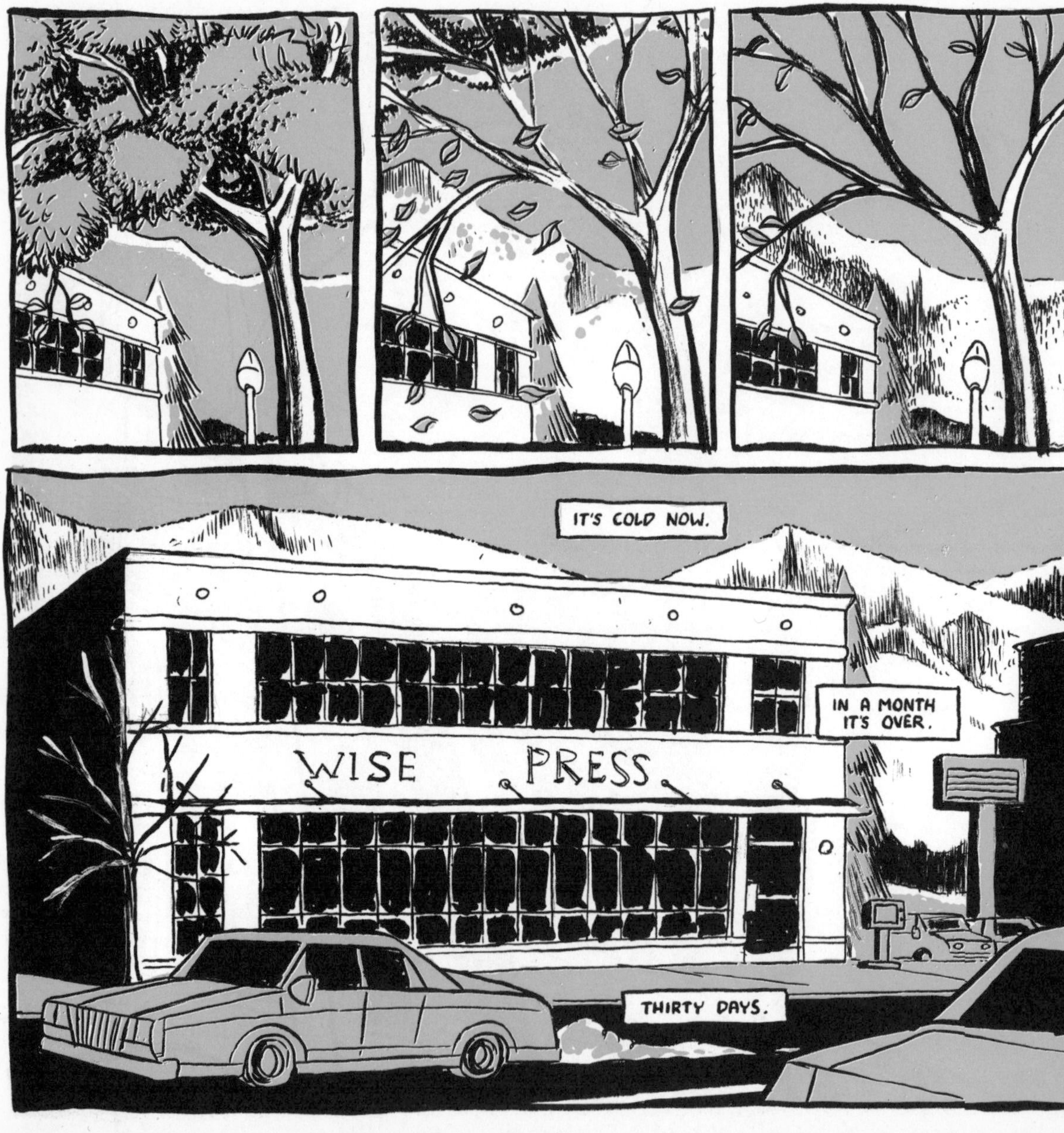
IT'S COLD NOW.
IN A MONTH IT'S OVER.
WISE PRESS
THIRTY DAYS.

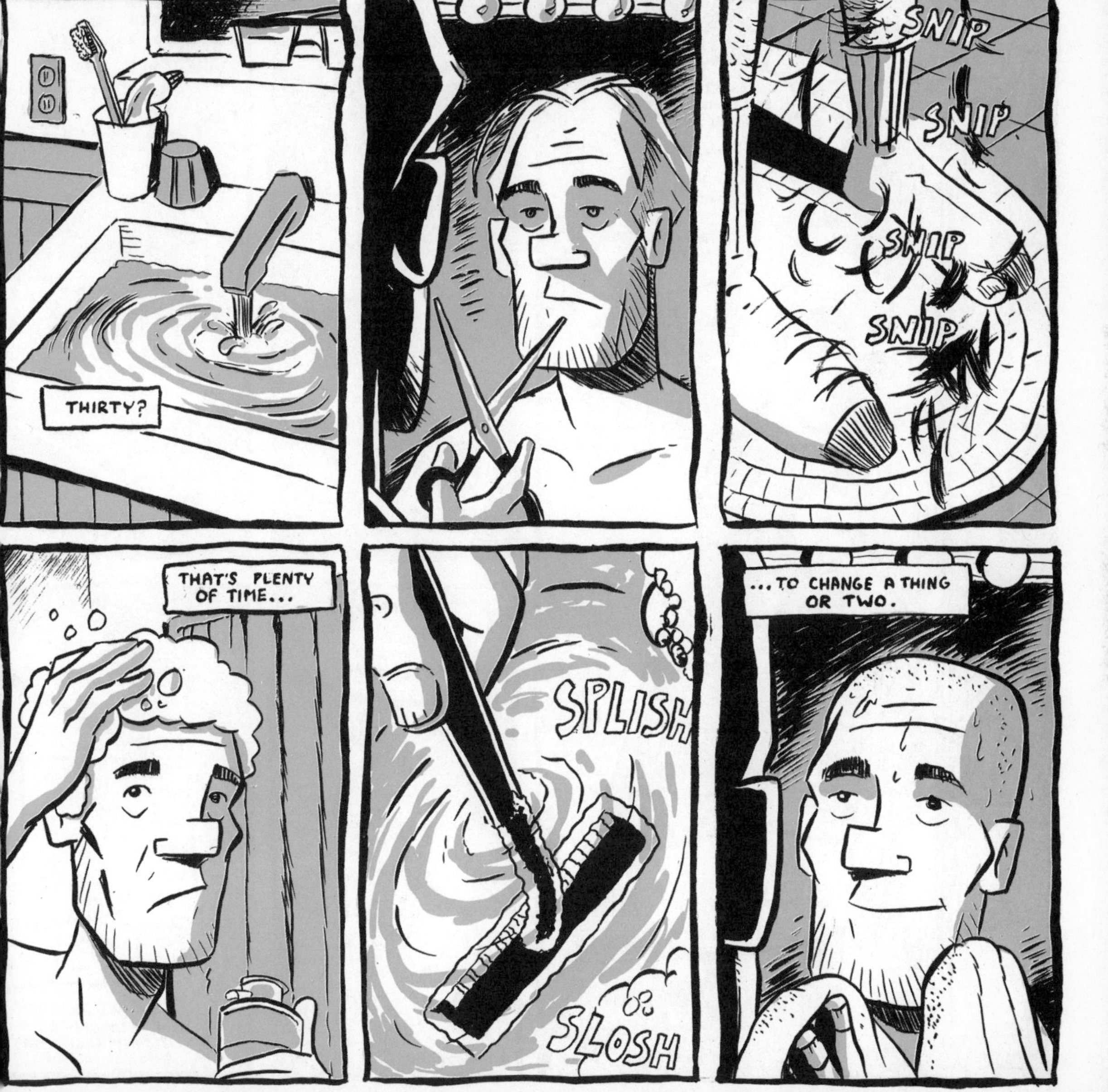
THIRTY?
SNIP
SNIP
SNIP
SNIP
THAT'S PLENTY OF TIME...
SPLISH
SLOSH
...TO CHANGE A THING OR TWO.

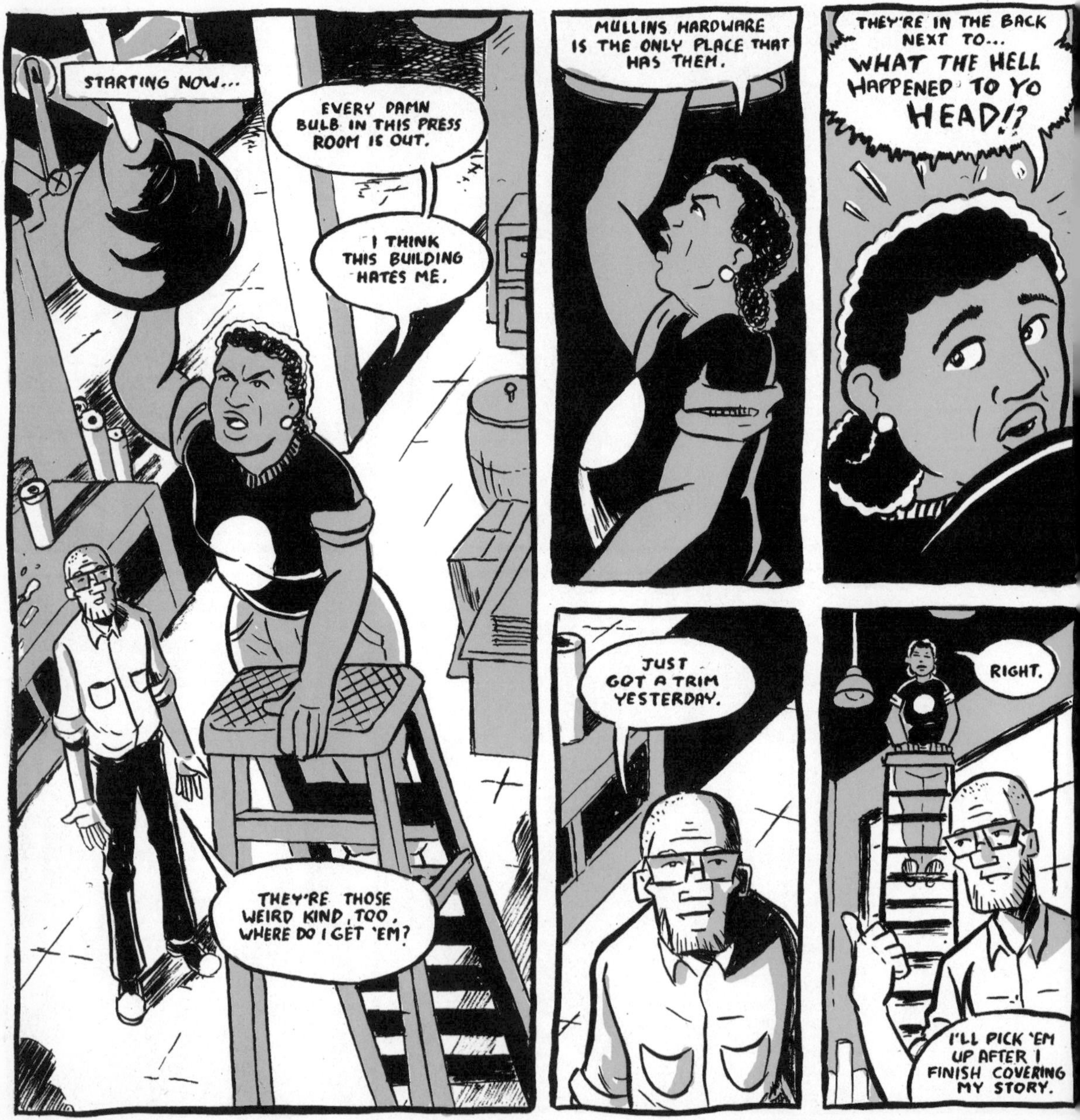
STARTING NOW...
EVERY DAMN BULB IN THIS PRESS ROOM IS OUT.
I THINK THIS BUILDING HATES ME.
THEY'RE THOSE WEIRD KIND, TOO. WHERE DO I GET 'EM?
MULLINS HARDWARE IS THE ONLY PLACE THAT HAS THEM.
THEY'RE IN THE BACK NEXT TO...
WHAT THE HELL HAPPENED TO YO HEAD!?
JUST GOT A TRIM YESTERDAY.
RIGHT.
I'LL PICK 'EM UP AFTER I FINISH COVERING MY STORY.

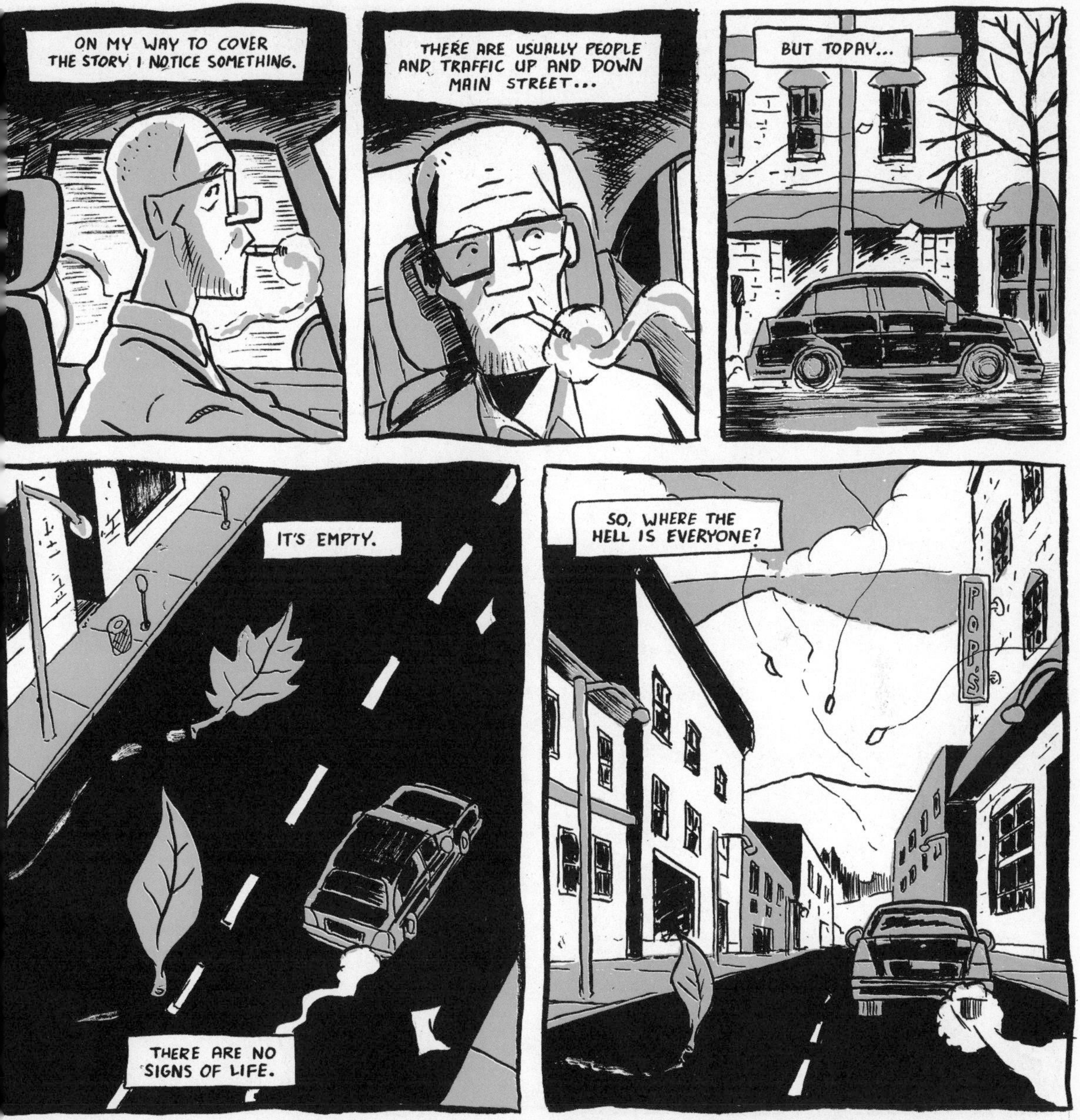
ON MY WAY TO COVER THE STORY I NOTICE SOMETHING.
THERE ARE USUALLY PEOPLE AND TRAFFIC UP AND DOWN MAIN STREET...
BUT TODAY...
IT'S EMPTY.
THERE ARE NO SIGNS OF LIFE.
SO, WHERE THE HELL IS EVERYONE?
POP'S

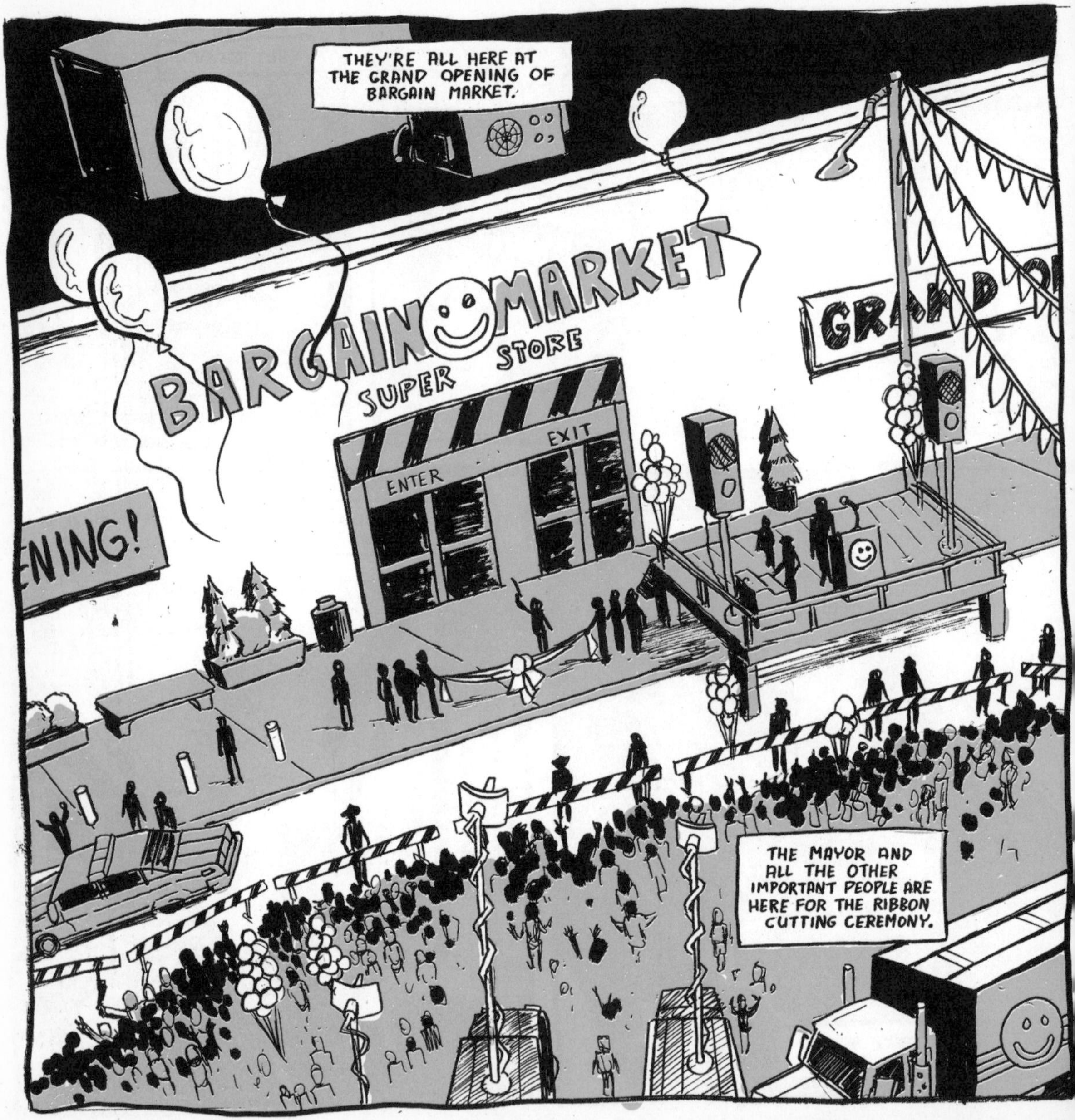
THEY'RE ALL HERE AT THE GRAND OPENING OF BARGAIN MARKET.
BARGAIN MARKET
SUPER STORE
ENTER
EXIT
GRAND
ENING!
THE MAYOR AND ALL THE OTHER IMPORTANT PEOPLE ARE HERE FOR THE RIBBON CUTTING CEREMONY.

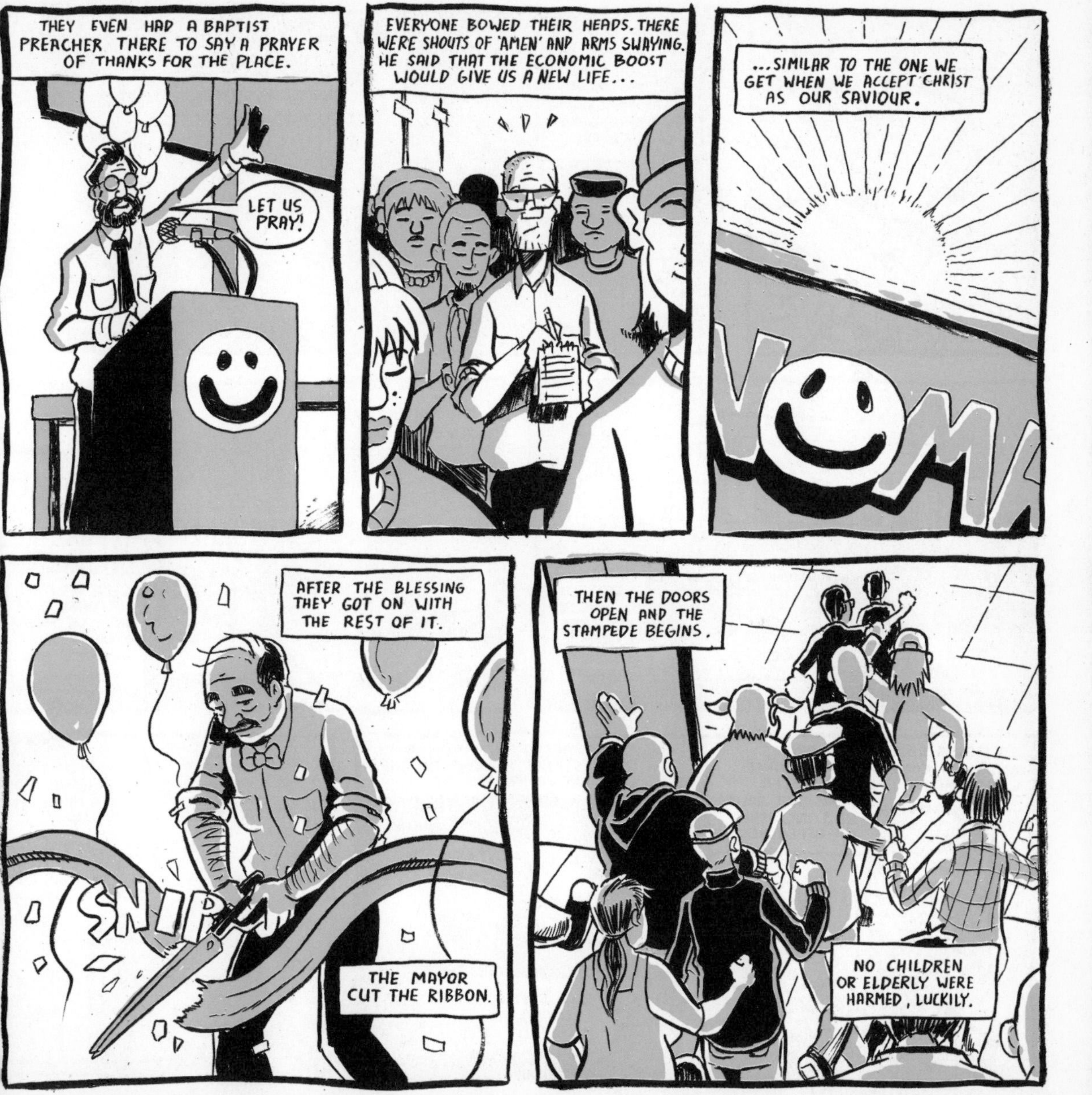
THEY EVEN HAD A BAPTIST PREACHER THERE TO SAY A PRAYER OF THANKS FOR THE PLACE.
LET US PRAY!
EVERYONE BOWED THEIR HEADS. THERE WERE SHOUTS OF 'AMEN' AND ARMS SWAYING. HE SAID THAT THE ECONOMIC BOOST WOULD GIVE US A NEW LIFE...
...SIMILAR TO THE ONE WE GET WHEN WE ACCEPT CHRIST AS OUR SAVIOUR.
AFTER THE BLESSING THEY GOT ON WITH THE REST OF IT.
SNIP
THE MAYOR CUT THE RIBBON.
THEN THE DOORS OPEN AND THE STAMPEDE BEGINS.
NO CHILDREN OR ELDERLY WERE HARMED, LUCKILY.

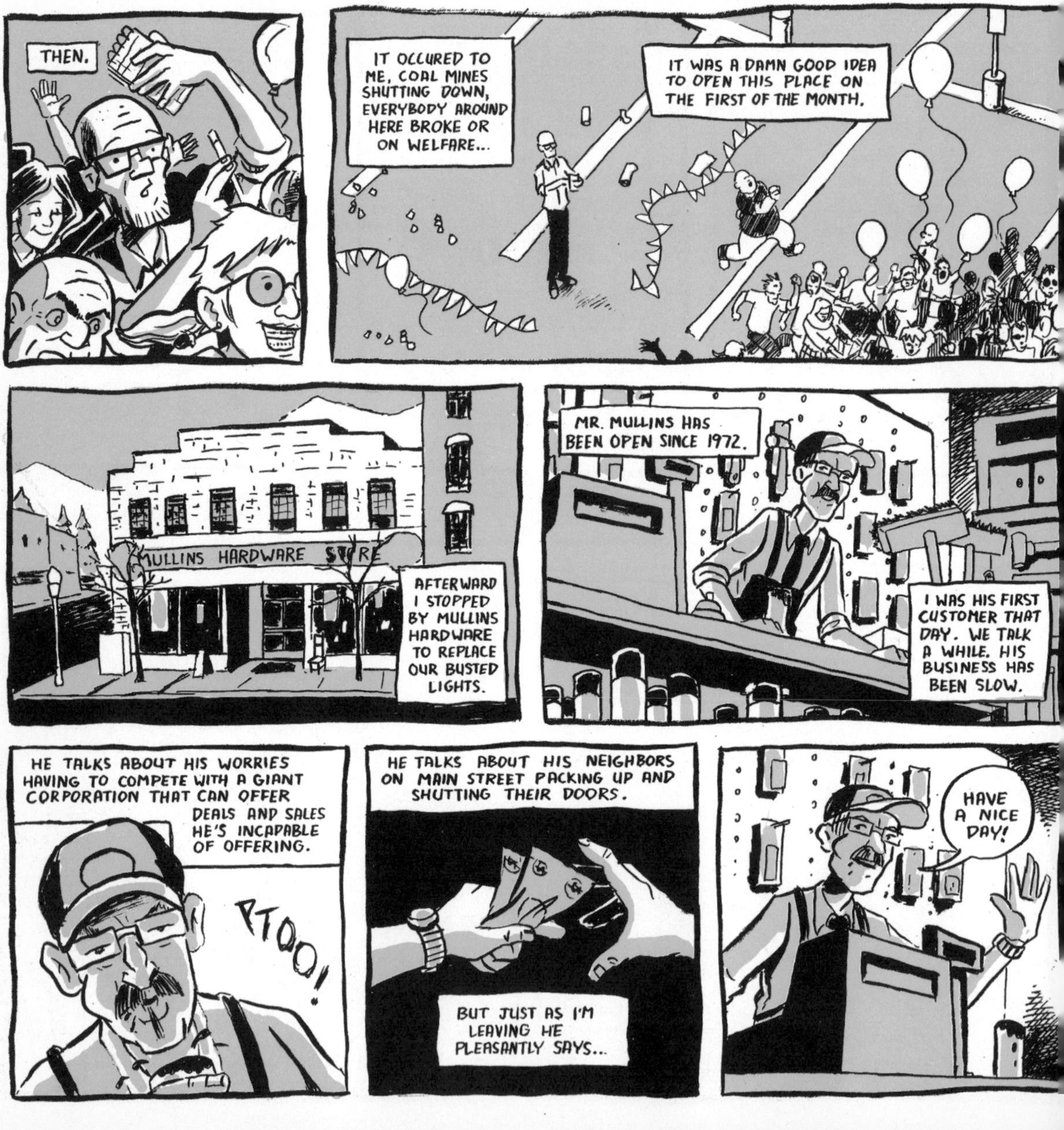
THEN.
IT OCCURED TO ME, COAL MINES SHUTTING DOWN, EVERYBODY AROUND HERE BROKE OR ON WELFARE...
IT WAS A DAMN GOOD IDEA TO OPEN THIS PLACE ON THE FIRST OF THE MONTH.
MULLINS HARDWARE STORE
AFTERWARD I STOPPED BY MULLINS HARDWARE TO REPLACE OUR BUSTED LIGHTS.
MR. MULLINS HAS BEEN OPEN SINCE 1972.
I WAS HIS FIRST CUSTOMER THAT DAY. WE TALK A WHILE. HIS BUSINESS HAS BEEN SLOW.
HE TALKS ABOUT HIS WORRIES HAVING TO COMPETE WITH A GIANT CORPORATION THAT CAN OFFER DEALS AND SALES HE'S INCAPABLE OF OFFERING.
PTOO!
HE TALKS ABOUT HIS NEIGHBORS ON MAIN STREET PACKING UP AND SHUTTING THEIR DOORS.
BUT JUST AS I'M LEAVING HE PLEASANTLY SAYS...
HAVE A NICE DAY!

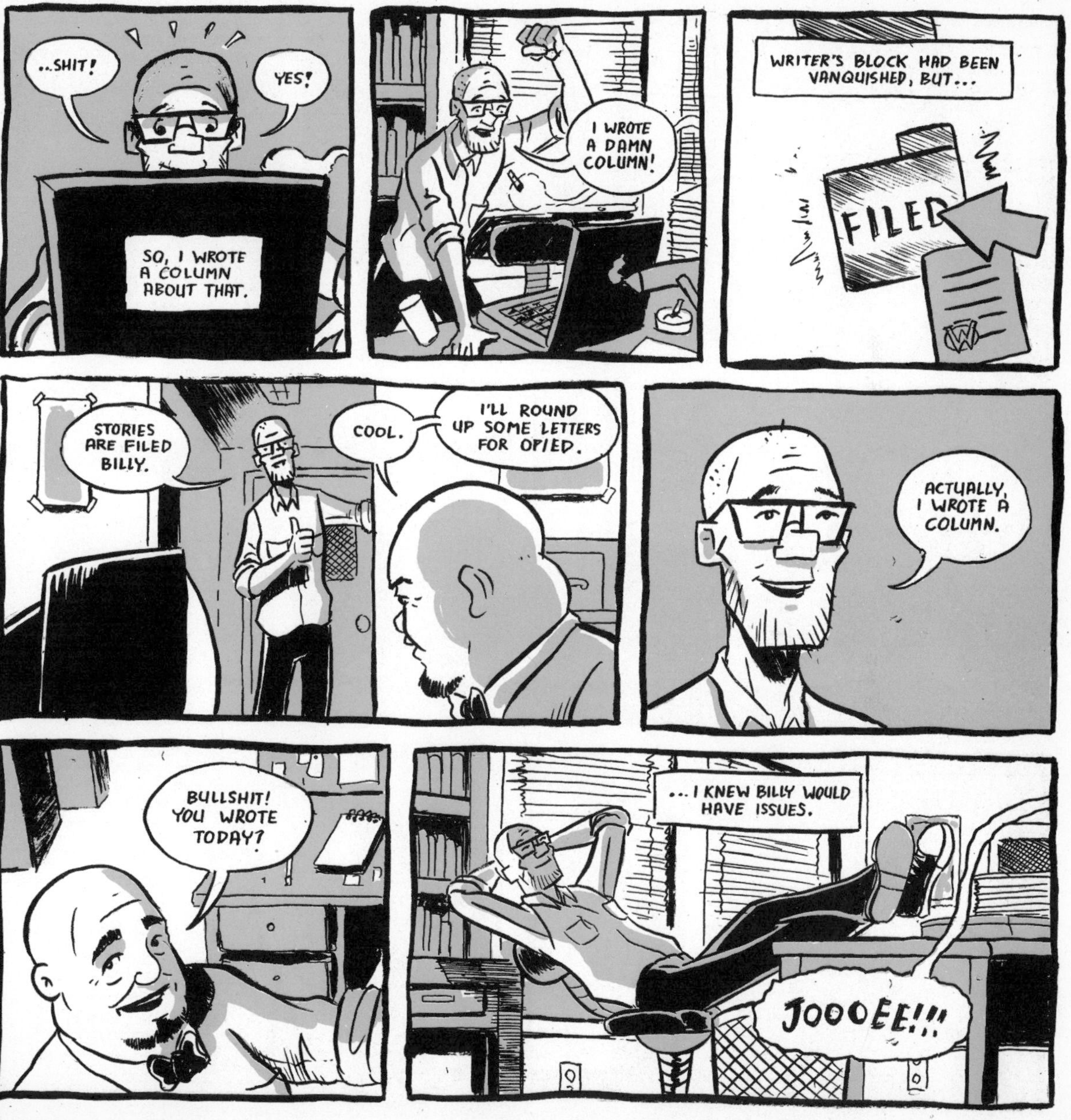
...SHIT!
YES!
SO, I WROTE A COLUMN ABOUT THAT.
I WROTE A DAMN COLUMN!
WRITER'S BLOCK HAD BEEN VANQUISHED, BUT...
FILED
STORIES ARE FILED BILLY.
COOL.
I'LL ROUND UP SOME LETTERS FOR OP/ED.
ACTUALLY, I WROTE A COLUMN.
BULLSHIT! YOU WROTE TODAY?
...I KNEW BILLY WOULD HAVE ISSUES.
JOOOEE!!!

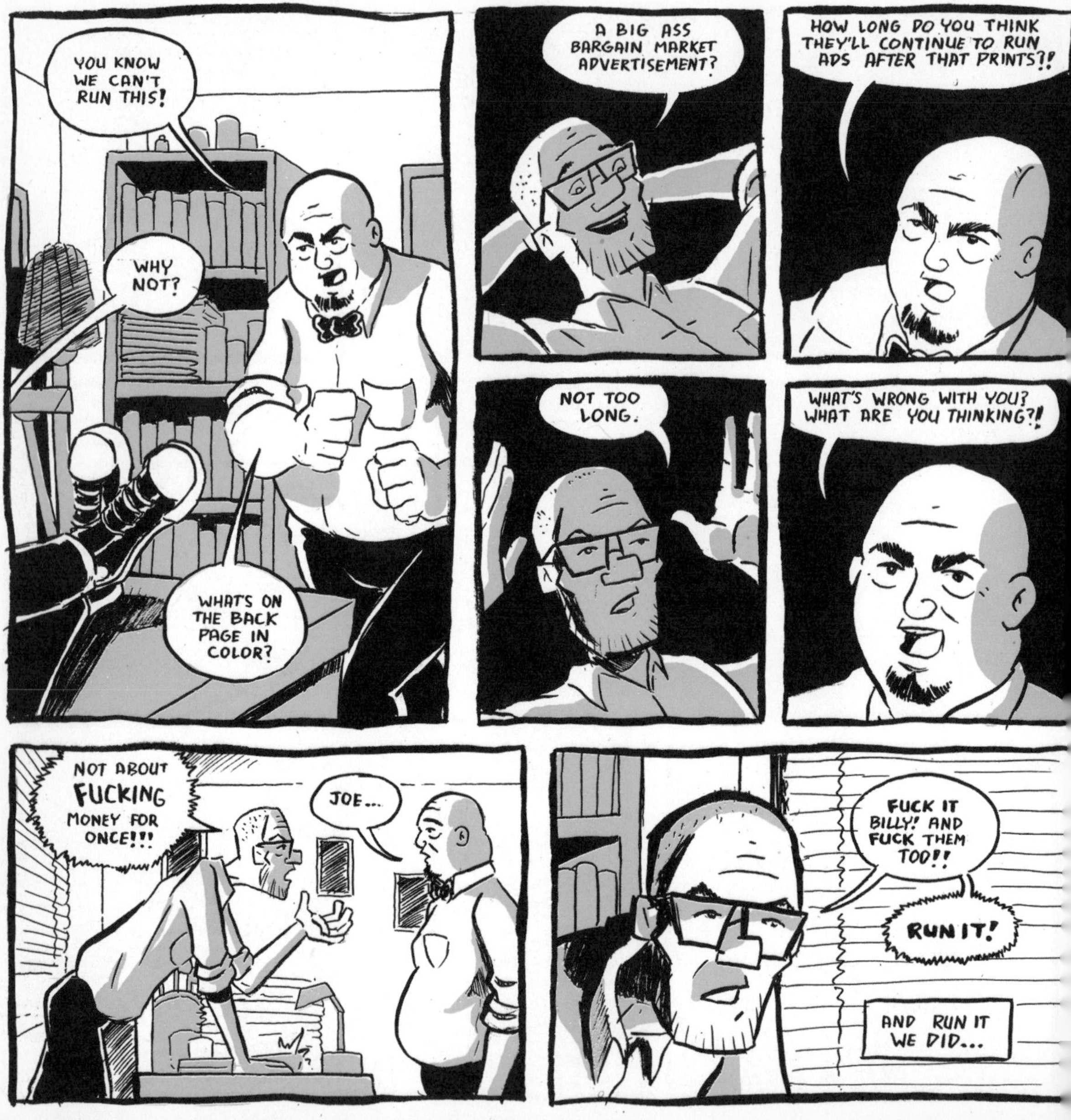
YOU KNOW WE CAN'T RUN THIS!
WHY NOT?
WHAT'S ON THE BACK PAGE IN COLOR?
A BIG ASS BARGAIN MARKET ADVERTISEMENT?
HOW LONG DO YOU THINK THEY'LL CONTINUE TO RUN ADS AFTER THAT PRINTS?!
NOT TOO LONG.
WHAT'S WRONG WITH YOU? WHAT ARE YOU THINKING?!
NOT ABOUT FUCKING MONEY FOR ONCE!!!
JOE...
FUCK IT BILLY! AND FUCK THEM TOO!!
RUN IT!
AND RUN IT WE DID...

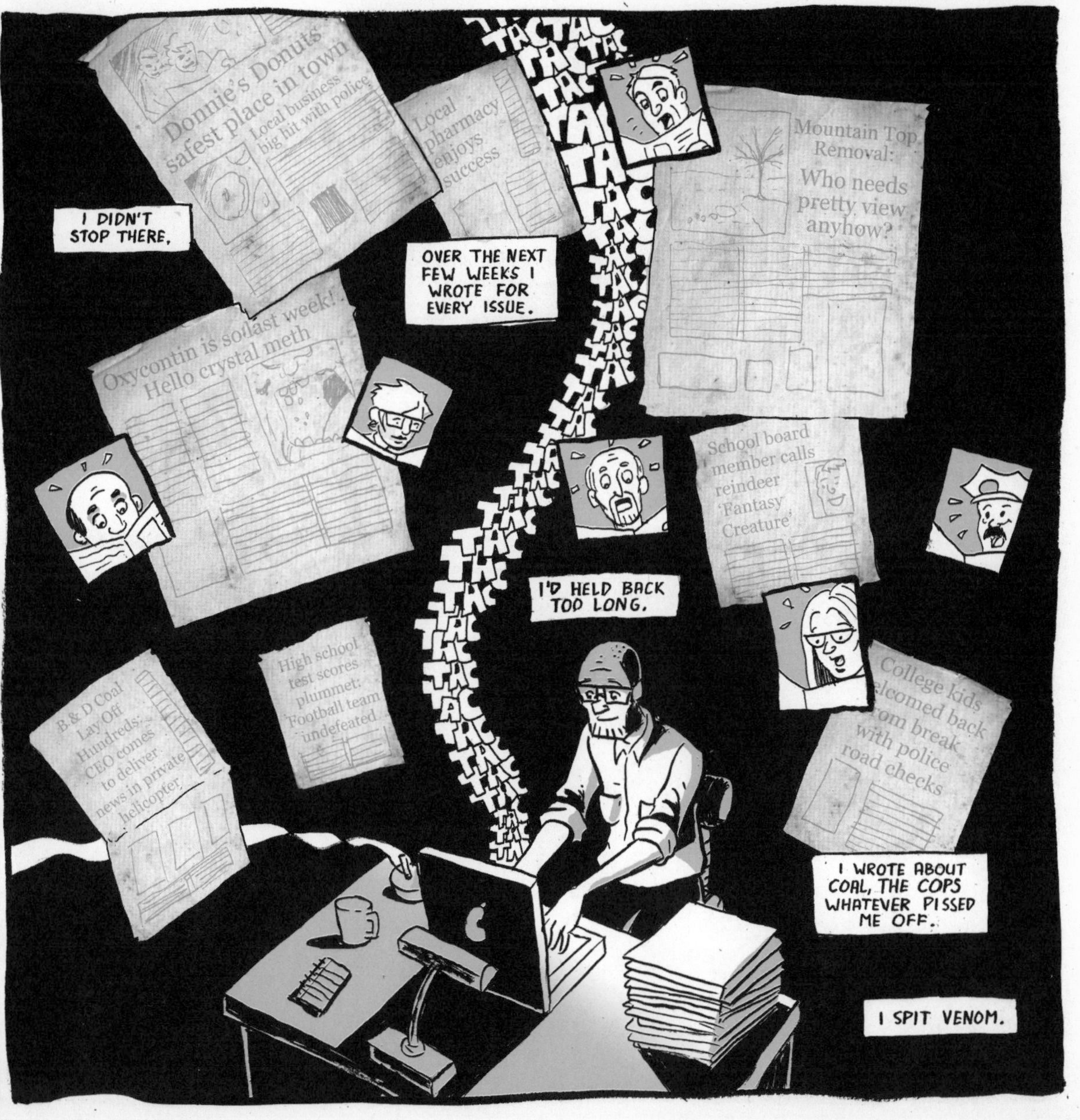

Donnie's Donuts safest place in town
Local business big hit with police
Local pharmacy enjoys success
TAC TAC TAC
Mountain Top Removal:
Who needs pretty view anyhow?
I DIDN'T STOP THERE.
OVER THE NEXT FEW WEEKS I WROTE FOR EVERY ISSUE.
Oxycontin is so last week! Hello crystal meth
School board member calls reindeer 'Fantasy Creature'
I'D HELD BACK TOO LONG.
B & D Coal Lay Off Hundreds; CEO comes to deliver news in private helicopter
High school test scores plummet; Football team undefeated
College kids
elcomed back
rom break
with police
road checks
I WROTE ABOUT COAL, THE COPS WHATEVER PISSED ME OFF.
I SPIT VENOM.

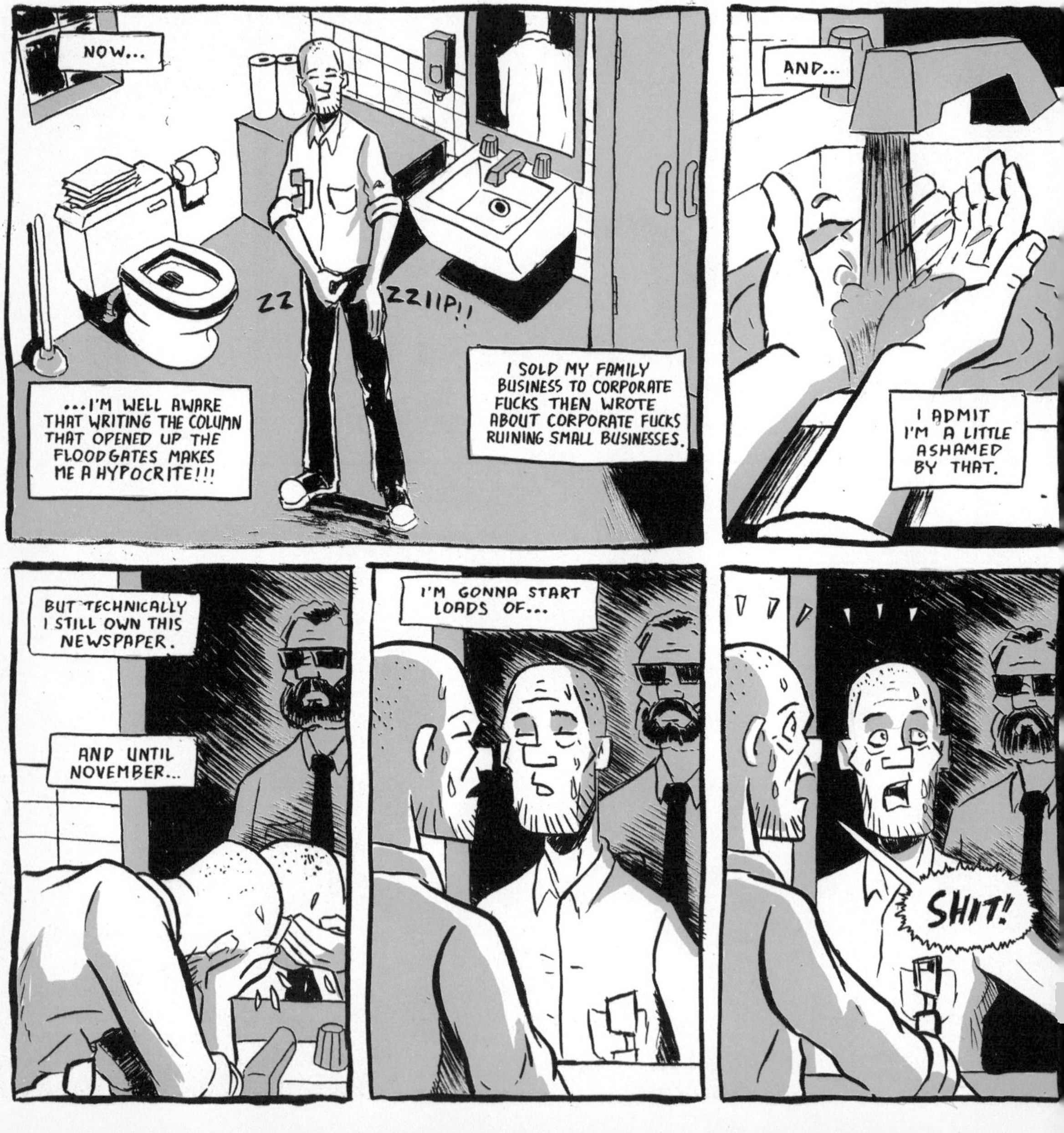
NOW...
ZZ ZZIIP!!
...I'M WELL AWARE THAT WRITING THE COLUMN THAT OPENED UP THE FLOODGATES MAKES ME A HYPOCRITE!!!
I SOLD MY FAMILY BUSINESS TO CORPORATE FUCKS THEN WROTE ABOUT CORPORATE FUCKS RUINING SMALL BUSINESSES.
AND...
I ADMIT I'M A LITTLE ASHAMED BY THAT.
BUT TECHNICALLY I STILL OWN THIS NEWSPAPER.
AND UNTIL NOVEMBER...
I'M GONNA START LOADS OF...
SHIT!

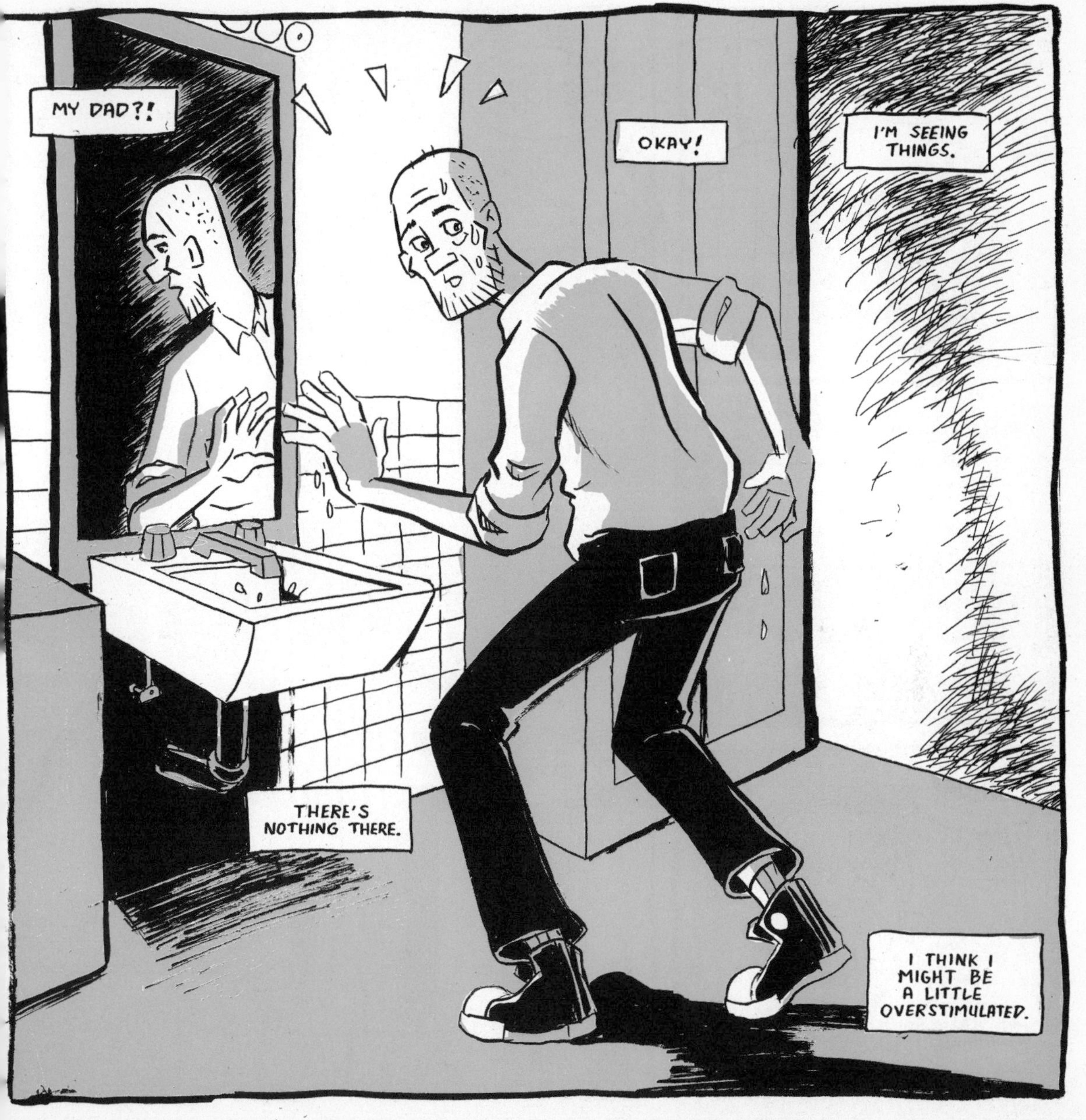
MY DAD?!
OKAY!
I'M SEEING THINGS.
THERE'S NOTHING THERE.
I THINK I MIGHT BE A LITTLE OVERSTIMULATED.

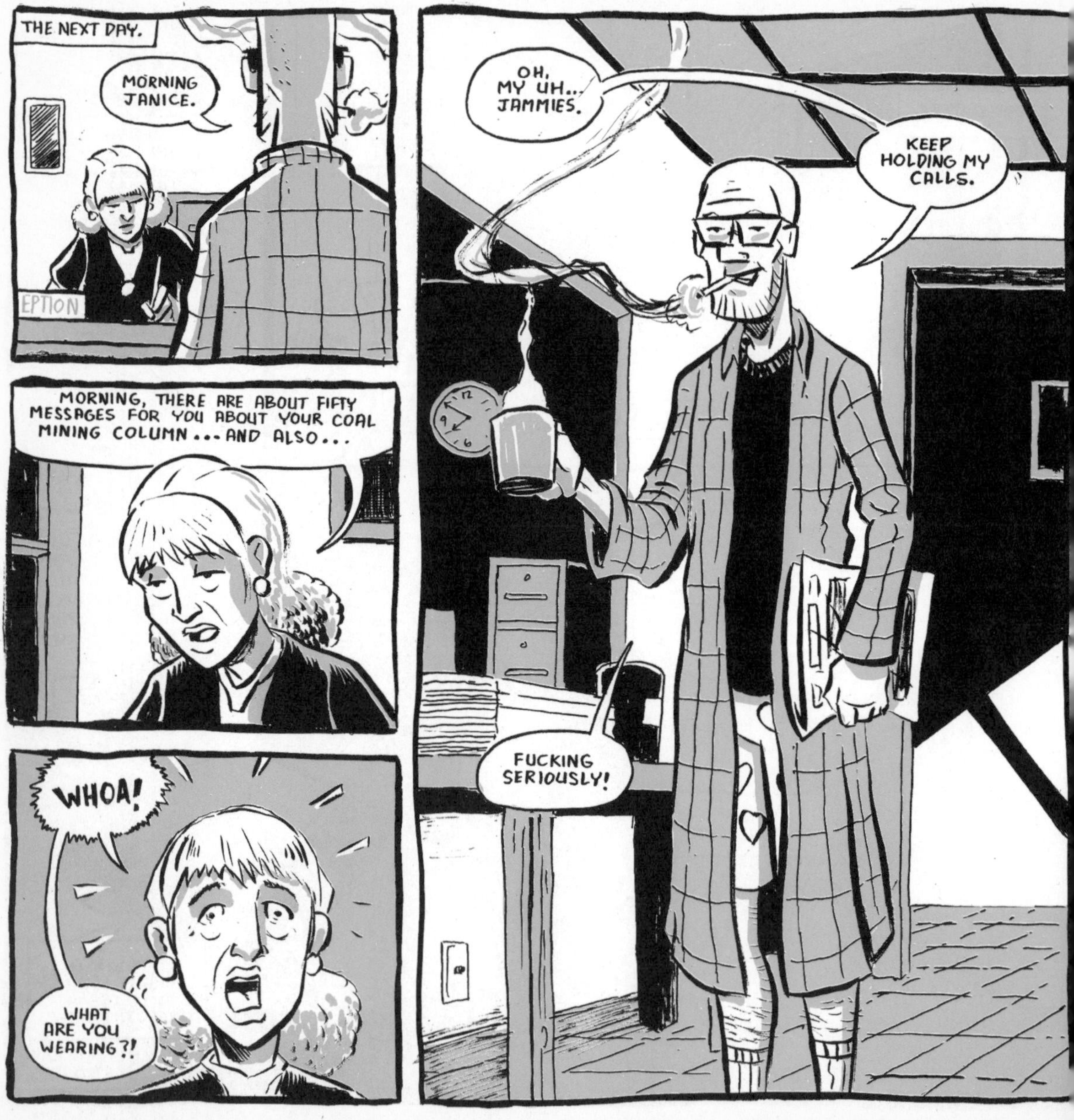
THE NEXT DAY.
MORNING JANICE.
EPTION
MORNING, THERE ARE ABOUT FIFTY MESSAGES FOR YOU ABOUT YOUR COAL MINING COLUMN ... AND ALSO ...
WHOA!
WHAT ARE YOU WEARING?!
OH, MY UH... JAMMIES.
KEEP HOLDING MY CALLS.
FUCKING SERIOUSLY!

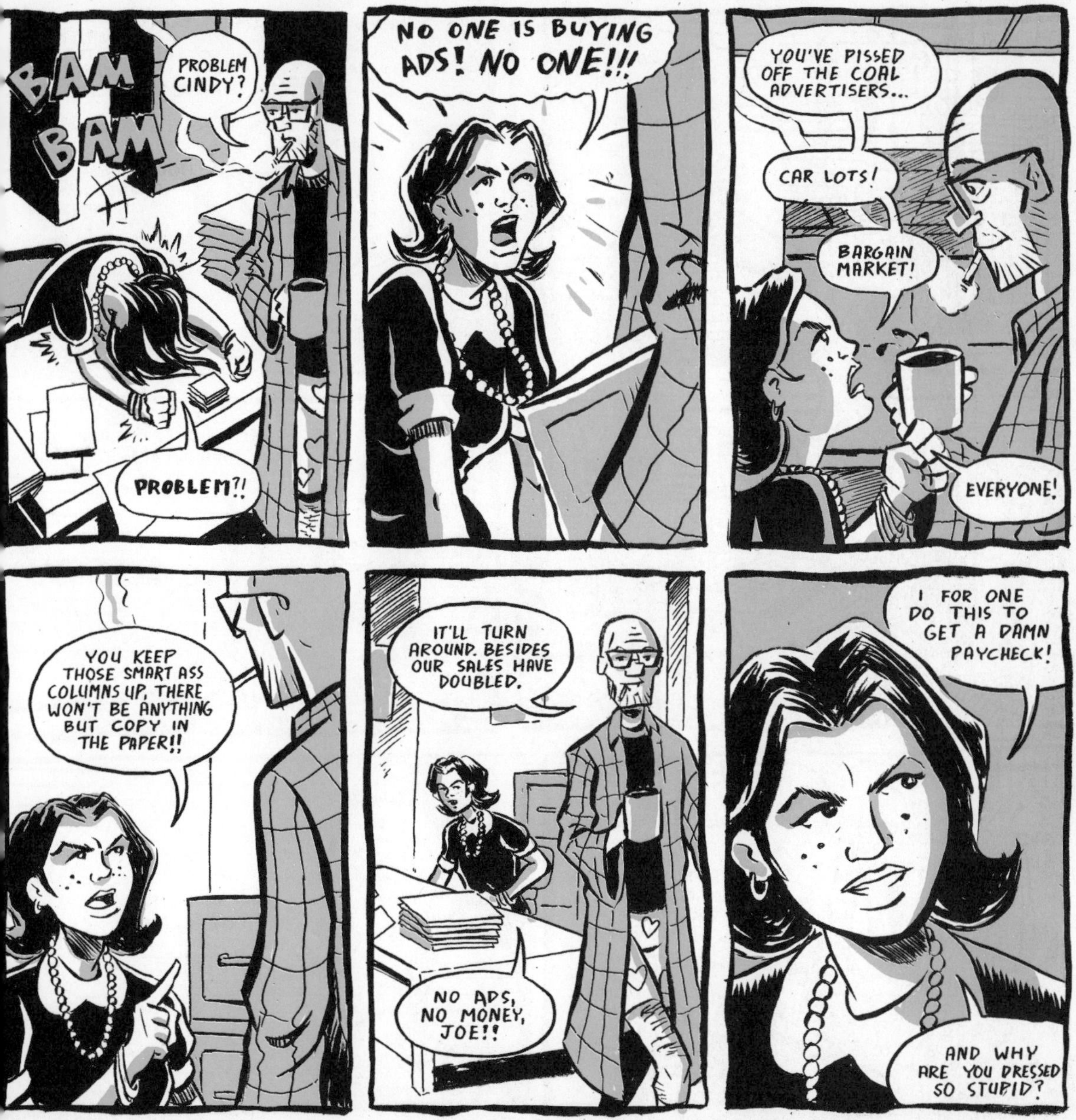
BAM
BAM
PROBLEM CINDY?
PROBLEM?!
NO ONE IS BUYING ADS! NO ONE!!!
YOU'VE PISSED OFF THE COAL ADVERTISERS...
CAR LOTS!
BARGAIN MARKET!
EVERYONE!
YOU KEEP THOSE SMART ASS COLUMNS UP, THERE WON'T BE ANYTHING BUT COPY IN THE PAPER!!
IT'LL TURN AROUND. BESIDES OUR SALES HAVE DOUBLED.
NO ADS, NO MONEY, JOE!!
I FOR ONE DO THIS TO GET A DAMN PAYCHECK!
AND WHY ARE YOU DRESSED SO STUPID?

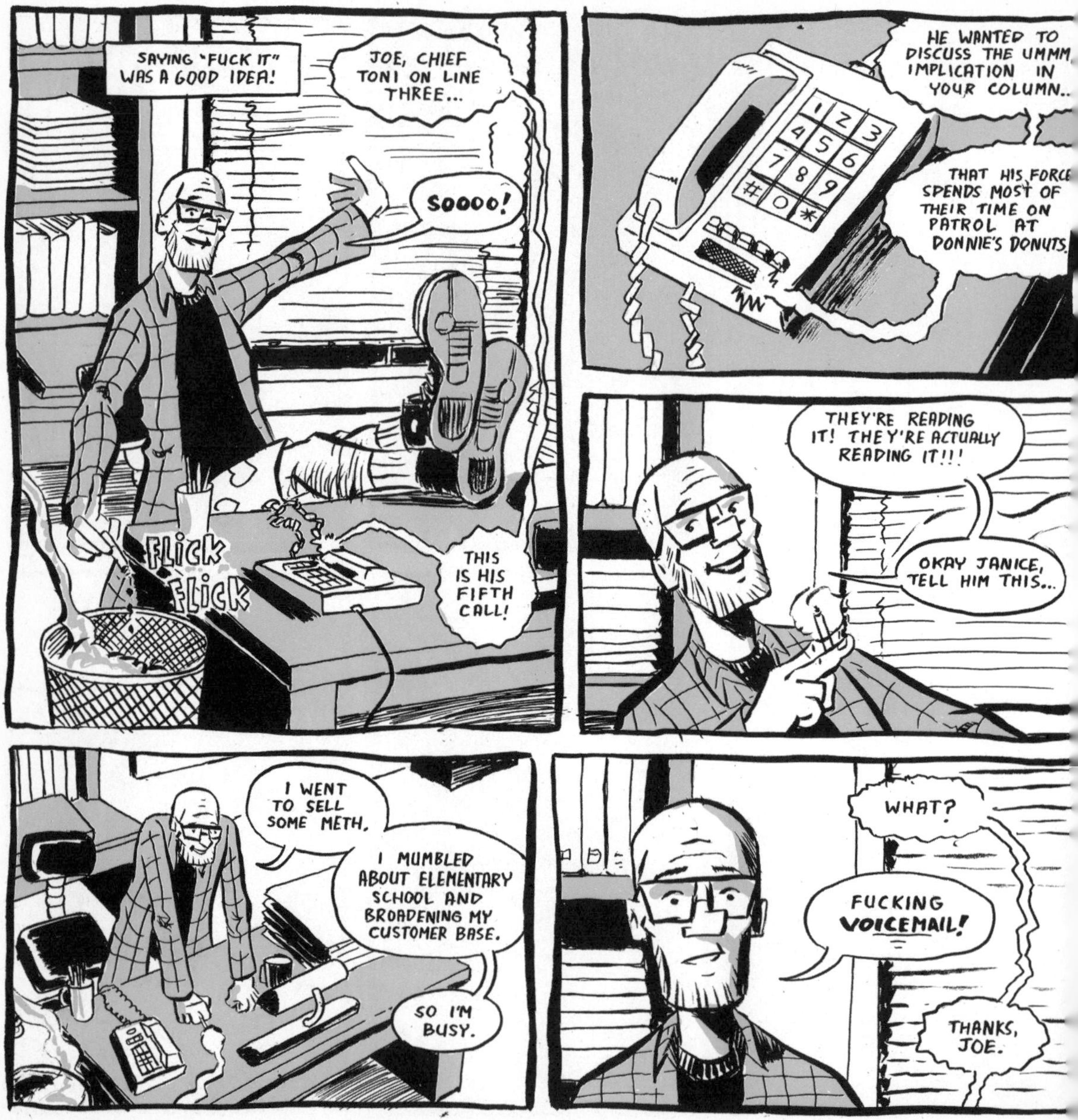
SAYING "FUCK IT" WAS A GOOD IDEA!
JOE, CHIEF TONI ON LINE THREE...
SOOOO!
FLICK FLICK
THIS IS HIS FIFTH CALL!
HE WANTED TO DISCUSS THE UMMM IMPLICATION IN YOUR COLUMN...
THAT HIS FORCE SPENDS MOST OF THEIR TIME ON PATROL AT DONNIE'S DONUTS.
THEY'RE READING IT! THEY'RE ACTUALLY READING IT!!!
OKAY JANICE, TELL HIM THIS...
I WENT TO SELL SOME METH.
I MUMBLED ABOUT ELEMENTARY SCHOOL AND BROADENING MY CUSTOMER BASE.
SO I'M BUSY.
WHAT?
FUCKING VOICEMAIL!
THANKS, JOE.

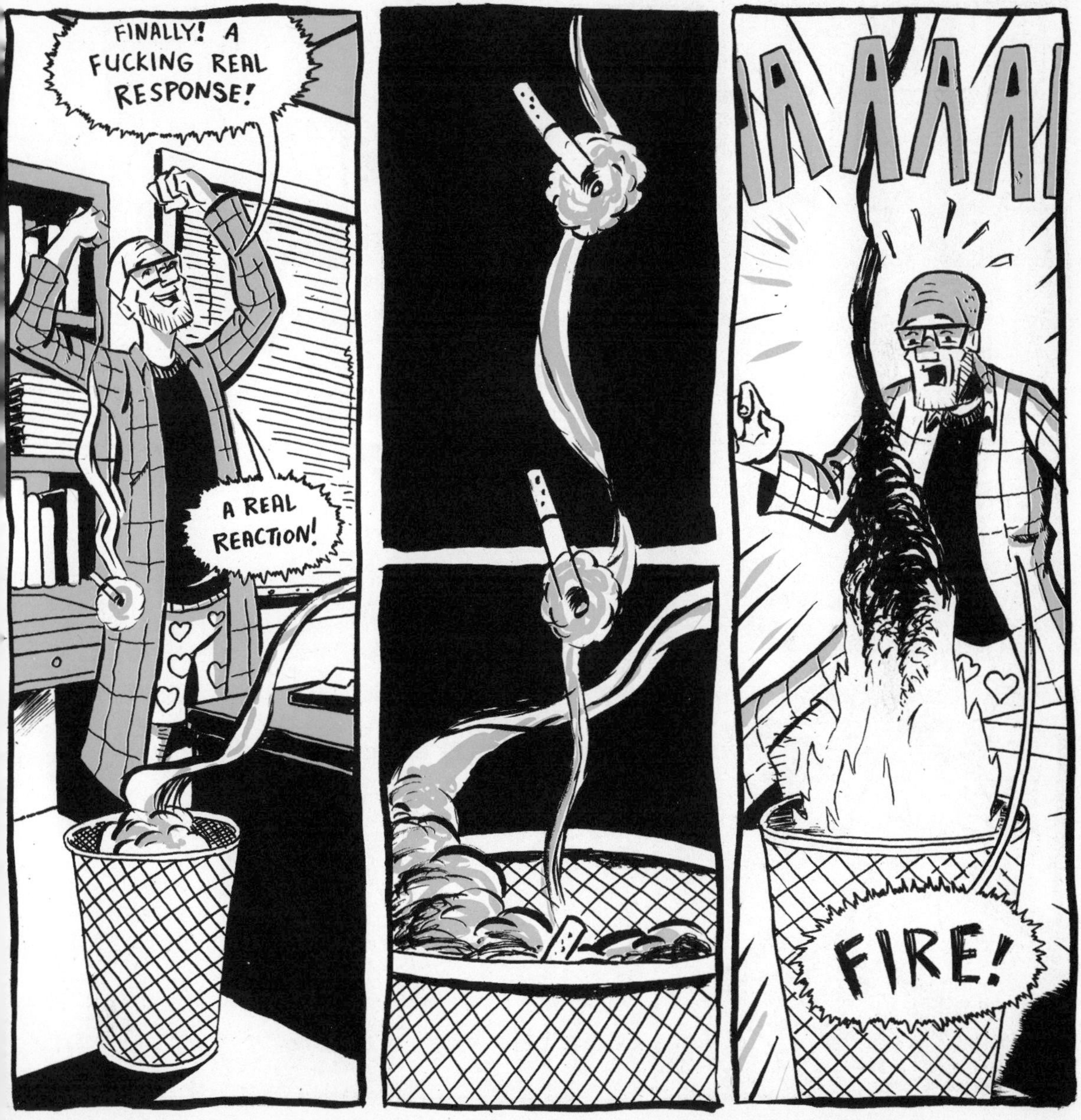
FINALLY! A FUCKING REAL RESPONSE!
A REAL REACTION!
AAAAA
FIRE!

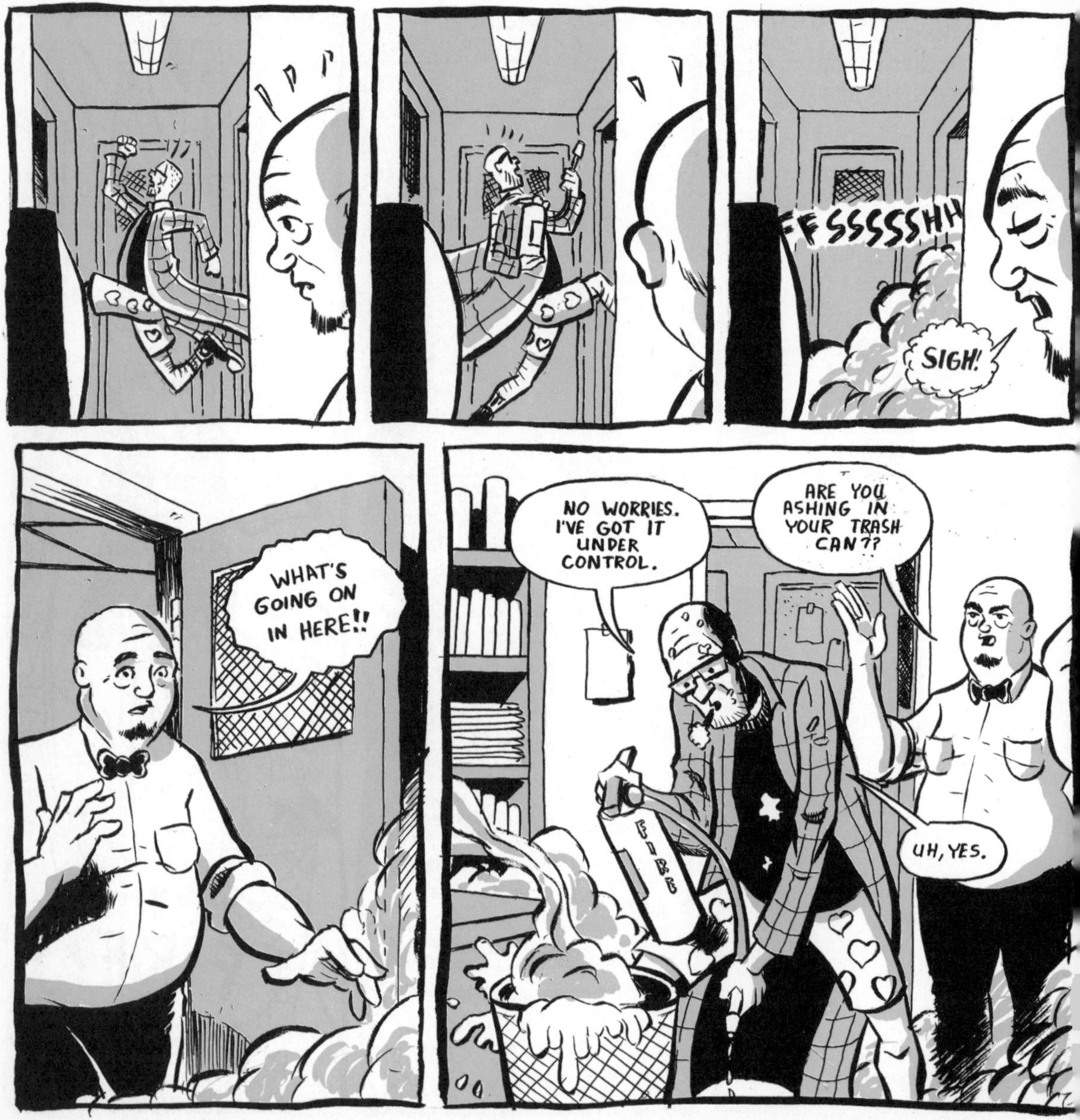
FFSSSSSHH
SIGH!
WHAT'S GOING ON IN HERE!!
NO WORRIES. I'VE GOT IT UNDER CONTROL.
ARE YOU ASHING IN YOUR TRASH CAN??
UH, YES.
FIRE

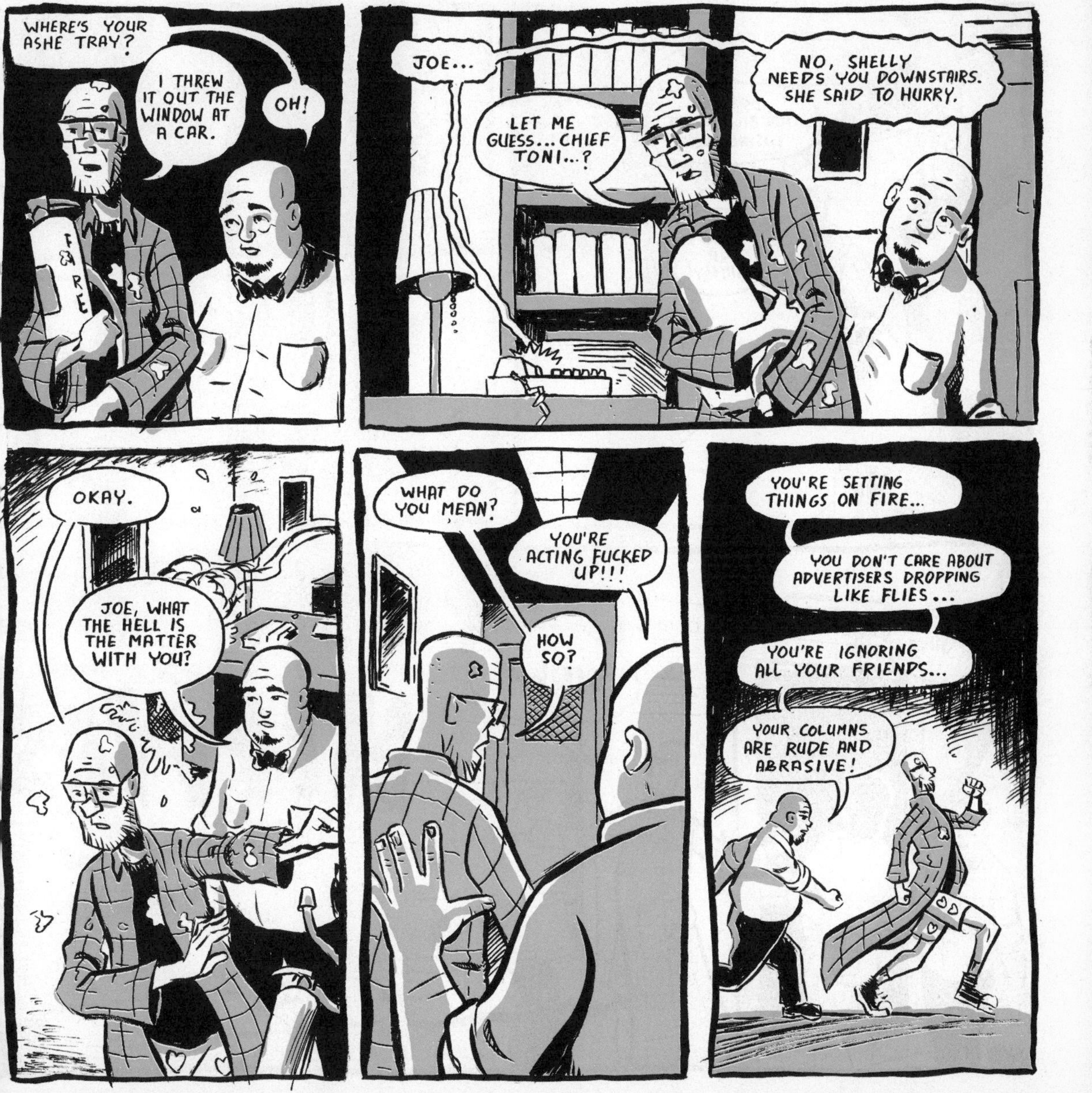
WHERE'S YOUR ASHE TRAY?
I THREW IT OUT THE WINDOW AT A CAR.
OH!
FIRE
JOE...
LET ME GUESS... CHIEF TONI...?
NO, SHELLY NEEDS YOU DOWNSTAIRS. SHE SAID TO HURRY.
OKAY.
JOE, WHAT THE HELL IS THE MATTER WITH YOU?
WHAT DO YOU MEAN?
YOU'RE ACTING FUCKED UP!!!
HOW SO?
YOU'RE SETTING THINGS ON FIRE...
YOU DON'T CARE ABOUT ADVERTISERS DROPPING LIKE FLIES...
YOU'RE IGNORING ALL YOUR FRIENDS...
YOUR COLUMNS ARE RUDE AND ABRASIVE!

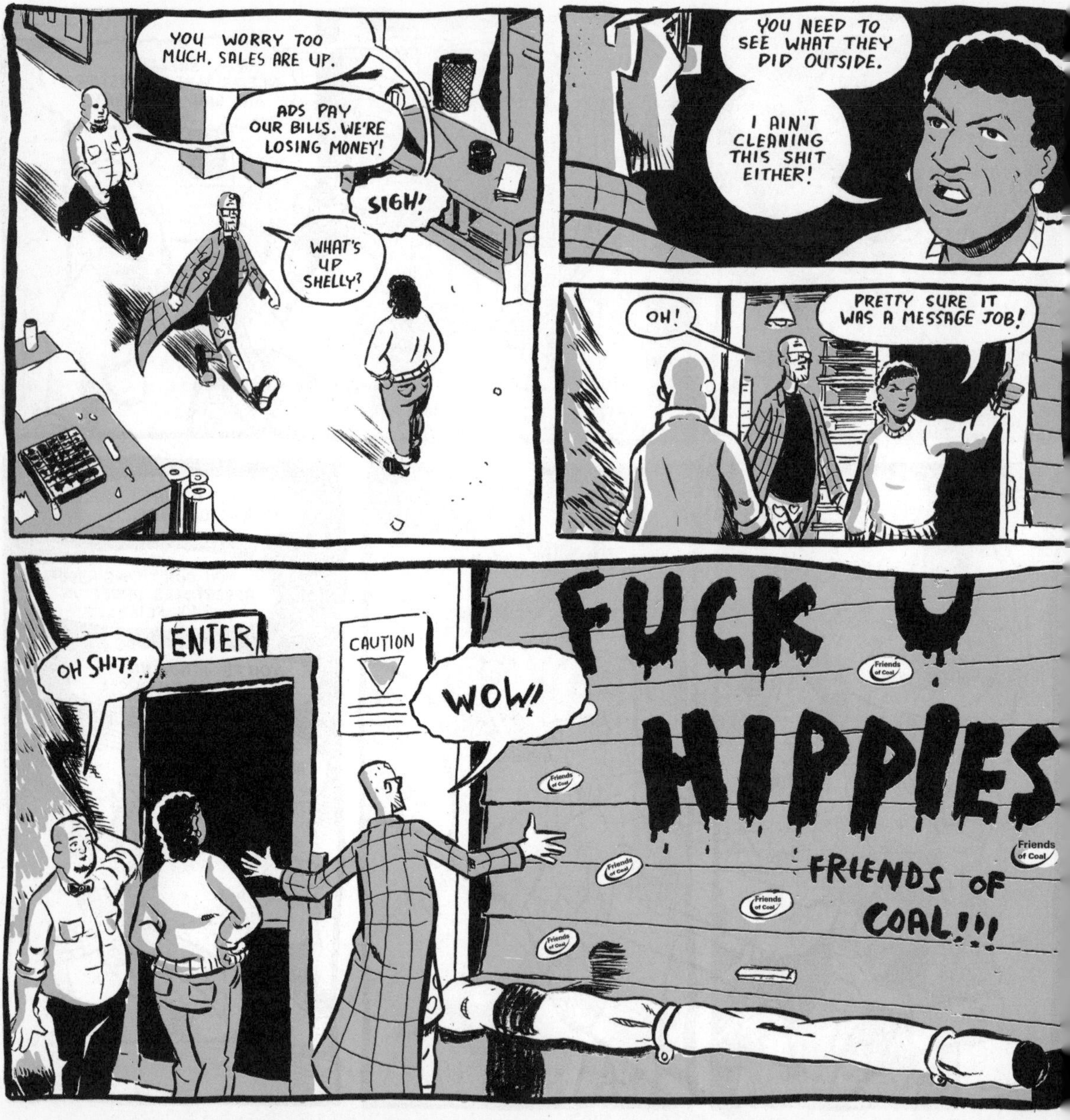
YOU WORRY TOO MUCH. SALES ARE UP.
ADS PAY OUR BILLS. WE'RE LOSING MONEY!
SIGH!
WHAT'S UP SHELLY?
YOU NEED TO SEE WHAT THEY DID OUTSIDE.
I AIN'T CLEANING THIS SHIT EITHER!
OH!
PRETTY SURE IT WAS A MESSAGE JOB!
ENTER
CAUTION
OH SHIT!..
WOW!
FUCK U
HIPPIES
FRIENDS OF COAL!!!
Friends of Coal

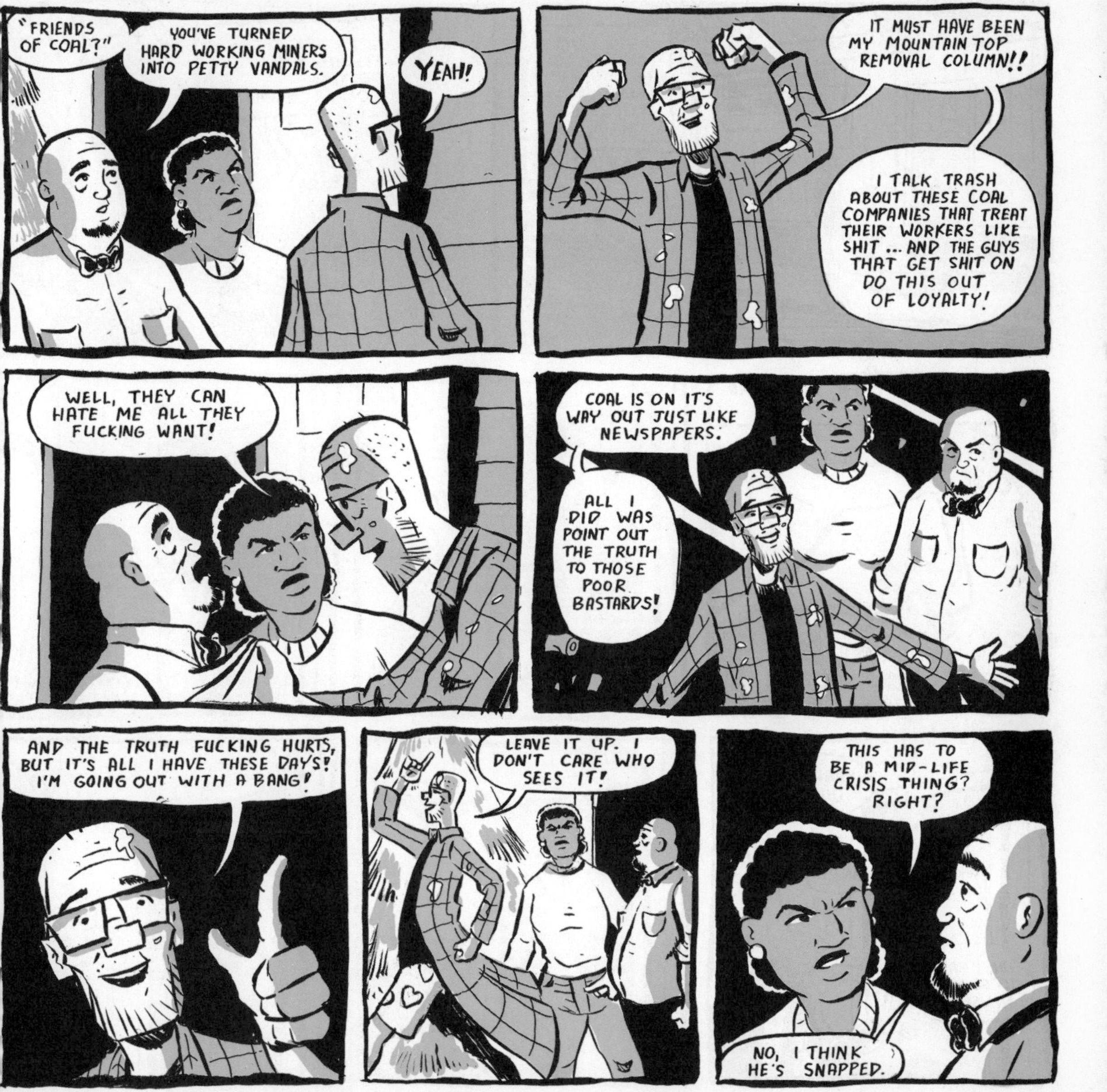
"FRIENDS OF COAL?"
YOU'VE TURNED HARD WORKING MINERS INTO PETTY VANDALS.
YEAH!
IT MUST HAVE BEEN MY MOUNTAIN TOP REMOVAL COLUMN!!
I TALK TRASH ABOUT THESE COAL COMPANIES THAT TREAT THEIR WORKERS LIKE SHIT ... AND THE GUYS THAT GET SHIT ON DO THIS OUT OF LOYALTY!
WELL, THEY CAN HATE ME ALL THEY FUCKING WANT!
COAL IS ON IT'S WAY OUT JUST LIKE NEWSPAPERS.
ALL I DID WAS POINT OUT THE TRUTH TO THOSE POOR BASTARDS!
AND THE TRUTH FUCKING HURTS, BUT IT'S ALL I HAVE THESE DAYS! I'M GOING OUT WITH A BANG!
LEAVE IT UP. I DON'T CARE WHO SEES IT!
THIS HAS TO BE A MID-LIFE CRISIS THING? RIGHT?
NO, I THINK HE'S SNAPPED.

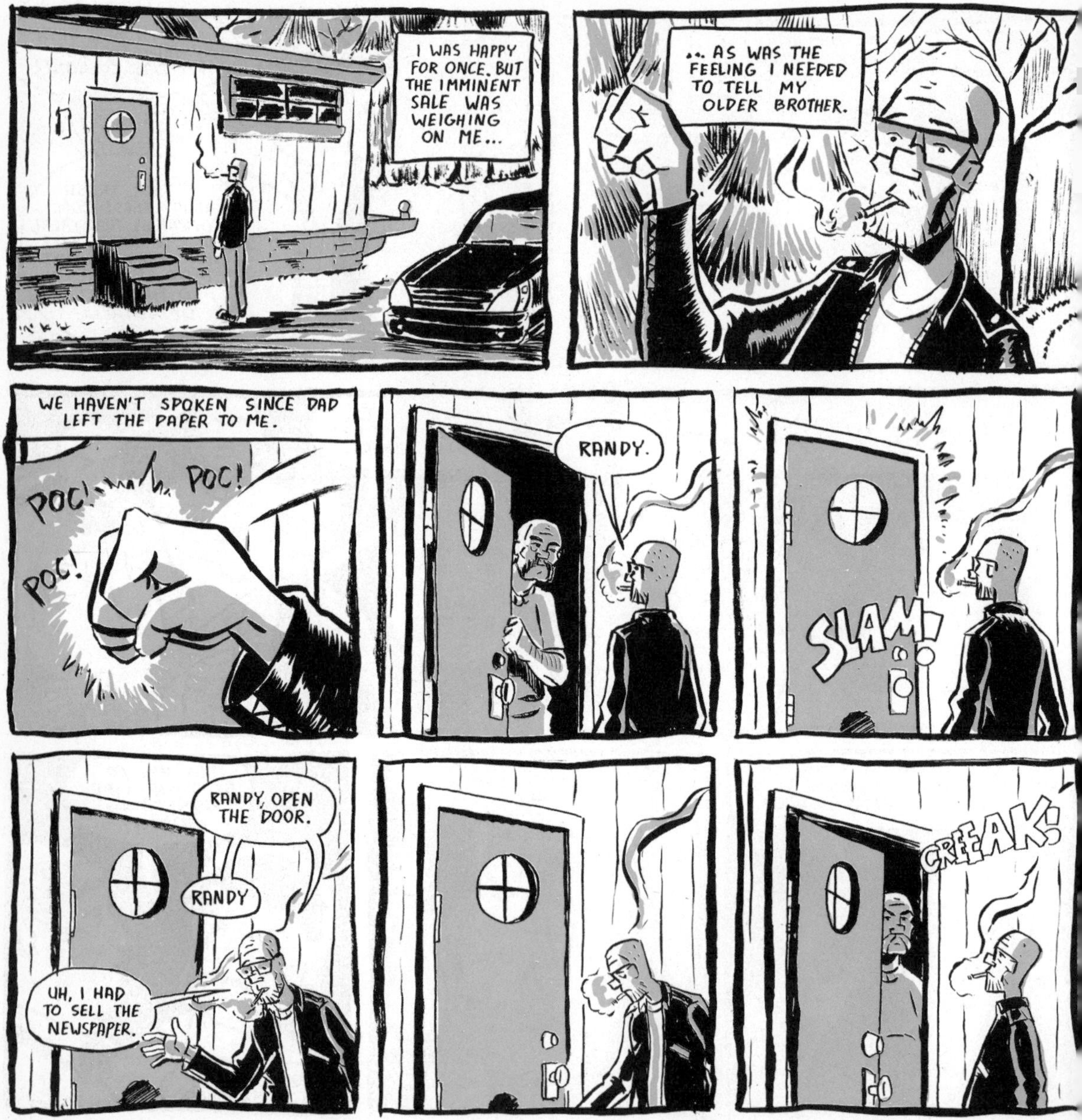
I WAS HAPPY FOR ONCE. BUT THE IMMINENT SALE WAS WEIGHING ON ME...
... AS WAS THE FEELING I NEEDED TO TELL MY OLDER BROTHER.
WE HAVEN'T SPOKEN SINCE DAD LEFT THE PAPER TO ME.
POC! POC!
POC!
RANDY.
SLAM!
RANDY, OPEN THE DOOR.
RANDY
UH, I HAD TO SELL THE NEWSPAPER.
CREEAK!

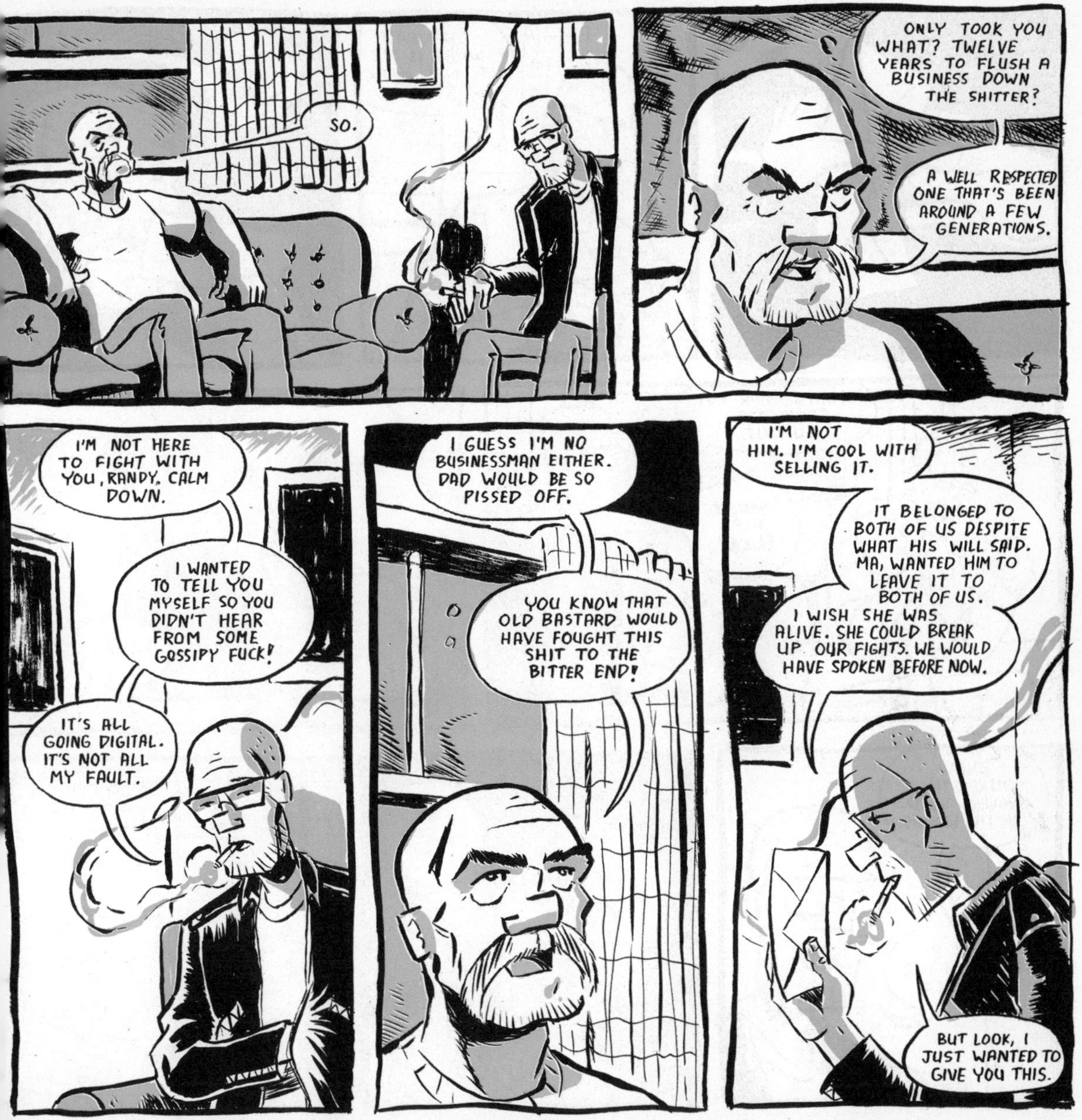
SO.
ONLY TOOK YOU WHAT? TWELVE YEARS TO FLUSH A BUSINESS DOWN THE SHITTER?
A WELL RESPECTED ONE THAT'S BEEN AROUND A FEW GENERATIONS.
I'M NOT HERE TO FIGHT WITH YOU, RANDY, CALM DOWN.
I WANTED TO TELL YOU MYSELF SO YOU DIDN'T HEAR FROM SOME GOSSIPY FUCK!
IT'S ALL GOING DIGITAL. IT'S NOT ALL MY FAULT.
I GUESS I'M NO BUSINESSMAN EITHER. DAD WOULD BE SO PISSED OFF.
YOU KNOW THAT OLD BASTARD WOULD HAVE FOUGHT THIS SHIT TO THE BITTER END!
I'M NOT HIM. I'M COOL WITH SELLING IT.
IT BELONGED TO BOTH OF US DESPITE WHAT HIS WILL SAID. MA, WANTED HIM TO LEAVE IT TO BOTH OF US.
I WISH SHE WAS ALIVE. SHE COULD BREAK UP OUR FIGHTS. WE WOULD HAVE SPOKEN BEFORE NOW.
BUT LOOK, I JUST WANTED TO GIVE YOU THIS.

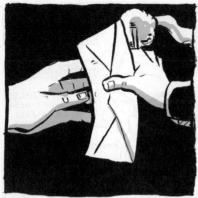

OH YEAH,
WHAT IS IT?
A HALLMARK
CARD?

NO, IT'S A CHECK.

THAT'S YOUR CUT FROM THE BUYOUT.

WHAT THE FUCK!

Y- YOU'RE JUST GONNA GIVE ME ALL THIS MONEY? LIKE THAT?

NO!

I KNOW YOU'RE STILL GROWING WEED IN THE WOODS.

I'D LIKE TO TRADE SOME FOR THAT CHECK.

HA! HA! HA!

LET'S SMOKE TO IT. I'LL GET MY BOWL.

PEACE PIPE.

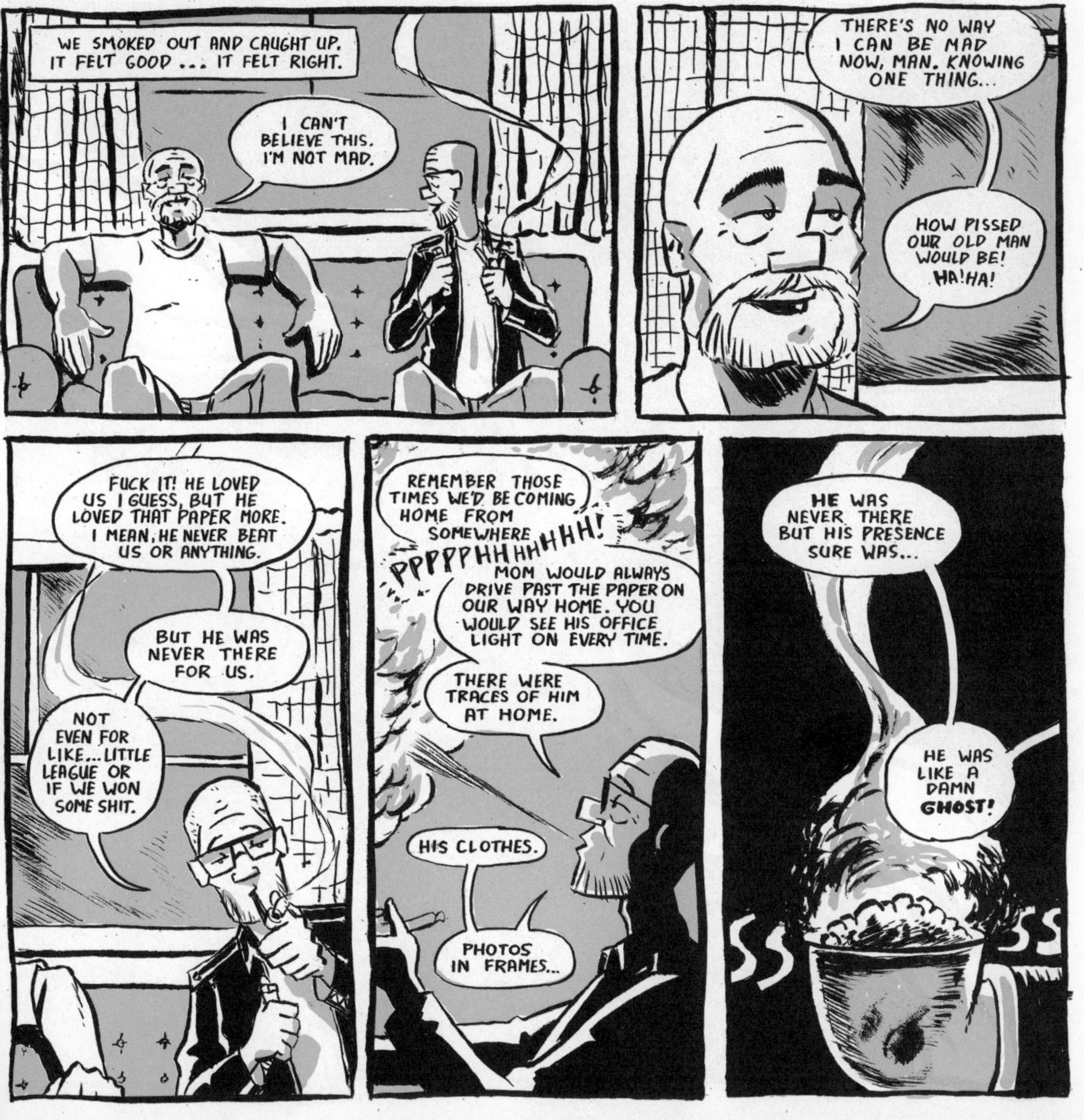
WE SMOKED OUT AND CAUGHT UP. IT FELT GOOD ... IT FELT RIGHT.
I CAN'T BELIEVE THIS. I'M NOT MAD.
THERE'S NO WAY I CAN BE MAD NOW, MAN. KNOWING ONE THING...
HOW PISSED OUR OLD MAN WOULD BE! HA! HA!
FUCK IT! HE LOVED US I GUESS, BUT HE LOVED THAT PAPER MORE. I MEAN, HE NEVER BEAT US OR ANYTHING.
BUT HE WAS NEVER THERE FOR US.
NOT EVEN FOR LIKE... LITTLE LEAGUE OR IF WE WON SOME SHIT.
REMEMBER THOSE TIMES WE'D BE COMING HOME FROM SOMEWHERE
PPPPPHHHHHHH!
MOM WOULD ALWAYS DRIVE PAST THE PAPER ON OUR WAY HOME. YOU WOULD SEE HIS OFFICE LIGHT ON EVERY TIME.
THERE WERE TRACES OF HIM AT HOME.
HIS CLOTHES.
PHOTOS IN FRAMES...
HE WAS NEVER THERE BUT HIS PRESENCE SURE WAS...
HE WAS LIKE A DAMN GHOST!
SS
SS

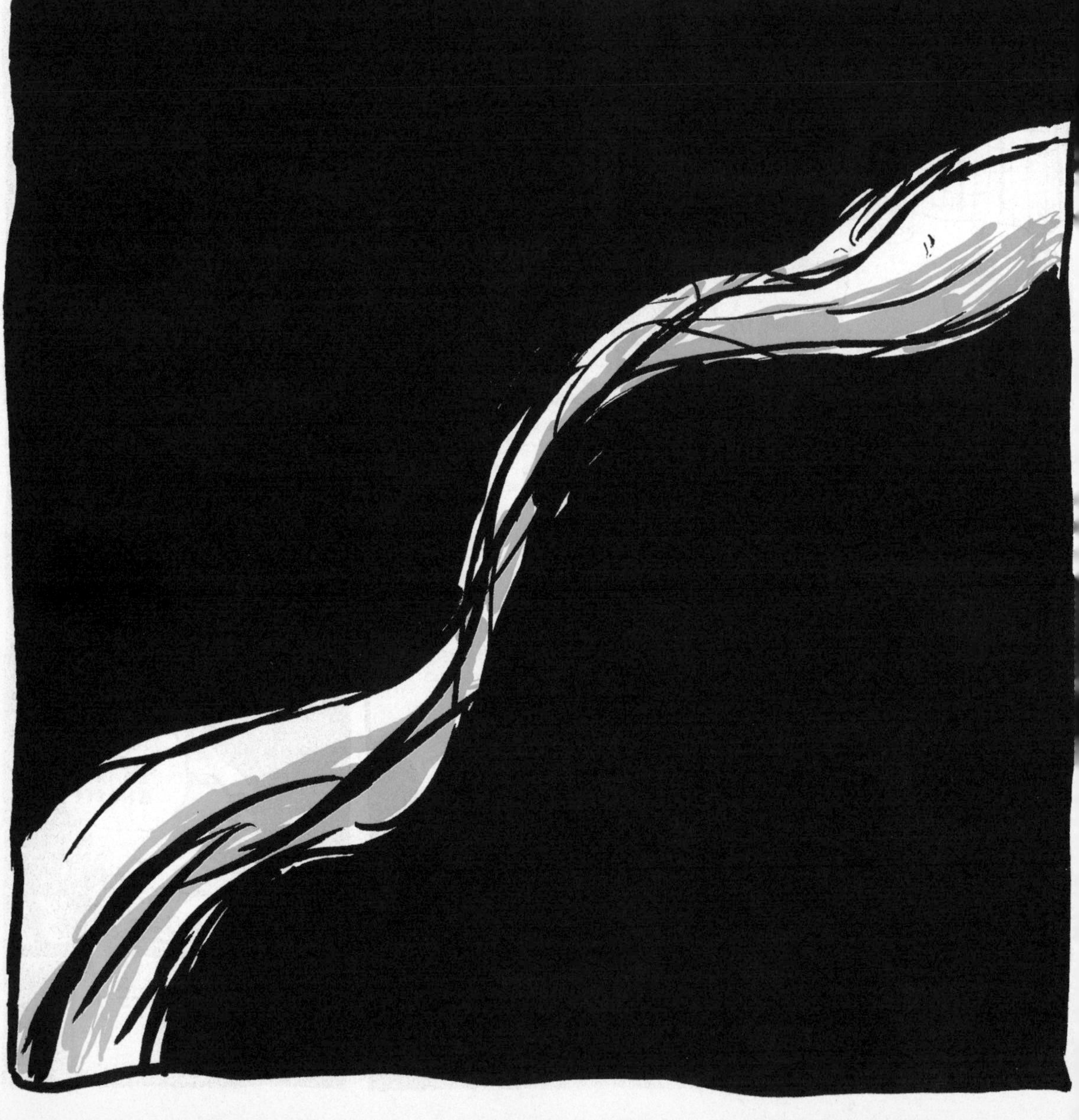

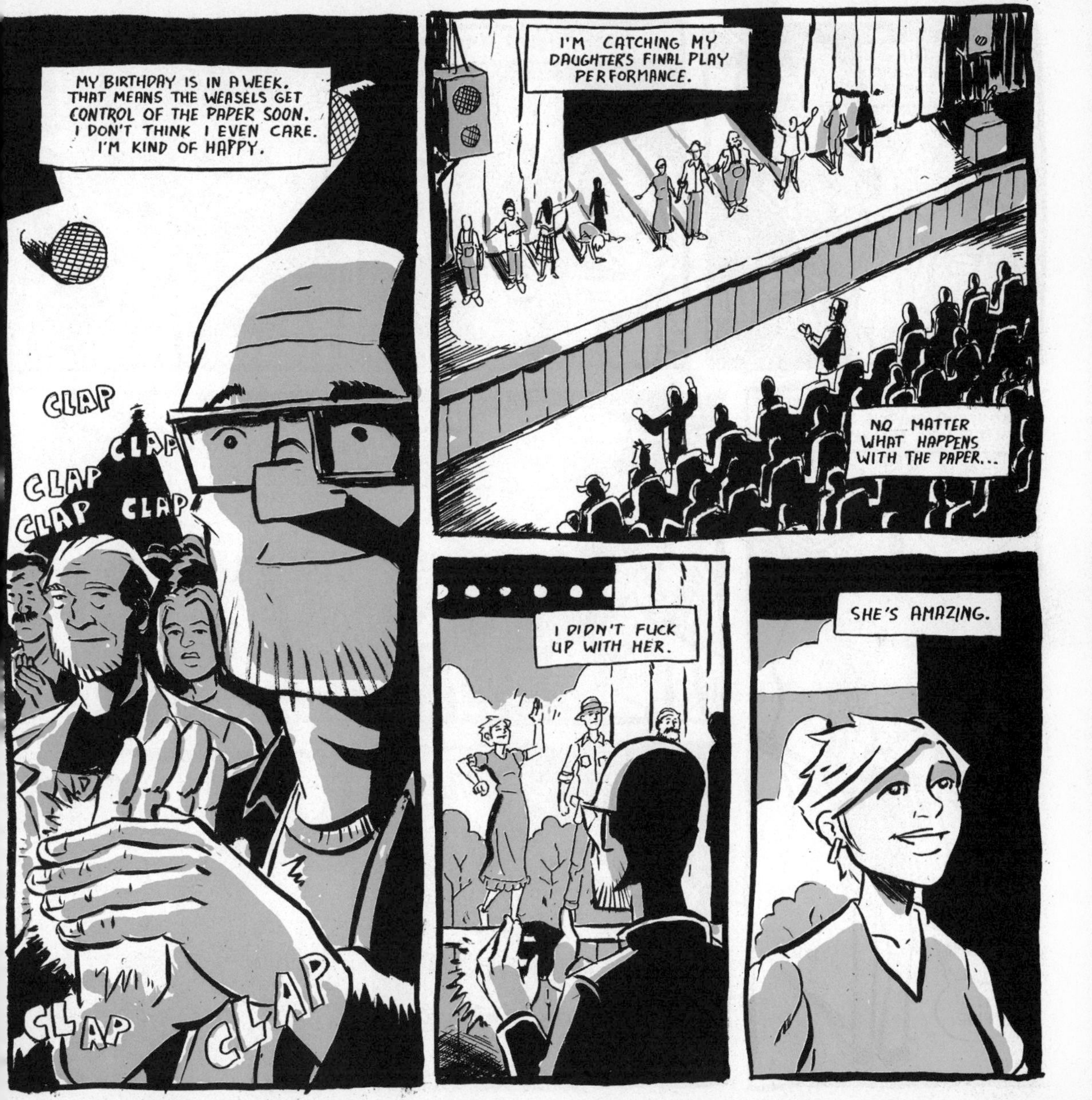
MY BIRTHDAY IS IN A WEEK. THAT MEANS THE WEASELS GET CONTROL OF THE PAPER SOON. I DON'T THINK I EVEN CARE. I'M KIND OF HAPPY.
CLAP
CLAP
CLAP
CLAP
CLAP
CLAP
CLAP
I'M CATCHING MY DAUGHTER'S FINAL PLAY PERFORMANCE.
NO MATTER WHAT HAPPENS WITH THE PAPER...
I DIDN'T FUCK UP WITH HER.
SHE'S AMAZING.

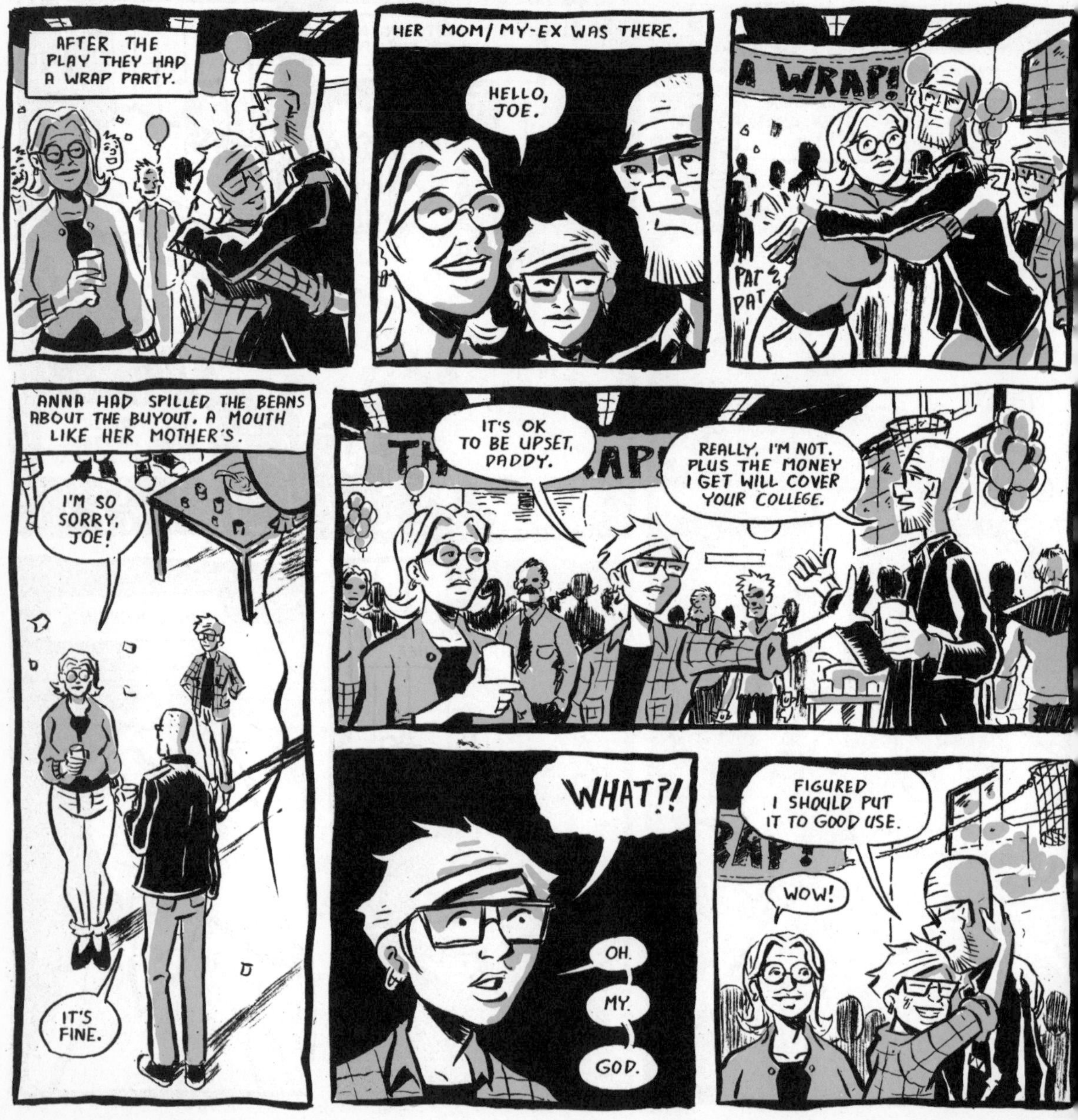

AFTER THE PLAY THEY HAD A WRAP PARTY.
HER MOM/MY-EX WAS THERE.
HELLO, JOE.
A WRAP!
PAT PAT
ANNA HAD SPILLED THE BEANS ABOUT THE BUYOUT. A MOUTH LIKE HER MOTHER'S.
I'M SO SORRY, JOE!
IT'S FINE.
IT'S OK TO BE UPSET, DADDY.
REALLY, I'M NOT. PLUS THE MONEY I GET WILL COVER YOUR COLLEGE.
WHAT?!
OH.
MY.
GOD.
FIGURED I SHOULD PUT IT TO GOOD USE.
WOW!

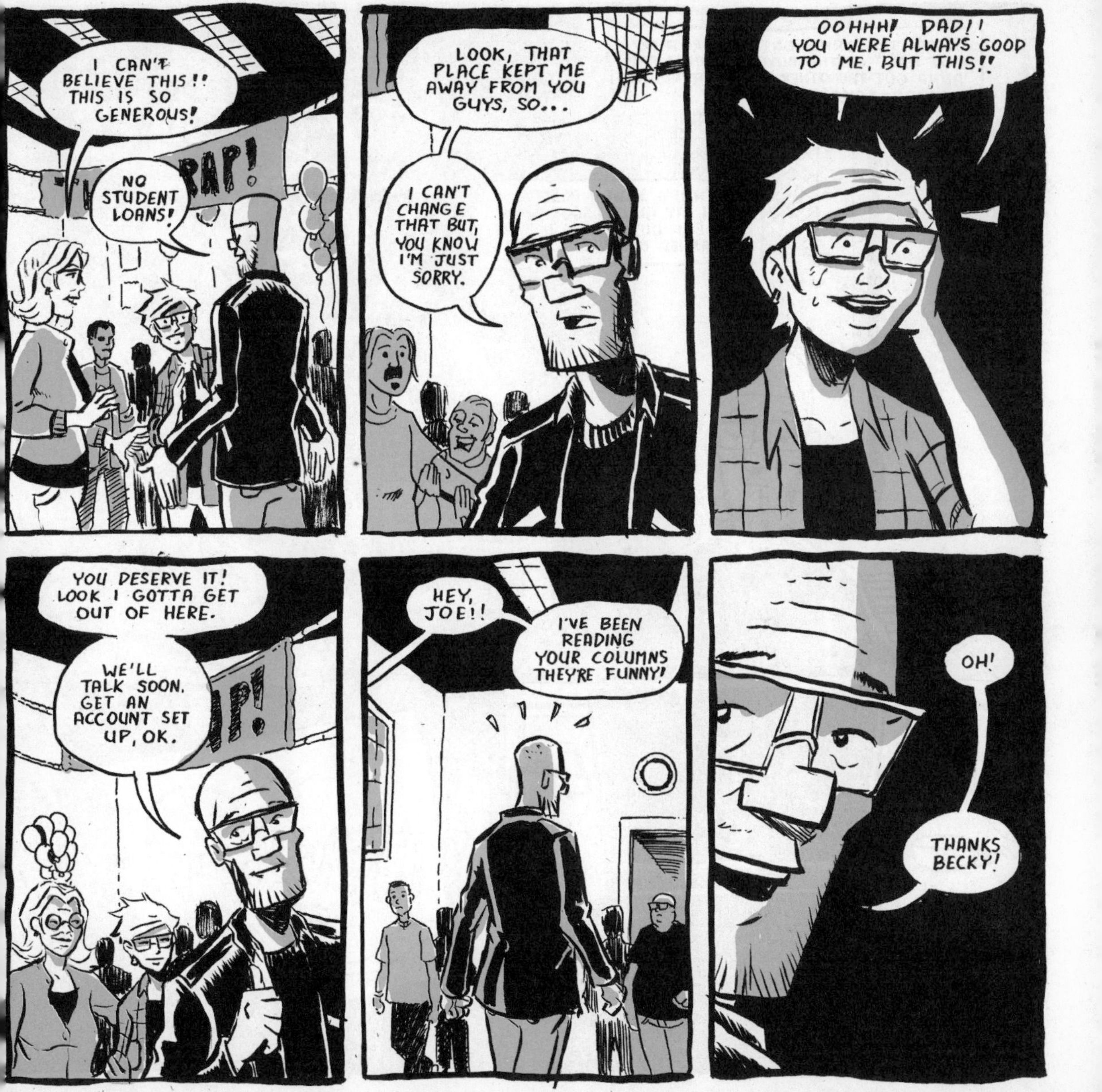
I CAN'T BELIEVE THIS!! THIS IS SO GENEROUS!
NO STUDENT LOANS!
LOOK, THAT PLACE KEPT ME AWAY FROM YOU GUYS, SO...
I CAN'T CHANGE THAT BUT, YOU KNOW I'M JUST SORRY.
OOHHH! DAD!! YOU WERE ALWAYS GOOD TO ME, BUT THIS!!
YOU DESERVE IT! LOOK I GOTTA GET OUT OF HERE.
WE'LL TALK SOON. GET AN ACCOUNT SET UP, OK.
HEY, JOE!!
I'VE BEEN READING YOUR COLUMNS THEY'RE FUNNY!
OH!
THANKS BECKY!

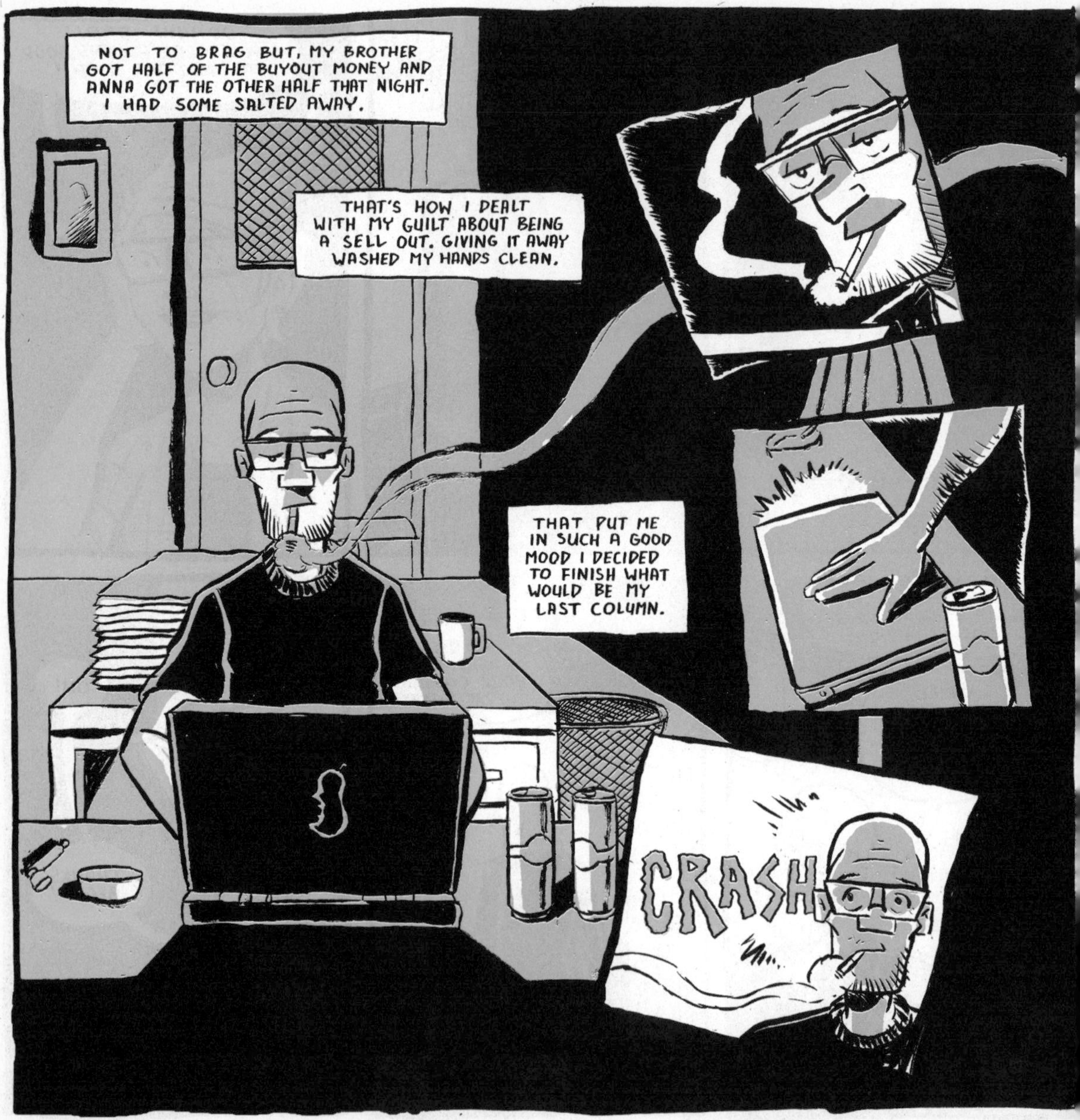
NOT TO BRAG BUT, MY BROTHER GOT HALF OF THE BUYOUT MONEY AND ANNA GOT THE OTHER HALF THAT NIGHT. I HAD SOME SALTED AWAY.
THAT'S HOW I DEALT WITH MY GUILT ABOUT BEING A SELL OUT. GIVING IT AWAY WASHED MY HANDS CLEAN.
THAT PUT ME IN SUCH A GOOD MOOD I DECIDED TO FINISH WHAT WOULD BE MY LAST COLUMN.
CRASH

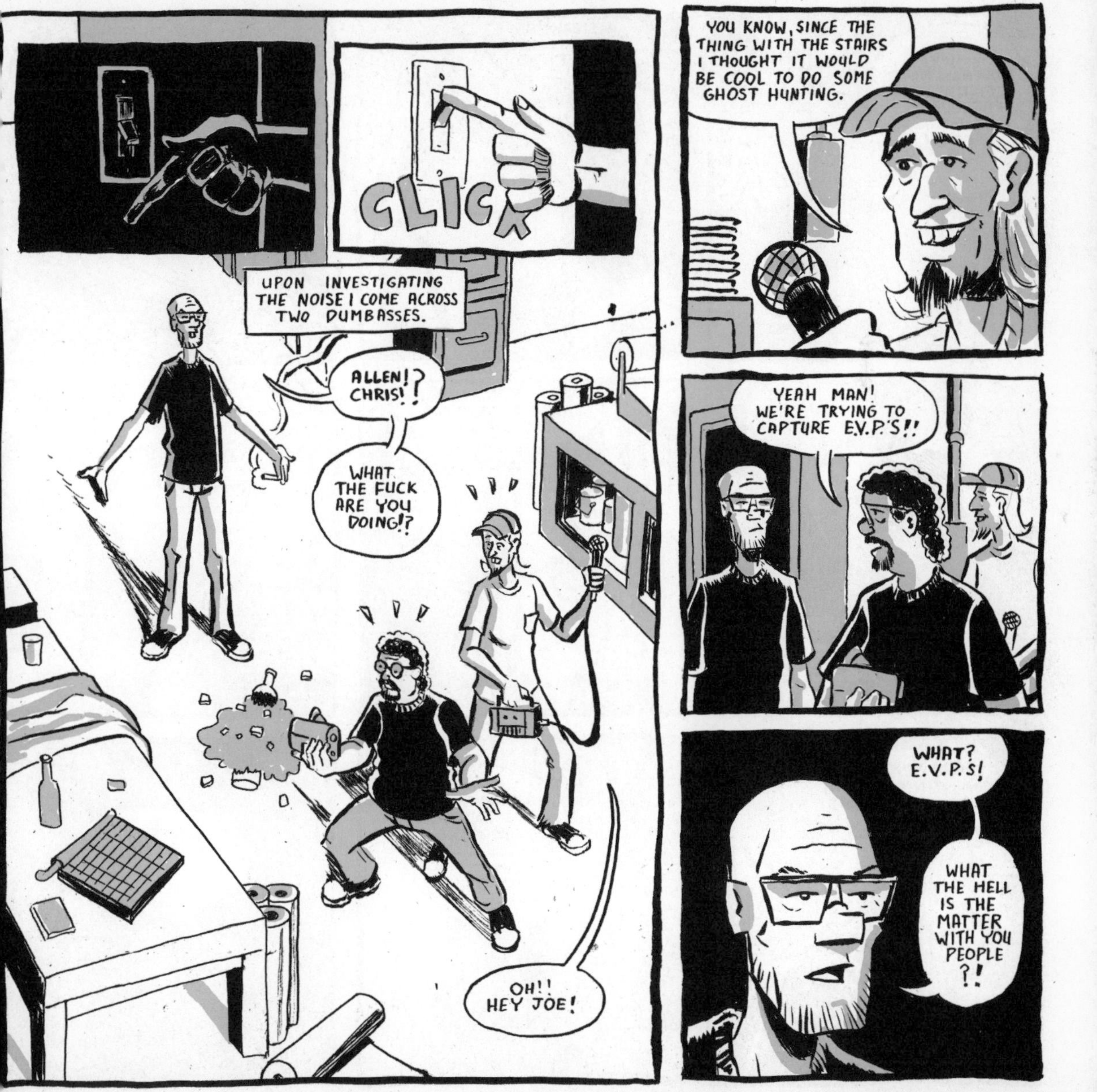
CLICK
UPON INVESTIGATING THE NOISE I COME ACROSS TWO DUMBASSES.
ALLEN!? CHRIS!?
WHAT THE FUCK ARE YOU DOING!?
OH!! HEY JOE!
YOU KNOW, SINCE THE THING WITH THE STAIRS I THOUGHT IT WOULD BE COOL TO DO SOME GHOST HUNTING.
YEAH MAN! WE'RE TRYING TO CAPTURE E.V.P.'S!!
WHAT? E.V.P.S!
WHAT THE HELL IS THE MATTER WITH YOU PEOPLE ?!

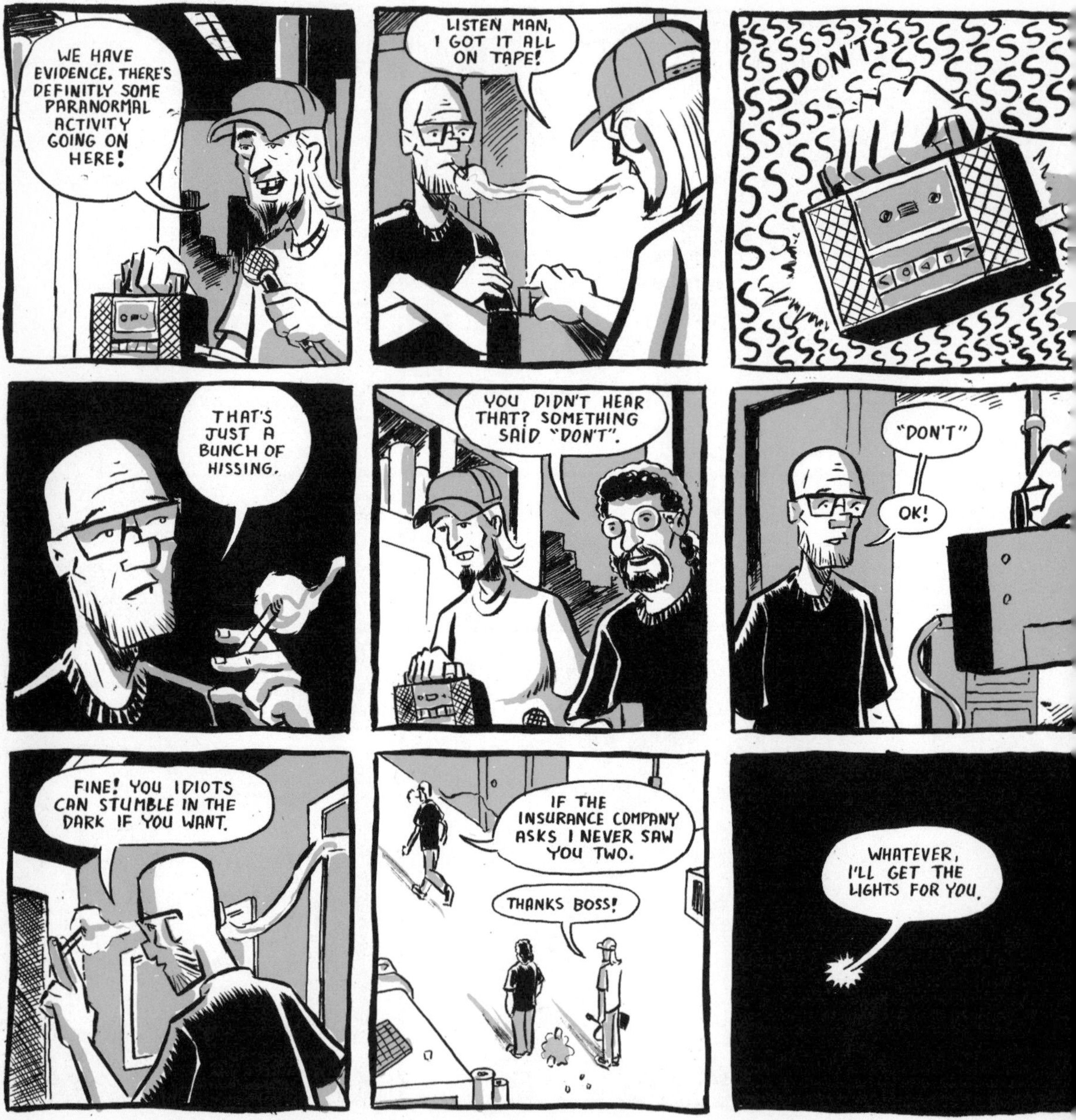
WE HAVE EVIDENCE. THERE'S DEFINITLY SOME PARANORMAL ACTIVITY GOING ON HERE!
LISTEN MAN, I GOT IT ALL ON TAPE!
SSSSSSSSSSSDON'TSSSSSSSSSS
THAT'S JUST A BUNCH OF HISSING.
YOU DIDN'T HEAR THAT? SOMETHING SAID "DON'T".
"DON'T"
OK!
FINE! YOU IDIOTS CAN STUMBLE IN THE DARK IF YOU WANT.
IF THE INSURANCE COMPANY ASKS I NEVER SAW YOU TWO.
THANKS BOSS!
WHATEVER, I'LL GET THE LIGHTS FOR YOU.

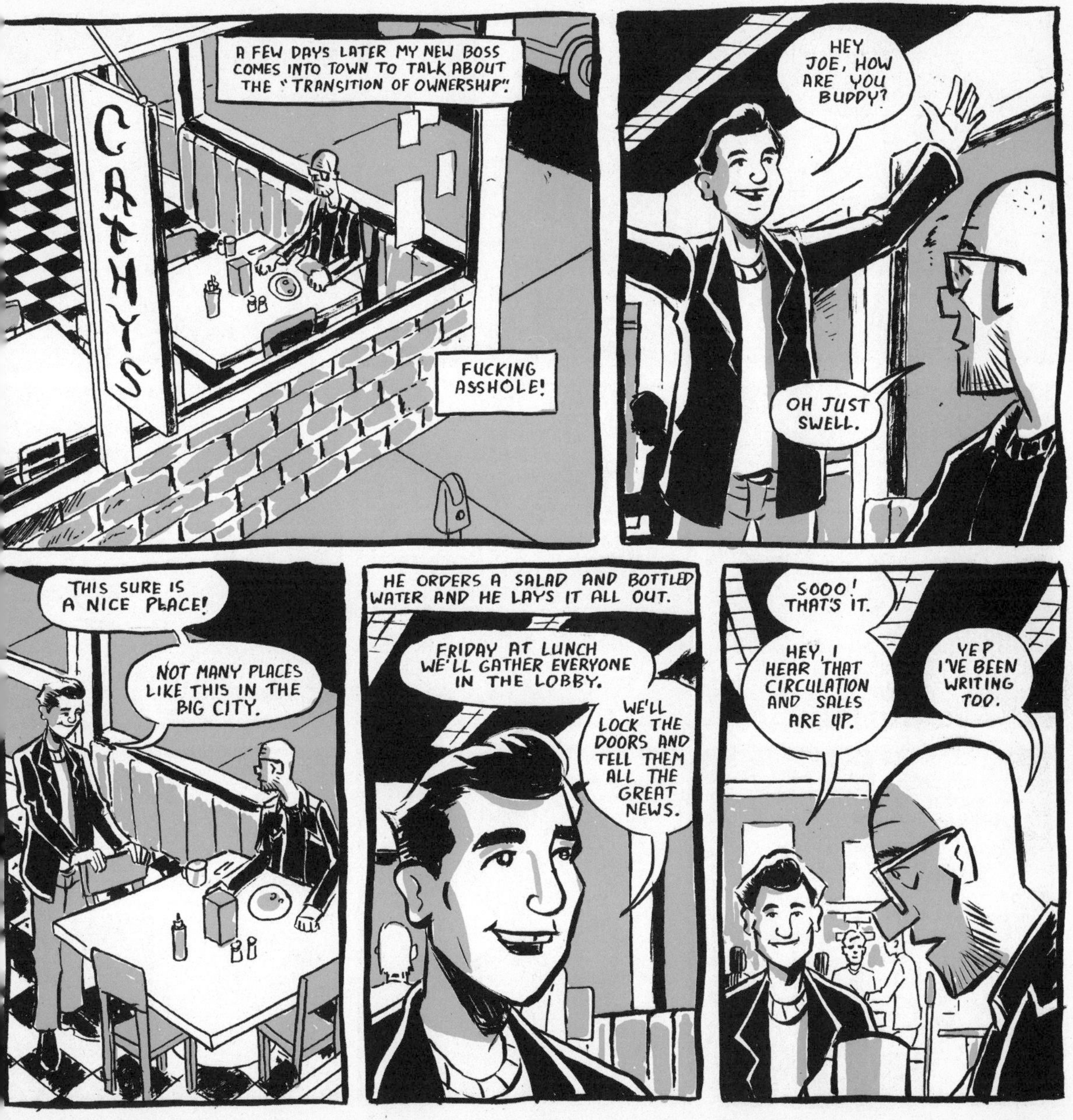
A FEW DAYS LATER MY NEW BOSS COMES INTO TOWN TO TALK ABOUT THE "TRANSITION OF OWNERSHIP".
CATHYS
FUCKING ASSHOLE!
HEY JOE, HOW ARE YOU BUDDY?
OH JUST SWELL.
THIS SURE IS A NICE PLACE!
NOT MANY PLACES LIKE THIS IN THE BIG CITY.
HE ORDERS A SALAD AND BOTTLED WATER AND HE LAYS IT ALL OUT.
FRIDAY AT LUNCH WE'LL GATHER EVERYONE IN THE LOBBY.
WE'LL LOCK THE DOORS AND TELL THEM ALL THE GREAT NEWS.
SOOO! THAT'S IT.
HEY, I HEAR THAT CIRCULATION AND SALES ARE UP.
YEP I'VE BEEN WRITING TOO.

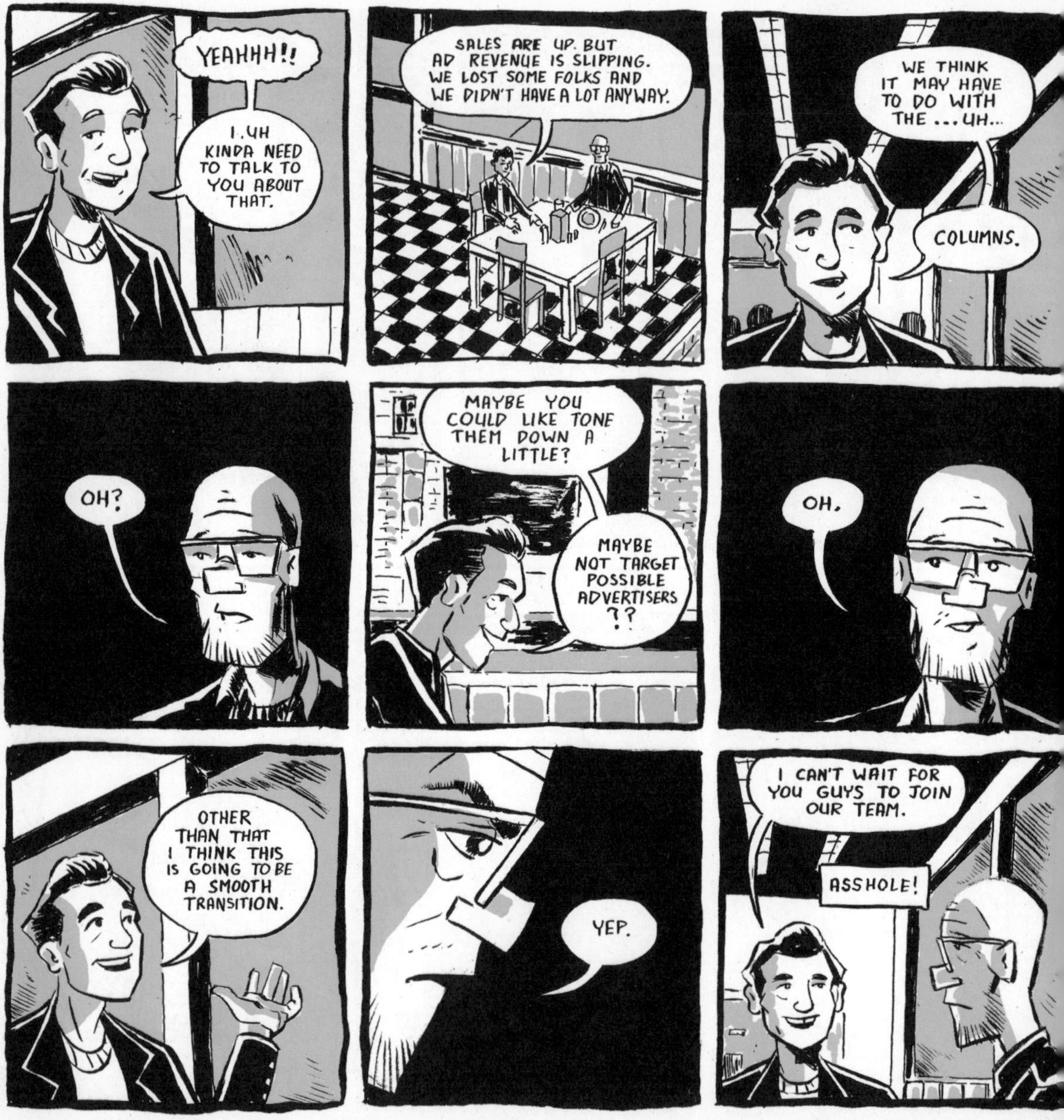
YEAHHH!!
I, UH KINDA NEED TO TALK TO YOU ABOUT THAT.
SALES ARE UP. BUT AD REVENUE IS SLIPPING. WE LOST SOME FOLKS AND WE DIDN'T HAVE A LOT ANYWAY.
WE THINK IT MAY HAVE TO DO WITH THE ... UH...
COLUMNS.
OH?
MAYBE YOU COULD LIKE TONE THEM DOWN A LITTLE?
MAYBE NOT TARGET POSSIBLE ADVERTISERS ??
OH.
OTHER THAN THAT I THINK THIS IS GOING TO BE A SMOOTH TRANSITION.
YEP.
I CAN'T WAIT FOR YOU GUYS TO JOIN OUR TEAM.
ASSHOLE!

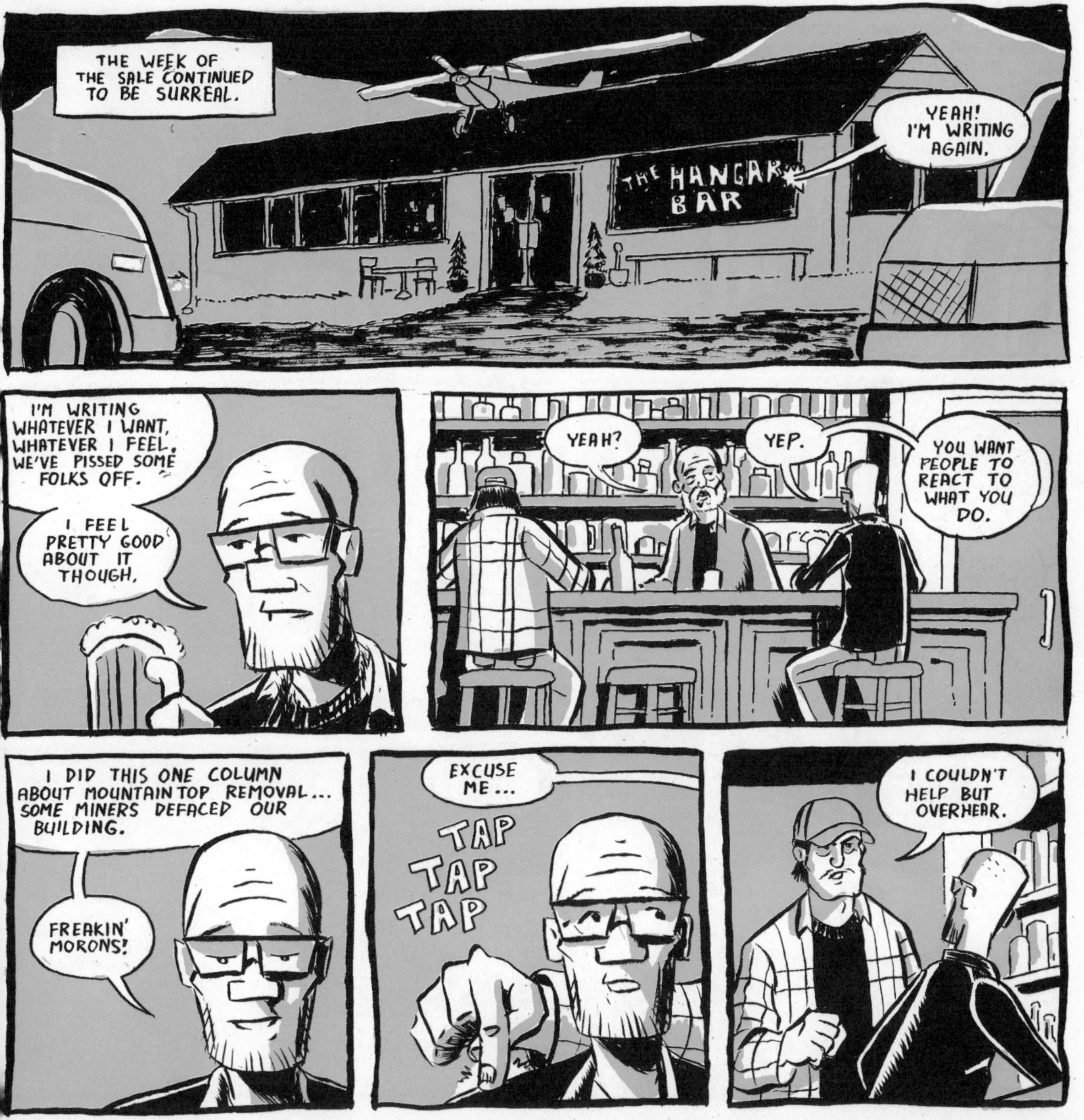
THE WEEK OF THE SALE CONTINUED TO BE SURREAL.
THE HANGAR BAR
YEAH! I'M WRITING AGAIN.
I'M WRITING WHATEVER I WANT, WHATEVER I FEEL. WE'VE PISSED SOME FOLKS OFF.
I FEEL PRETTY GOOD ABOUT IT THOUGH.
YEAH?
YEP.
YOU WANT PEOPLE TO REACT TO WHAT YOU DO.
I DID THIS ONE COLUMN ABOUT MOUNTAIN TOP REMOVAL... SOME MINERS DEFACED OUR BUILDING.
FREAKIN' MORONS!
EXCUSE ME...
TAP
TAP
TAP
I COULDN'T HELP BUT OVERHEAR.

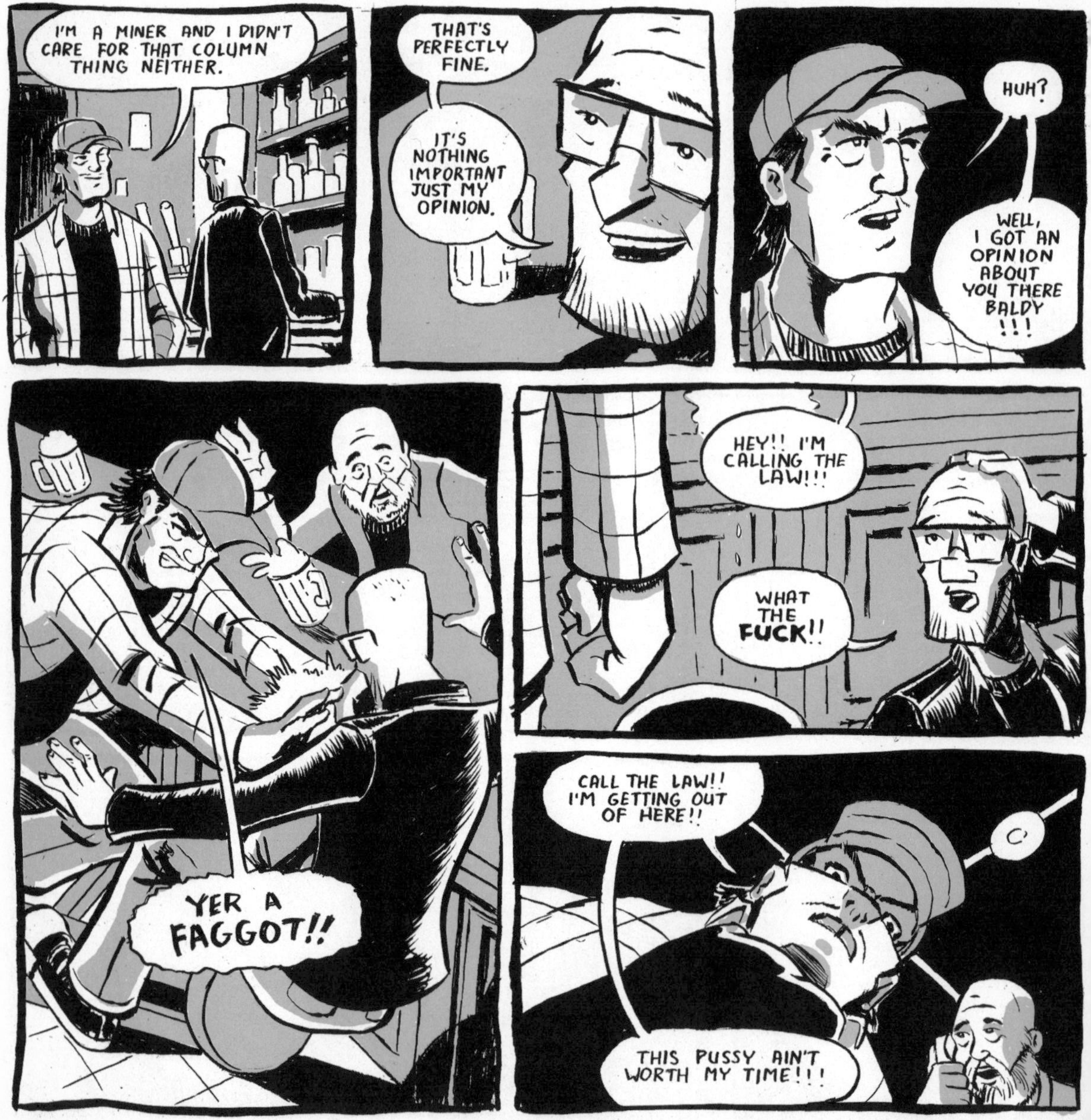

I'M A MINER AND I DIDN'T CARE FOR THAT COLUMN THING NEITHER.
THAT'S PERFECTLY FINE.
IT'S NOTHING IMPORTANT JUST MY OPINION.
HUH?
WELL, I GOT AN OPINION ABOUT YOU THERE BALDY !!!
YER A FAGGOT!!
HEY!! I'M CALLING THE LAW!!!
WHAT THE FUCK!!
CALL THE LAW!! I'M GETTING OUT OF HERE!!
THIS PUSSY AIN'T WORTH MY TIME!!!

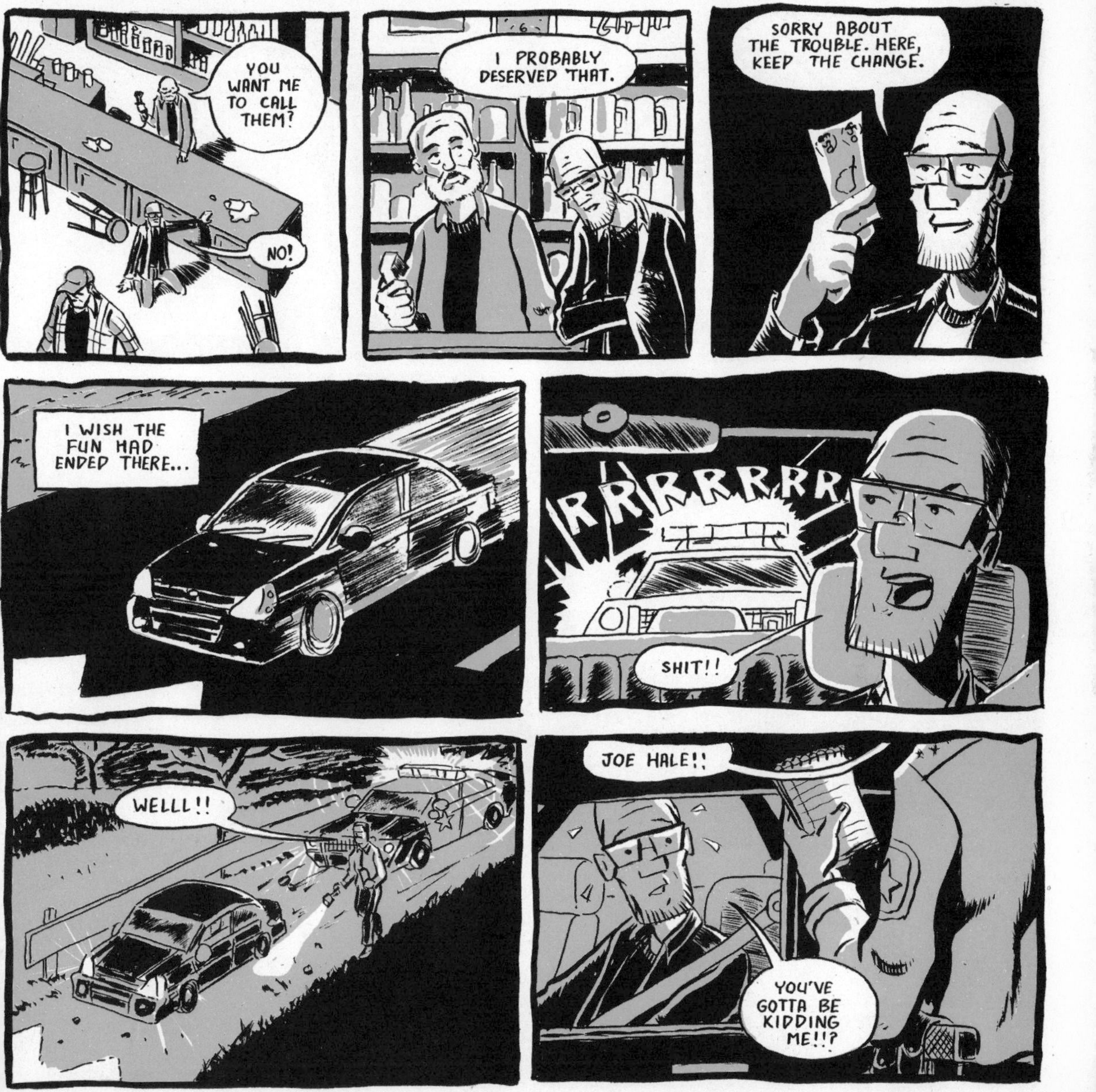
YOU WANT ME TO CALL THEM?
NO!
I PROBABLY DESERVED THAT.
SORRY ABOUT THE TROUBLE. HERE, KEEP THE CHANGE.
I WISH THE FUN HAD ENDED THERE...
RRRRRRRR
SHIT!!
WELLL!!
JOE HALE!!
YOU'VE GOTTA BE KIDDING ME!!?

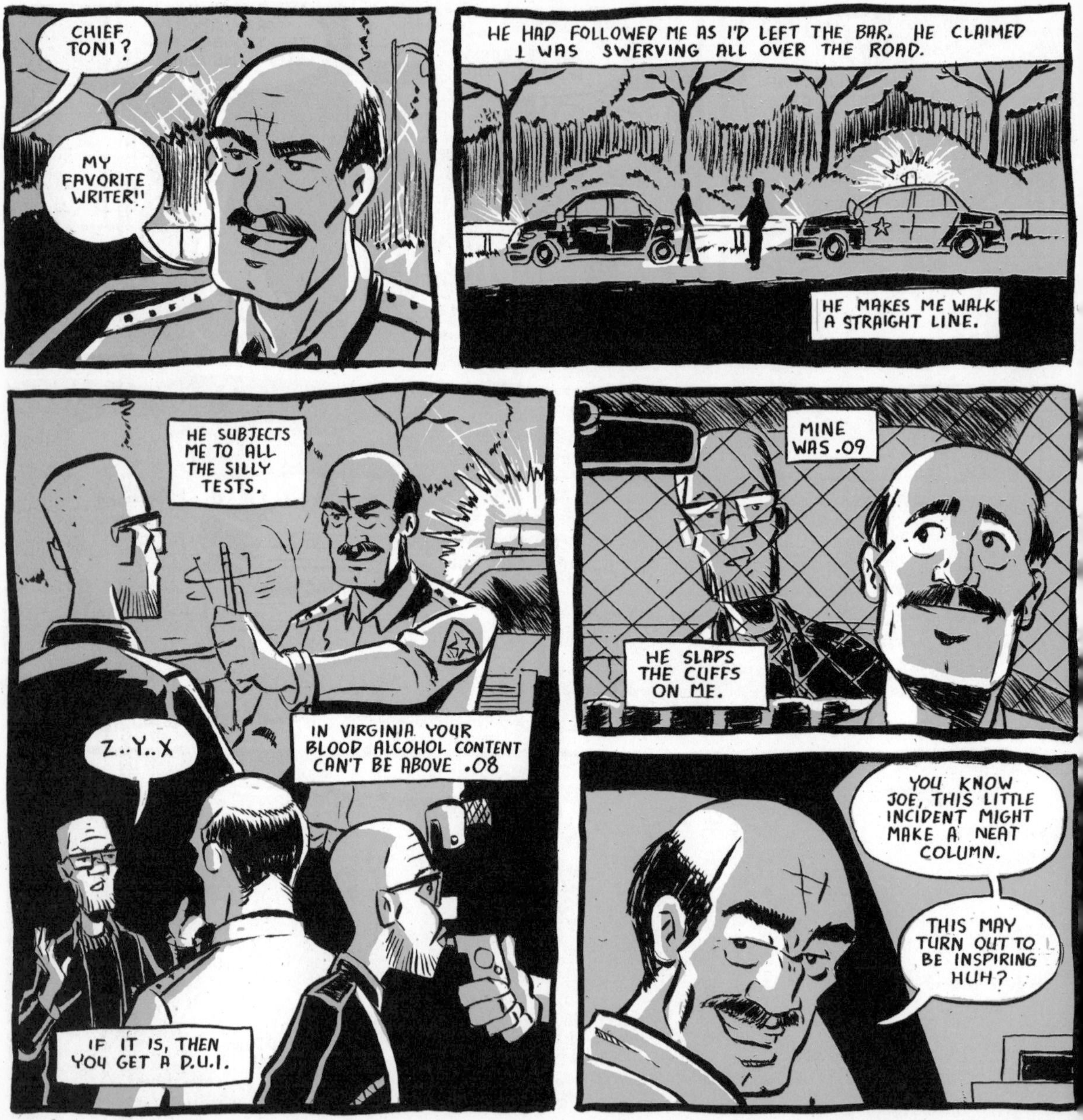
CHIEF TONI?
MY FAVORITE WRITER!!
HE HAD FOLLOWED ME AS I'D LEFT THE BAR. HE CLAIMED I WAS SWERVING ALL OVER THE ROAD.
HE MAKES ME WALK A STRAIGHT LINE.
HE SUBJECTS ME TO ALL THE SILLY TESTS.
Z..Y..X
IN VIRGINIA YOUR BLOOD ALCOHOL CONTENT CAN'T BE ABOVE .08
IF IT IS, THEN YOU GET A D.U.I.
MINE WAS .09
HE SLAPS THE CUFFS ON ME.
YOU KNOW JOE, THIS LITTLE INCIDENT MIGHT MAKE A NEAT COLUMN.
THIS MAY TURN OUT TO BE INSPIRING HUH?

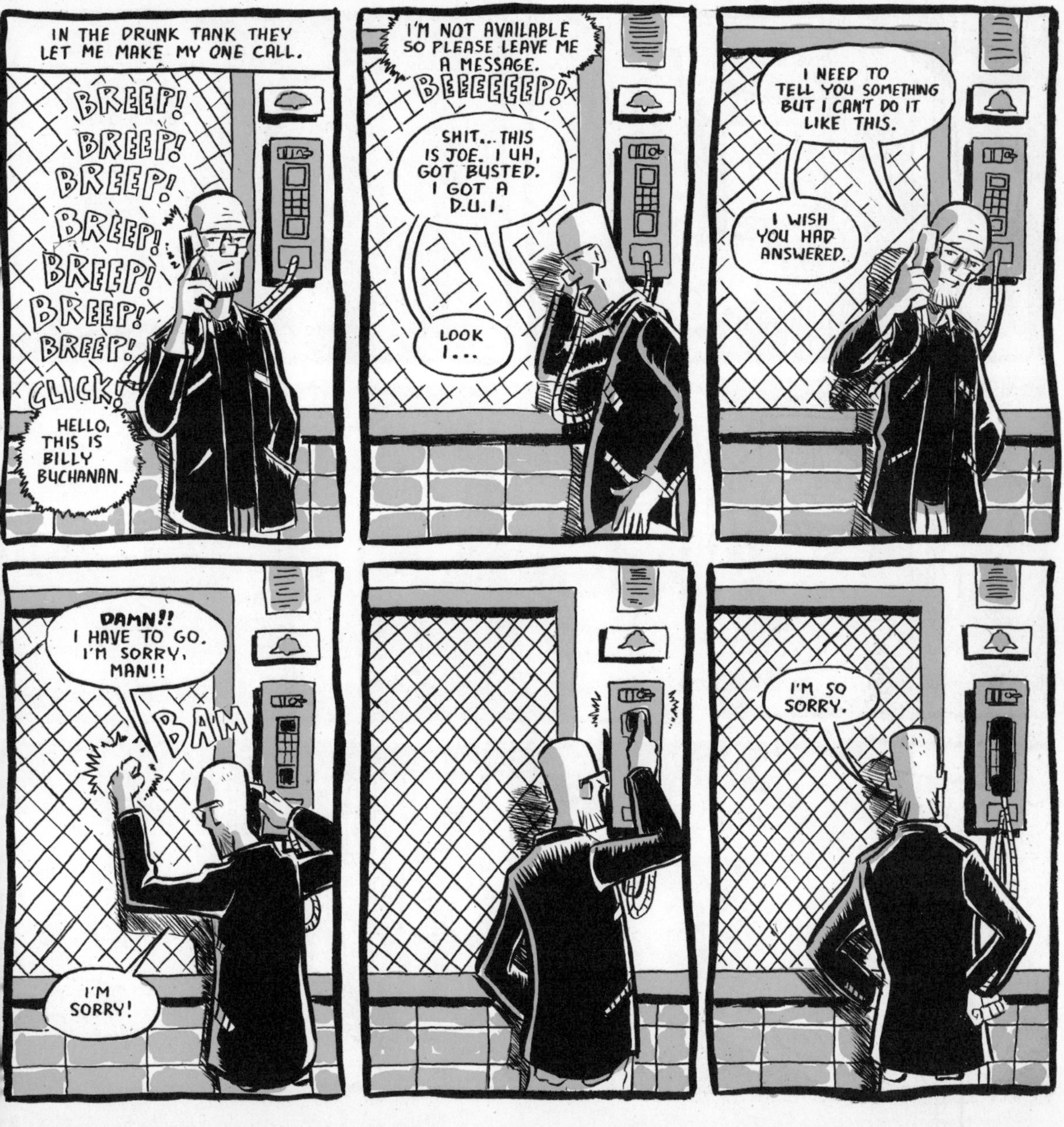
IN THE DRUNK TANK THEY LET ME MAKE MY ONE CALL.
BREEP!
BREEP!
BREEP!
BREEP!
BREEP!
BREEP!
BREEP!
CLICK!
HELLO, THIS IS BILLY BUCHANAN.
I'M NOT AVAILABLE SO PLEASE LEAVE ME A MESSAGE.
BEEEEEEP!
SHIT... THIS IS JOE. I UH, GOT BUSTED. I GOT A D.U.I.
LOOK I...
I NEED TO TELL YOU SOMETHING BUT I CAN'T DO IT LIKE THIS.
I WISH YOU HAD ANSWERED.
DAMN!! I HAVE TO GO. I'M SORRY, MAN!!
BAM
I'M SORRY!
I'M SO SORRY.

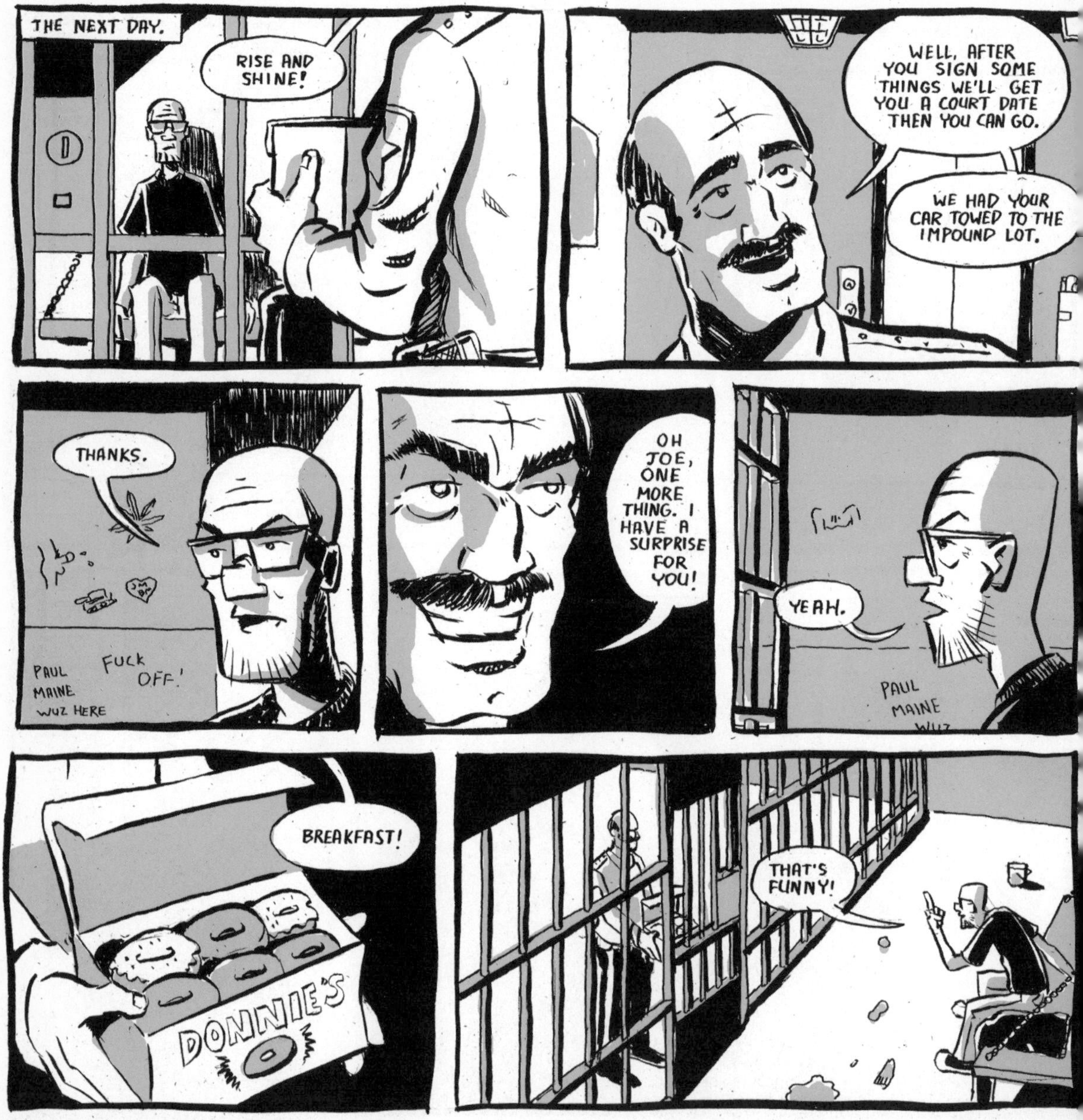
THE NEXT DAY.
RISE AND SHINE!
WELL, AFTER YOU SIGN SOME THINGS WE'LL GET YOU A COURT DATE THEN YOU CAN GO.
WE HAD YOUR CAR TOWED TO THE IMPOUND LOT.
THANKS.
PAUL MAINE WUZ HERE
FUCK OFF!
OH JOE, ONE MORE THING. I HAVE A SURPRISE FOR YOU!
YEAH.
PAUL MAINE
BREAKFAST!
DONNIE'S
THAT'S FUNNY!

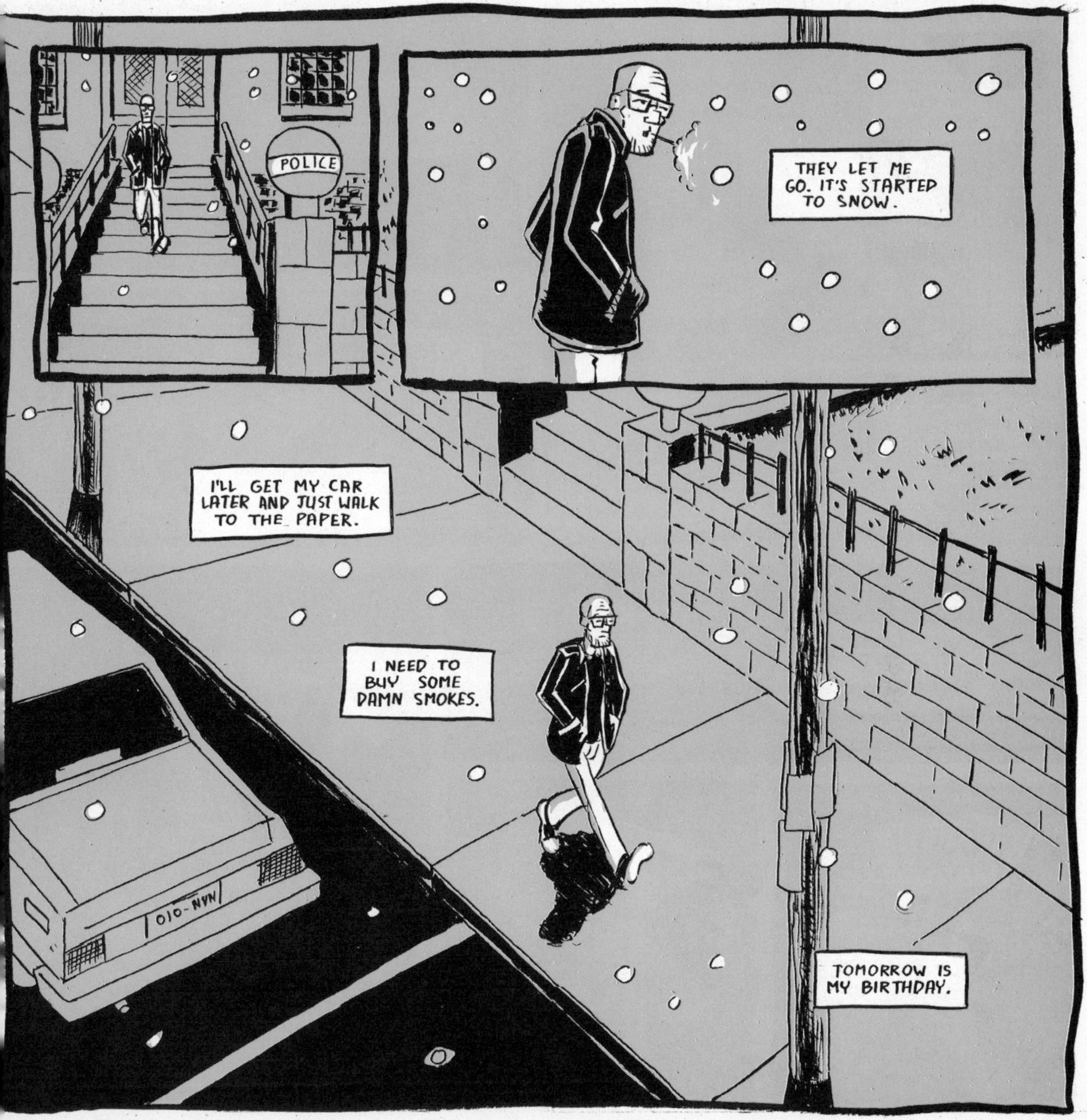
POLICE
THEY LET ME GO. IT'S STARTED TO SNOW.
I'LL GET MY CAR LATER AND JUST WALK TO THE PAPER.
I NEED TO BUY SOME DAMN SMOKES.
TOMORROW IS MY BIRTHDAY.
010-NVN

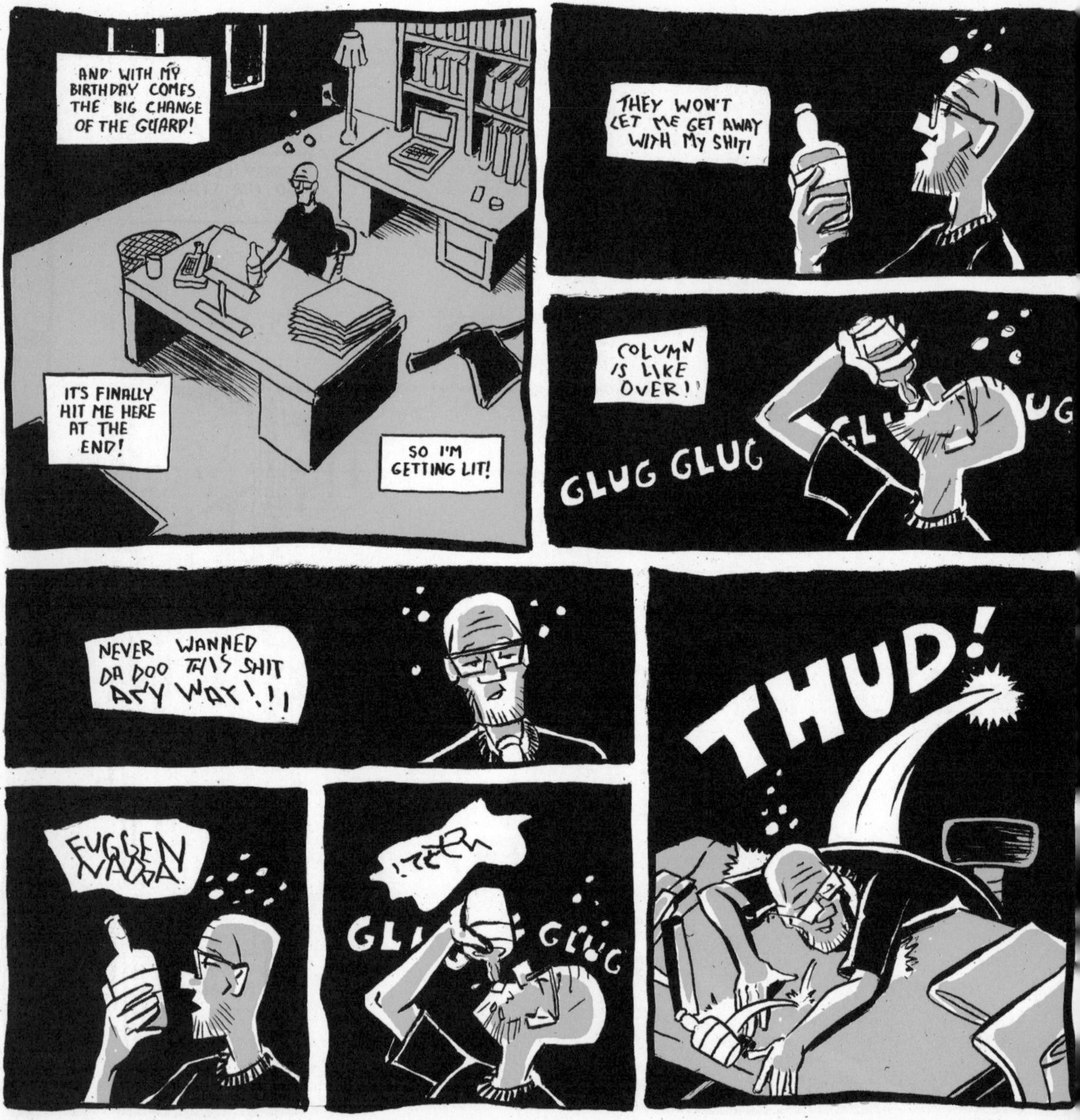
AND WITH MY BIRTHDAY COMES THE BIG CHANGE OF THE GUARD!
IT'S FINALLY HIT ME HERE AT THE END!
SO I'M GETTING LIT!
THEY WON'T LET ME GET AWAY WITH MY SHIT!
COLUMN IS LIKE OVER!!
GLUG GLUG
NEVER WANNED DA DOO THIS SHIT ANY WAY!!!
FUGGEN NAGGA!
GLUG
THUD!

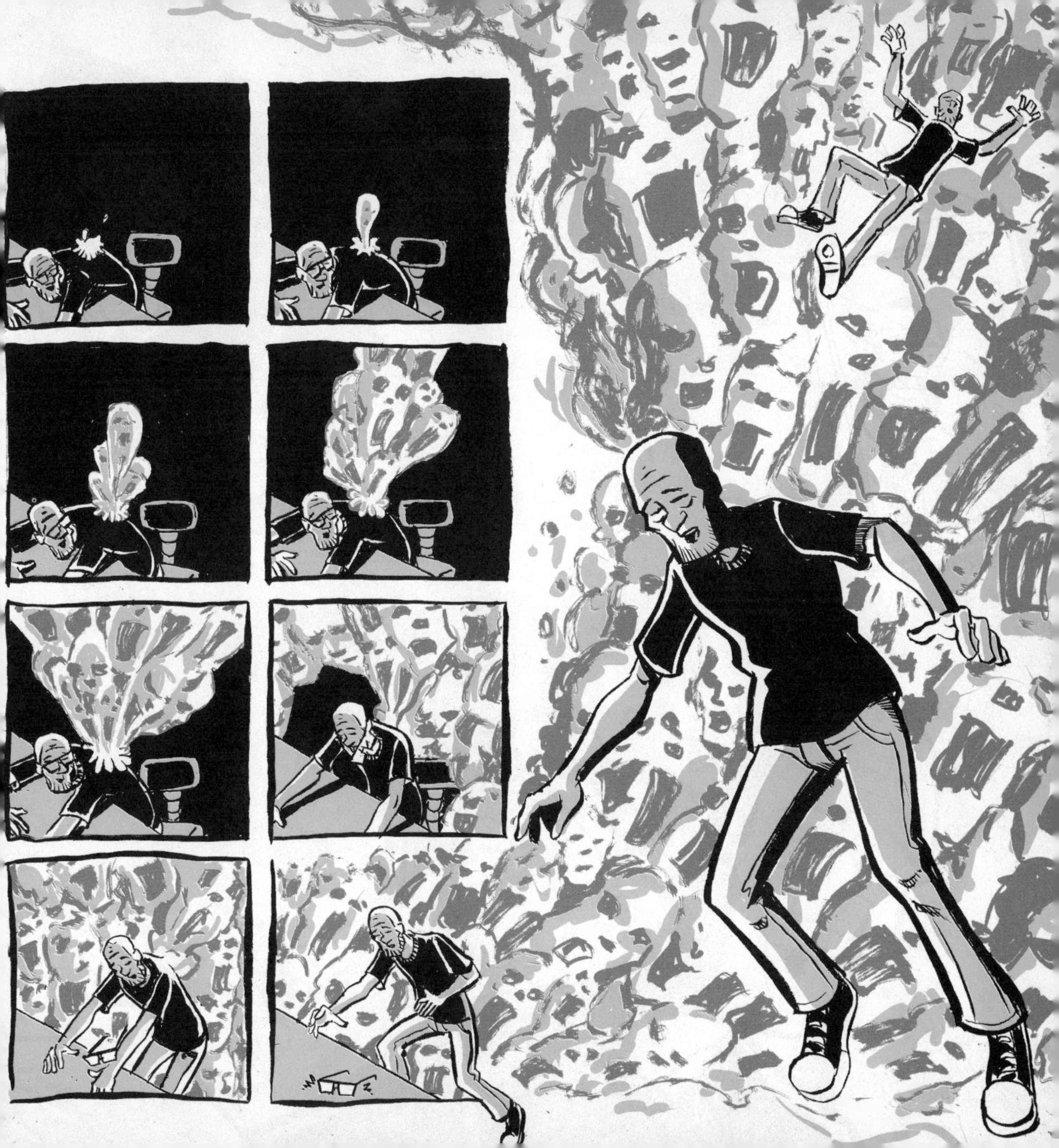

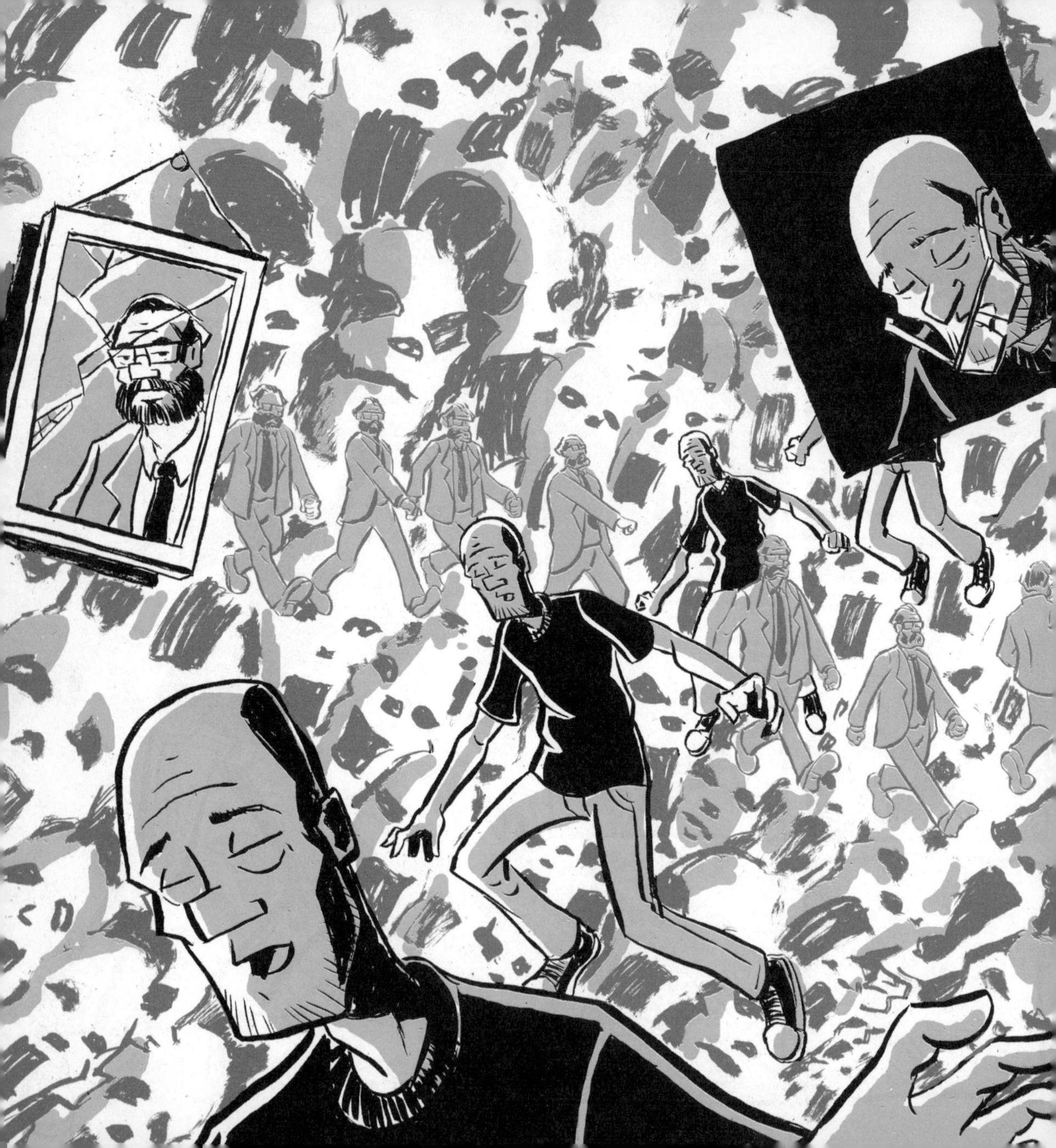

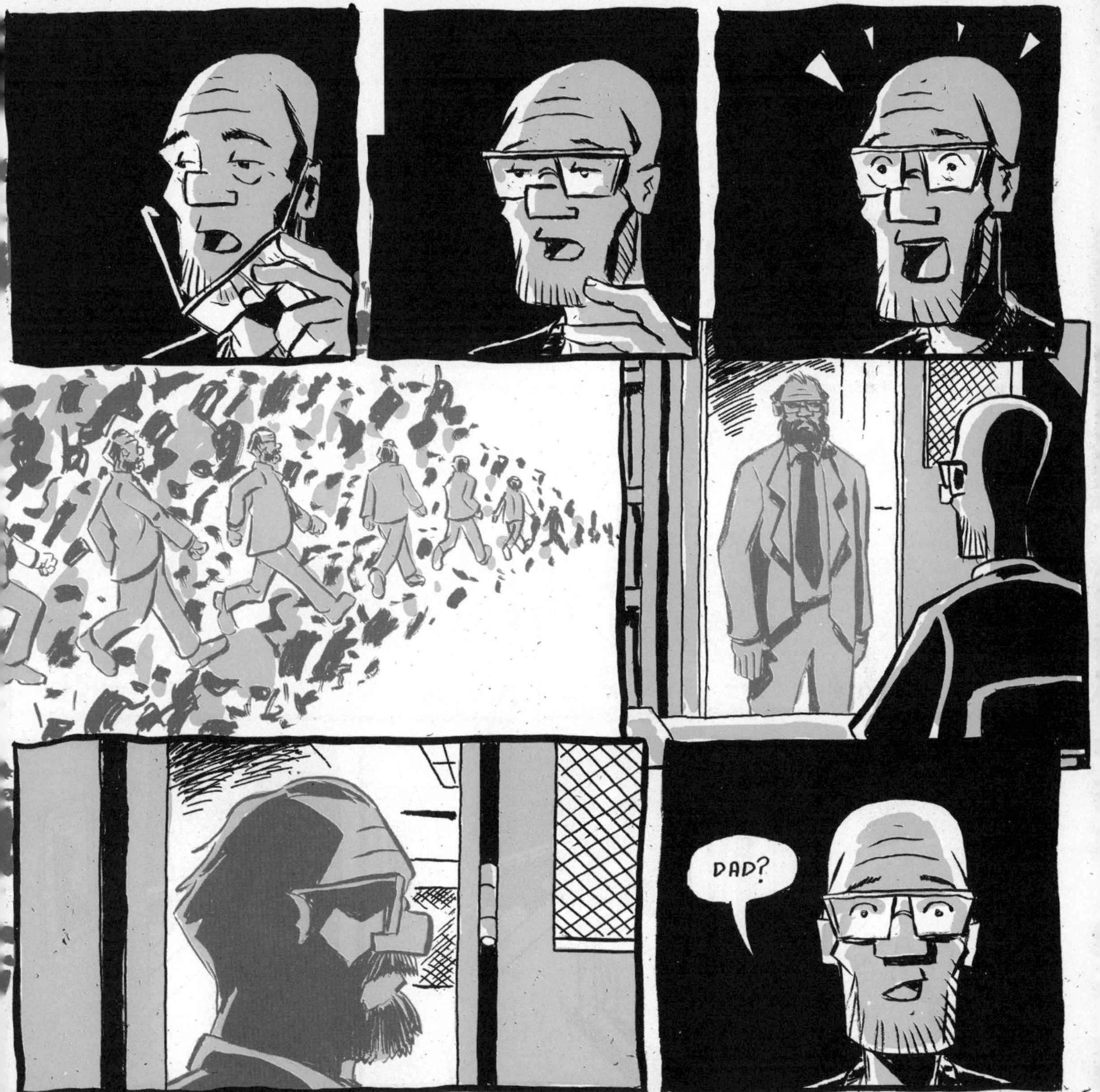
DAD?

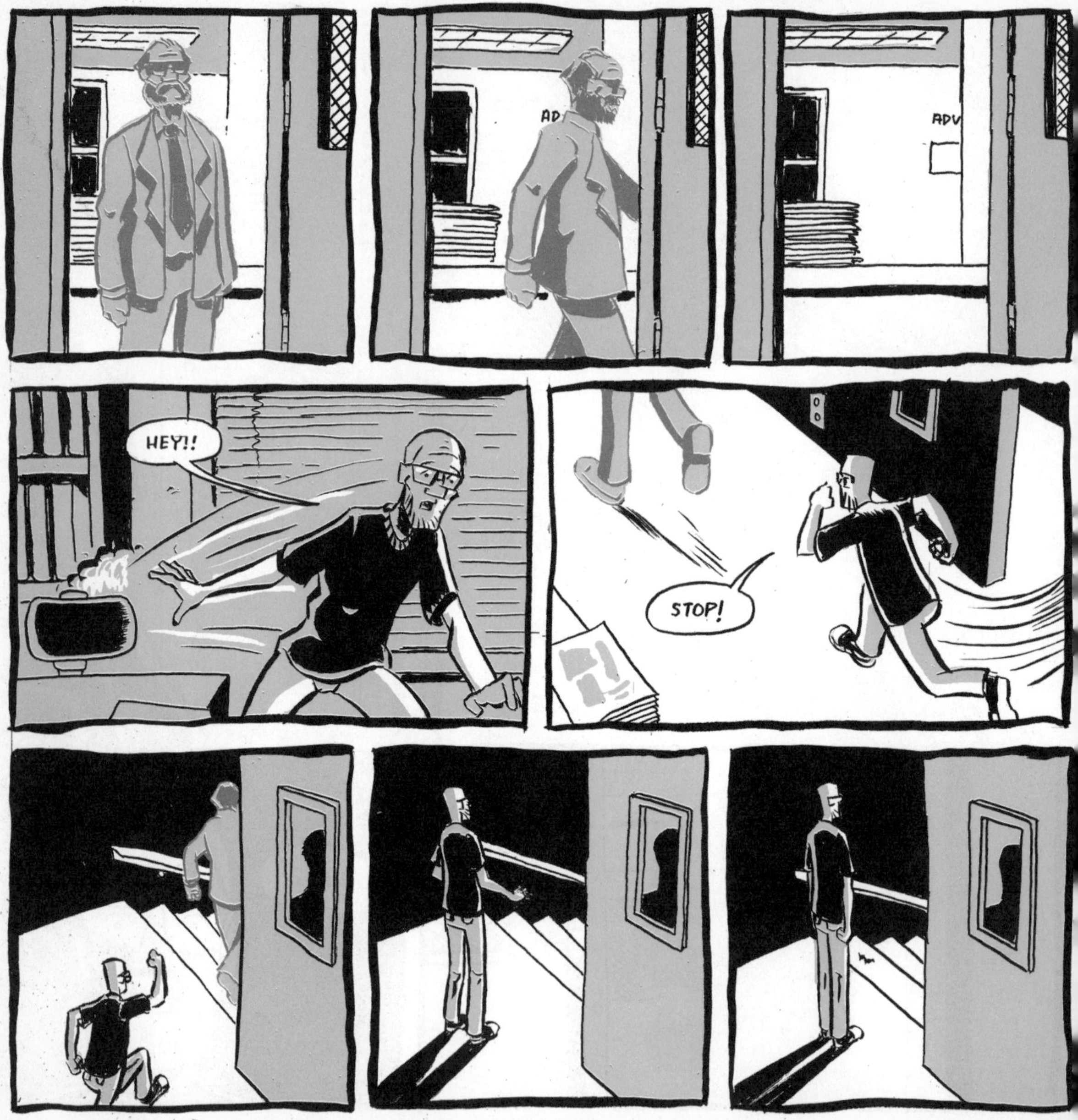
AD
ADV
HEY!!
STOP!

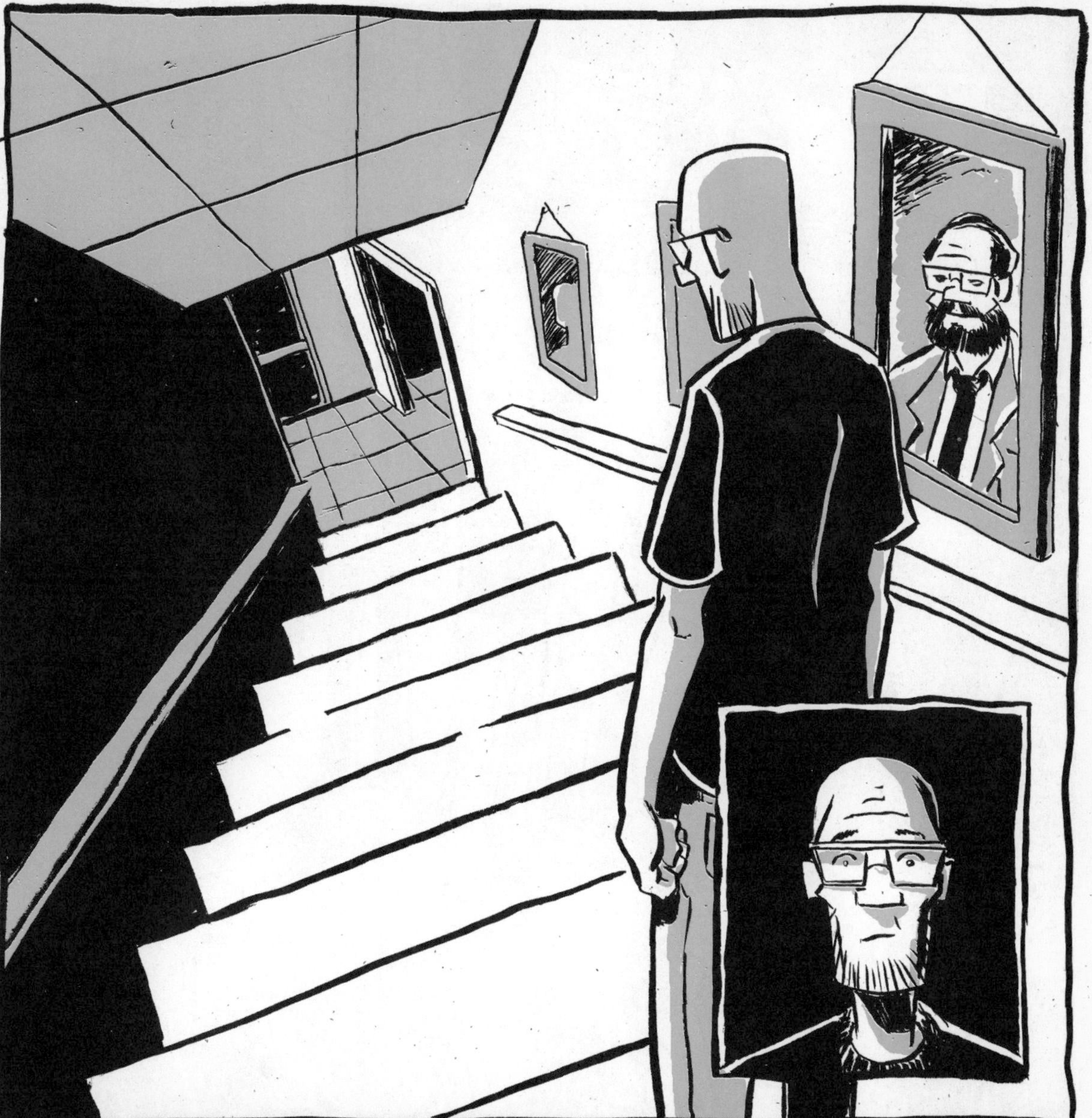

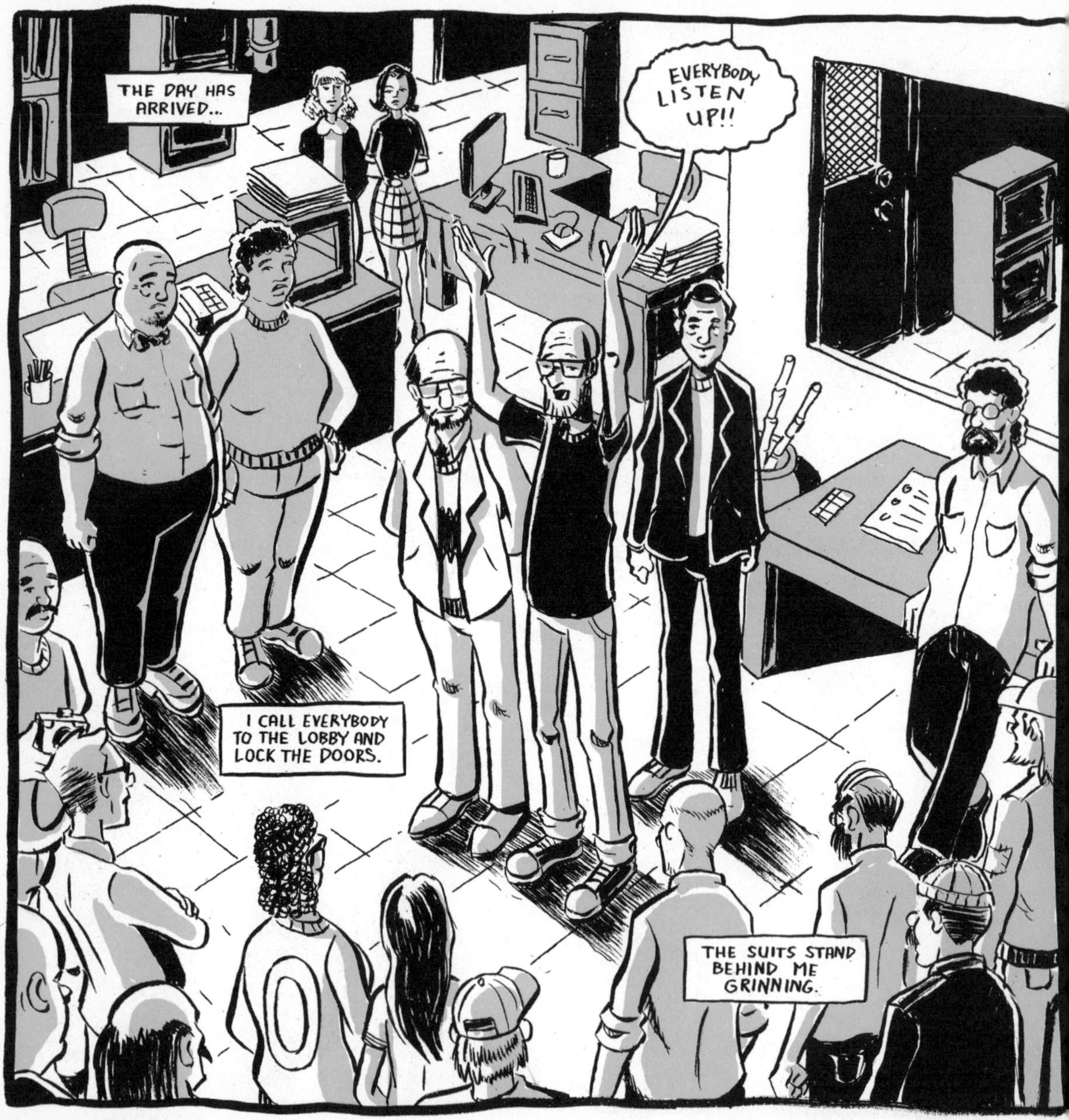
THE DAY HAS ARRIVED...
EVERYBODY LISTEN UP!!
I CALL EVERYBODY TO THE LOBBY AND LOCK THE DOORS.
THE SUITS STAND BEHIND ME GRINNING.

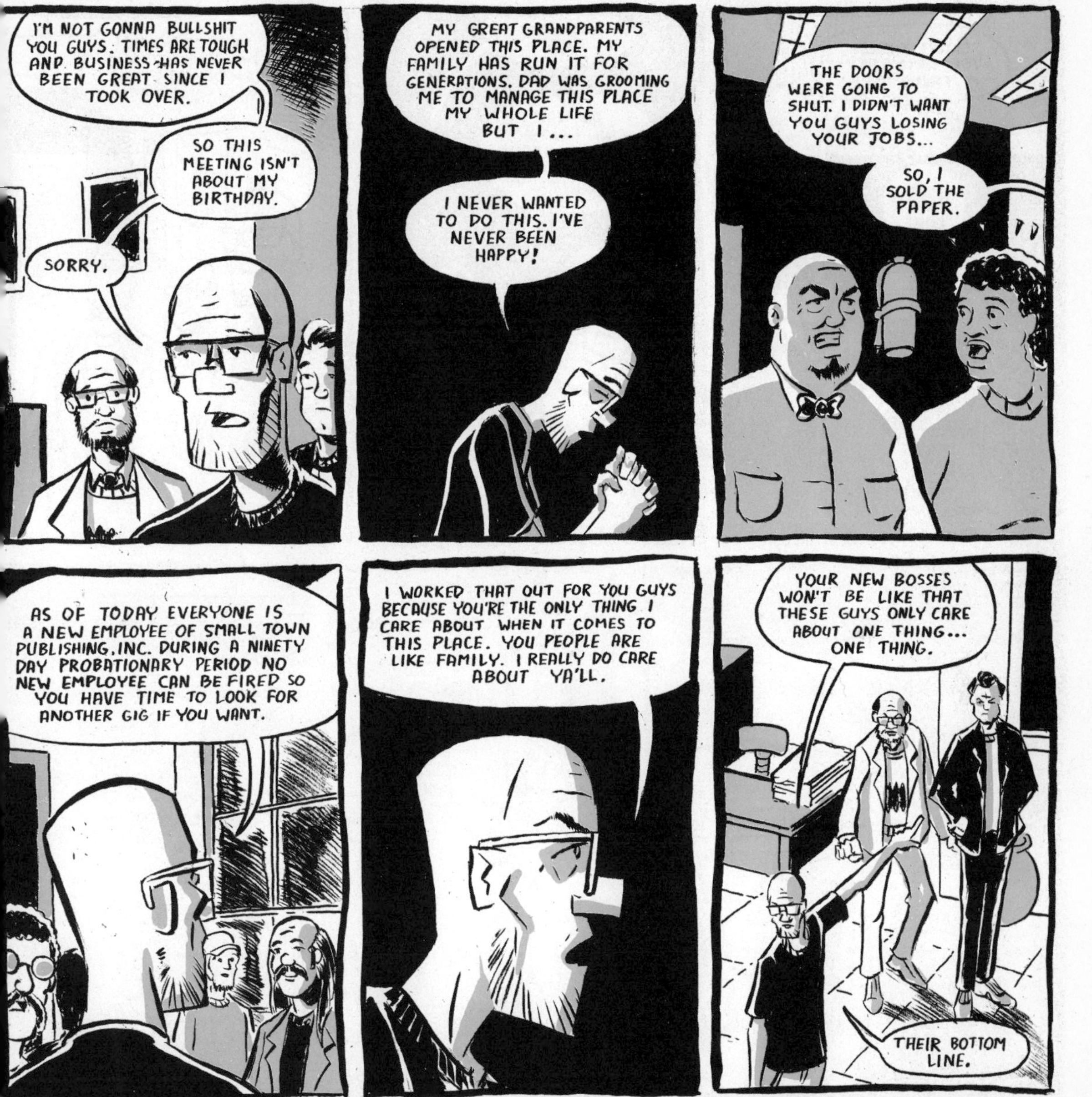
I'M NOT GONNA BULLSHIT YOU GUYS. TIMES ARE TOUGH AND BUSINESS HAS NEVER BEEN GREAT SINCE I TOOK OVER.
SO THIS MEETING ISN'T ABOUT MY BIRTHDAY.
SORRY.
MY GREAT GRANDPARENTS OPENED THIS PLACE. MY FAMILY HAS RUN IT FOR GENERATIONS. DAD WAS GROOMING ME TO MANAGE THIS PLACE MY WHOLE LIFE BUT I...
I NEVER WANTED TO DO THIS. I'VE NEVER BEEN HAPPY!
THE DOORS WERE GOING TO SHUT. I DIDN'T WANT YOU GUYS LOSING YOUR JOBS...
SO, I SOLD THE PAPER.
AS OF TODAY EVERYONE IS A NEW EMPLOYEE OF SMALL TOWN PUBLISHING, INC. DURING A NINETY DAY PROBATIONARY PERIOD NO NEW EMPLOYEE CAN BE FIRED SO YOU HAVE TIME TO LOOK FOR ANOTHER GIG IF YOU WANT.
I WORKED THAT OUT FOR YOU GUYS BECAUSE YOU'RE THE ONLY THING I CARE ABOUT WHEN IT COMES TO THIS PLACE. YOU PEOPLE ARE LIKE FAMILY. I REALLY DO CARE ABOUT YA'LL.
YOUR NEW BOSSES WON'T BE LIKE THAT. THESE GUYS ONLY CARE ABOUT ONE THING... ONE THING.
THEIR BOTTOM LINE.

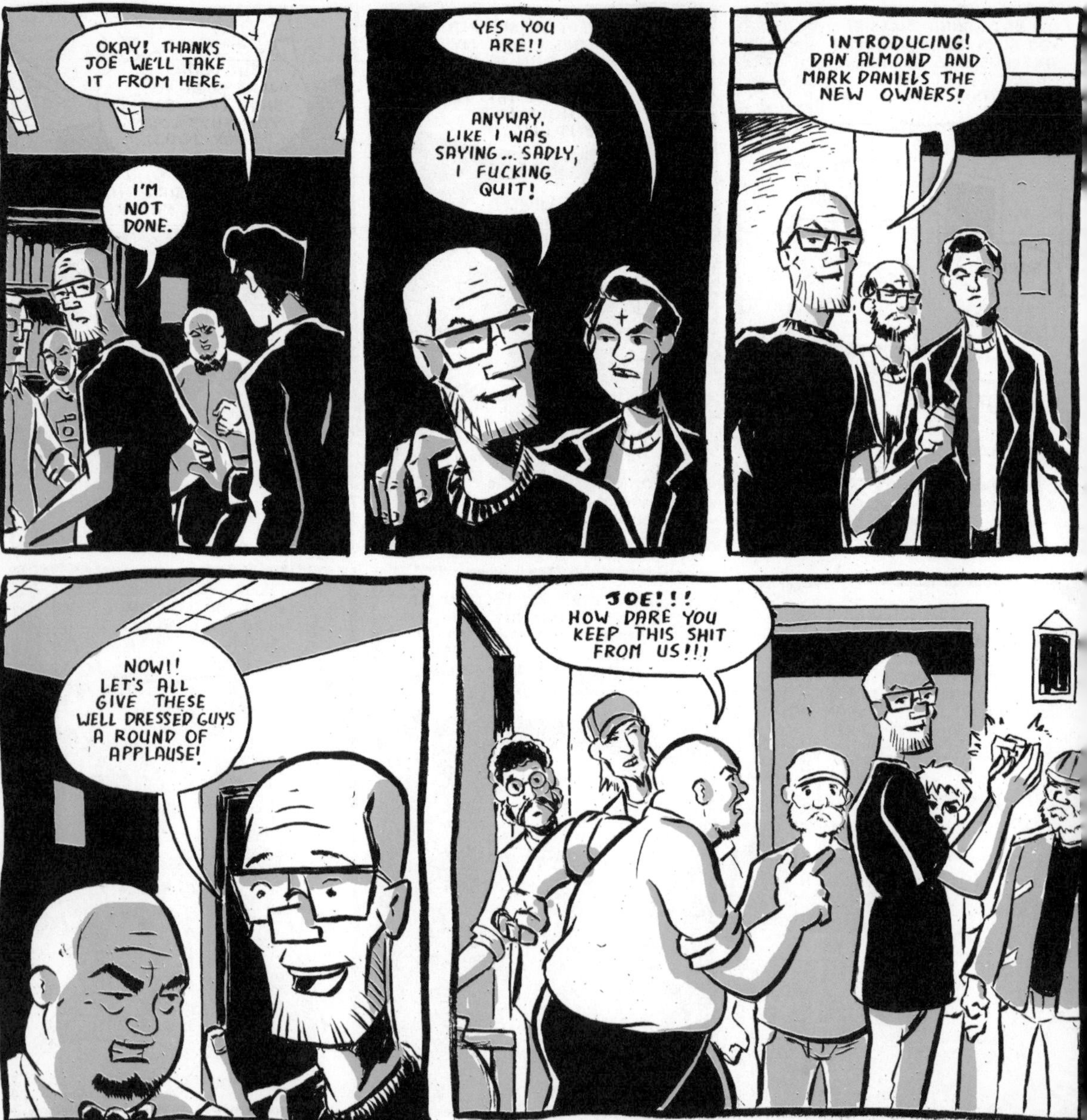
OKAY! THANKS JOE WE'LL TAKE IT FROM HERE.
I'M NOT DONE.
YES YOU ARE!!
ANYWAY, LIKE I WAS SAYING... SADLY, I FUCKING QUIT!
INTRODUCING! DAN ALMOND AND MARK DANIELS THE NEW OWNERS!
NOW!! LET'S ALL GIVE THESE WELL DRESSED GUYS A ROUND OF APPLAUSE!
JOE!!! HOW DARE YOU KEEP THIS SHIT FROM US!!!

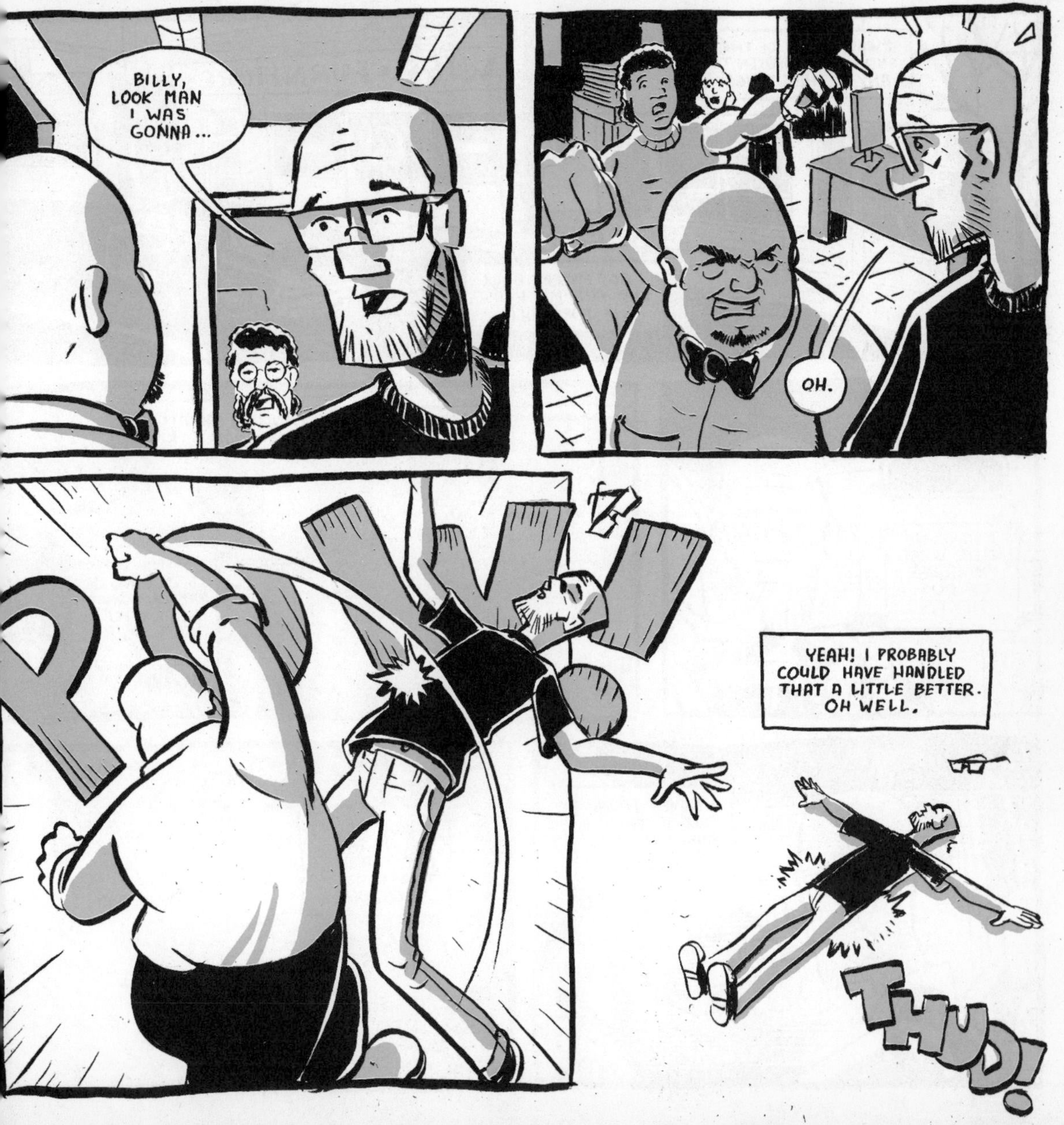
BILLY, LOOK MAN I WAS GONNA...
OH.
YEAH! I PROBABLY COULD HAVE HANDLED THAT A LITTLE BETTER. OH WELL.
THUD!

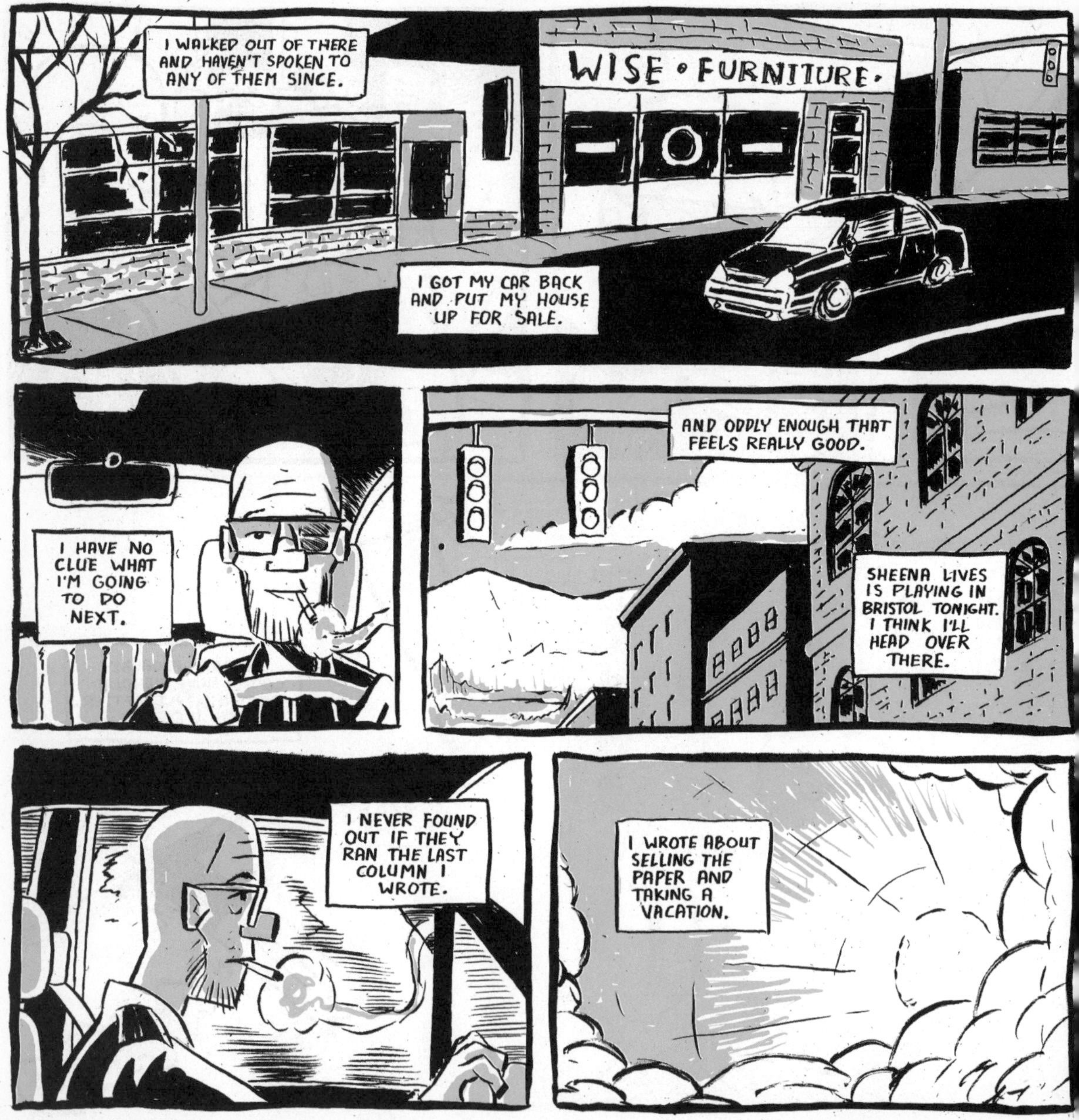
I WALKED OUT OF THERE AND HAVEN'T SPOKEN TO ANY OF THEM SINCE.
WISE • FURNITURE •
I GOT MY CAR BACK AND PUT MY HOUSE UP FOR SALE.
I HAVE NO CLUE WHAT I'M GOING TO DO NEXT.
AND ODDLY ENOUGH THAT FEELS REALLY GOOD.
SHEENA LIVES IS PLAYING IN BRISTOL TONIGHT. I THINK I'LL HEAD OVER THERE.
I NEVER FOUND OUT IF THEY RAN THE LAST COLUMN I WROTE.
I WROTE ABOUT SELLING THE PAPER AND TAKING A VACATION.

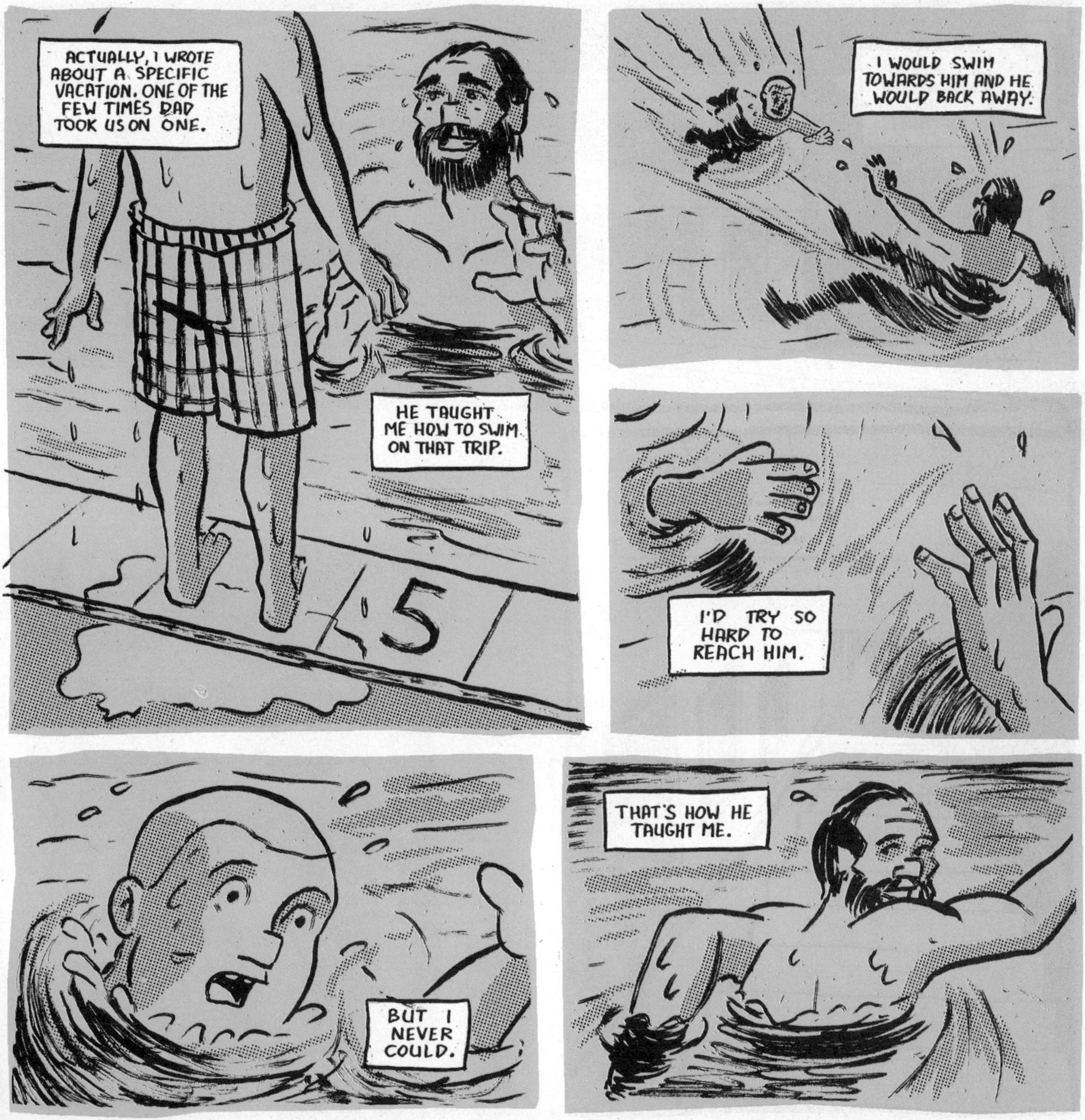
ACTUALLY, I WROTE ABOUT A SPECIFIC VACATION. ONE OF THE FEW TIMES DAD TOOK US ON ONE.
HE TAUGHT ME HOW TO SWIM ON THAT TRIP.
I WOULD SWIM TOWARDS HIM AND HE WOULD BACK AWAY.
I'D TRY SO HARD TO REACH HIM.
BUT I NEVER COULD.
THAT'S HOW HE TAUGHT ME.

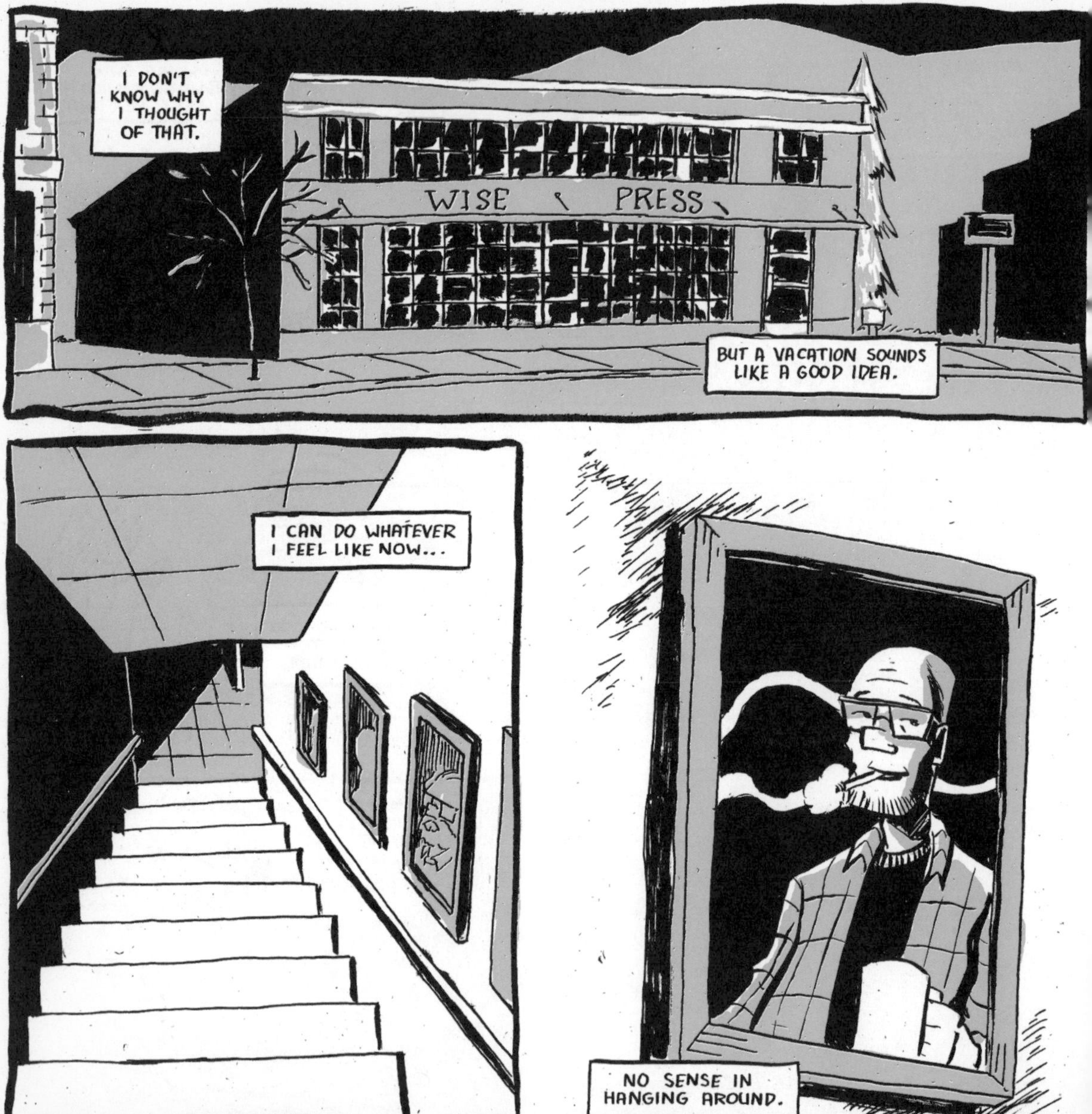
I DON'T KNOW WHY I THOUGHT OF THAT.
WISE PRESS
BUT A VACATION SOUNDS LIKE A GOOD IDEA.
I CAN DO WHATEVER I FEEL LIKE NOW...
NO SENSE IN HANGING AROUND.

END

THIS BOOK IS A WORK OF FICTION
ANY SIMILARITY TO THOSE LIVING OR
DEAD (GHOSTS AND WHAT NOT) IS
PURELY COINCIDENTAL.

ALL MY GHOSTS
9781934985502
2016 FIRST PRINTING
PUBLISHED BY ALTERNA COMICS, INC.
ALTERNA COMICS AND ITS LOGOS ARE ™ AND © 2007-2016 ALTERNA COMICS, INC. ALL RIGHTS
RESERVED. ALL MY GHOSTS AND ALL RELATED CHARACTERS ARE ™ AND © 2016 JEREMY MASSIE.
ALL RIGHTS RESERVED. WITH THE EXCEPTION OF ARTWORK USED FOR REVIEW PURPOSES, NO
PORTION OF THIS PUBLICATION MAY BE REPRODUCED BY ANY MEANS WITHOUT THE EXPRESSED
WRITTEN CONSENT OF THE COPYRIGHT HOLDER. PRINTED IN TAIWAN BY KRAKENPRINT.

A VERY SPECIAL THANKS TO THE KICKSTARTER BACKERS

BRIAR ROSE
ADAM DAUGHHETEE
JESSIE MASSIE
REALITY HAPPENS
WILLIAM SIMS
SIERRA J. SMITH
GREY GORILLA JERKY
HALEY MULLINS COLLINS
JEFF ZWIREK
MATTHEW SMITH
JASON LIEBIG
LINDA STEVENS
A K
STEPHANIE MAY
JILL
RANDALL NICHOLS
OLIVER KRANKHFELD
ROBERT PILKINGTON
RICHARD ZIMMER
NATE WHELAN
BRAD BURDICK
ELIZABETH SHEPARD
BRETT COOK
JORDAN WILLIAMS
JOURDAN McCLAIN
WILLIAM PENTECOST-BRATTON
SETH OSBORN
MICHAEL KOVAKS
JOSH HASKINS
T-RAY MAINE
STEVEN KNISLEY
KARL M.
MATTHEW REX
DCQ
RANDY BELENGER
DENA D.
CHRIS HAYWARD
TY HUDSON
VES
SCOTT EARLY
CAMERON DEKRUIP
JOHN HERSHEY
HOWL COMICS
BRUCE
OLIVER MERTZ
SHELLEY HARLAN
ATHERIS GAMES
ELI NEUGEBOREN
CHRISTINE BRUNSON
KIRK LUND

LETI KOSTELECKY
JUSTIN
KENJI CHAPA
BRIAN
BEN MITCHELL
T. L. HOWL
PATRICK McELREARY
TP GARY
JAMES MEDINA
WALTER HAYES
CHRIS KIER CONROY
JONATHAN HILL
ERIL SCHAEFGES
BRUCE DUNN
ROBBIE HAMILTON
AMOMEGA
GEOFF ARBUCKLE
BRENT WHITE
MIKE BARON
DEVON BARLOW
RONSCHILD
JOHN McLEOD
EDWARD POTTER
KARL WIESER
TOM PLASKON
PAINTED HEROES
JOHN YORK
COURTNEY G.
CHRIS LOEFFLER
SCHALA
AMELIA
PHILLIP RADCLIFFE
PATRICK BOBELL
DSHAWN
TRENT MOORE
ROBIN
ROBERT CURD
MY Q. KAPLAN
CHAD LAMBERT
OWEN RYAN
PETER L BROWN
SALLY JOE CUNNINGHAM
NICK MELLISH
MARGARET MCFEE
JEFF KNIGHT
DOUG VARNER
THOMAS CALVER
SAMUEL FREDERICK
STUART DAVIES
BEREEN GREENSPAN
JAMES McCULLOCH

SCOTT HARRIMAN
MICHAEL PEARSON
PAULISH MH
OTTERO
JAMES HALLAM
DANIELLE CHRISTMAS
CAELA MENDINI
DOLEV AMITAI
INGO LEMBCKE
RYAN WING
TONY KEAR
GERD HASSELKUSS
CRAIG GALLOWAY
CRYSTAL MONEY
WOLF GETER
ZACHARY CAILEN
ALLEN BOYD
CLEMENS SOL-LÜER
KEN N.
ALICIA MUNDINGER
CALLIE McNEIL
KYLE GODFREY
JEFF BRAWNER
TOR VIDAR BORKAMO
JARED GAFFORD
N.R. JENZEN JONES
DAVID CLARKE
CHRIS THOMPSON
COURTNEY ARMSTRONG
IAN AHL
RODRIGUEZ 1879
TJ
BRETT RAPP
DANIEL STANLEY
BRADLEY 'DR' NOE
ANDREW MILLER
GABRIEL JAGUSH
ANNA
KENN MINTER
LESLIE SULLIVAN
JAMES IASRAL MACFARLANE
GARY SCOTT BEATTY
PARK CIRCLE COMICS
DANIEL LOYD
THE COOPERSTEINS
CHARLES PRINCE
BRANDON BARROWS
JEFF
JASON MURRELL
JESSICA GOH
GREG M.

ANDY CHUNG
WALLER HASTINGS
CYNTHIA LEIKER
MAGNUE H BLYSTAD
MICHAEL FARAH
NIKKI SHERMAN
BAY AREA COMICS ANTHOLOGY
MICHAEL SCHEVERMANN
KATE SKEBER
AGOSTINO DAMIANO
DONALD MICHAEL McCARTY
KAYLA HALLEUR
BRYAN BROWN
BRIAN FRACOLLI
C JOKES
JEN O'L
EL TIBURON
RUS WOOTEN
ALFRED D. III
JANNA SOLIS
MATTHEW CURRY
MARK HIRST
JASMINA BRICIL
ROBERT F. DANIEL
OLIVIA ROHAN
ROK TEASLEY
STEFANI MANARD
THOMAS CHILDERS
MELODIE WONG
MICHAEL
LAURA
HAYDEN MILES
JASON ISODA
JASON RAINEY
ALEXANDER LYLE
SERGIO DELGADO
DEBRA S.
ANTONIO
BEN STERLING
CARLOS G. GANANIAN
JADIE LADY
SHANNON SMITH
RICHARD PHILLIPS
STRAIGHT WHITE TEETH
MOSHIN REZA
MATT HANSEN
JAMES BLACKBURN
AUSTIN MURPHY
JUSTIN JONES

THANKS...

• JEREMY MASSIE •

'ALL MY GHOSTS' IS JEREMY'S
THIRD BOOK WITH ALTERNA.
HIS FIRST WAS 'THE DEADBEAT'
FOLLOWED BY 'BEE STING'
WRITTEN BY MATTHEW D. SMITH
WHICH WAS ADAPTED INTO A
LOW BUDGET SLASHER FILM.
HE RESIDES IN THE APPALACHIAN
MOUNTAINS OF VIRGINIA AND
SPENDS HIS NON COMIC MAKING
TIME WITH HIS WIFE AND
TWO CHILDREN AND ALSO
PLAYS MUSIC WITH A BAND
CALLED, SPACE JUNK.
FOLLOW HIM ON TWITTER
AND FACEBOOK @
WWW.TWITTER.COM/JEREMY_MASSIE
WWW.FACEBOOK.COM/ALLMYGHOSTSCOMIC